TO THE
GREATEST
HEIGHTS

TO THE
GREATEST
HEIGHTS

Facing Danger, Finding Humility,
and Climbing a Mountain of Truth

— A MEMOIR —

VANESSA O'BRIEN

EMILY BESTLER BOOKS

ATRIA

New York   London   Toronto   Sydney   New Delhi

An Imprint of Simon & Schuster, Inc.
1230 Avenue of the Americas
New York, NY 10020

Some names and identifying details have been changed and some individuals and events have been composited.

First Emily Bestler Books/Atria Books hardcover edition March 2021

EMILY BESTLER BOOKS / ATRIA BOOKS and colophon
are trademarks of Simon & Schuster, Inc.

For information about special discounts for bulk purchases, please contact Simon & Schuster Special Sales at 1-866-506-1949 or business@simonandschuster.com.

The Simon & Schuster Speakers Bureau can bring authors to your live event. For more information or to book an event, contact the Simon & Schuster Speakers Bureau at 1-866-248-3049 or visit our website at www.simonspeakers.com.

Interior design by Jill Putorti

Manufactured in the United States of America

1 3 5 7 9 10 8 6 4 2

Library of Congress Cataloging-in-Publication Data has been applied for.

ISBN 978-1-9821-2378-9
ISBN 978-1-9821-2380-2 (ebook)

To all those with the courage to embrace change.

PROLOGUE

*Mountain climbing is extended periods of intense
boredom interrupted by occasional moments of sheer terror.*
—ANONYMOUS

I scrambled over a rocky moraine onto the Godwin-Austen Glacier high in the Himalayas. K2 towered over me, marbled white and black against blue sky, an almost perfect triangle, like a mountain drawn by a child. I tried to focus on my feet, but the summit teased the corner of my eye and made me feel a bit off-kilter. It dodged in and out, playing hide-and-seek with the midsummer cirrus clouds and crystalline snow plumes that rode a relentless wind. I don't recall the exact song I heard in my earbuds. It may have been the Rolling Stones singing about the difference between getting what you want and getting what you need, or maybe the Sex Pistols singing about the difference between what you want and what you get. Every expedition has its own soundtrack, and either one of those would be appropriate for my second attempt on K2.

Straddling the border between Pakistan and China, K2 is the highest point in the Karakoram Range, the second-highest mountain on the planet, at 28,251 feet and around 11,850 feet from Base Camp to summit. Its brutal cold, constant avalanches and falling rock, tricky technical climbs, and predictably dire weather conditions are legendary. It's a grueling test of physical endurance and mental will. Nothing keeps you there but sheer determination, because going there puts you and everyone who loves you in an excruciatingly uncomfortable position, as my husband, Jonathan, can confirm without complaining.

In 2013, three years before my second attempt on K2, a father and son were swept away by an avalanche near Camp 3, around 24,275 feet. On a bluebird day, I could just about see where they would have been. I had made a promise to the surviving wife and mother and her daughter, Sequoia Schmidt, that I would keep an eye out for any signs of either of them, so ever since we'd arrived at Base Camp and begun seeing the evidence of what various avalanches had been pulling down the mountains, I'd been investigating shredded summit suits, pieces of torn clothing, and yes, even the odd fragments of human remains. When I heard through the grapevine that another team had spotted two different boots side by side sticking out of an ebbing glacier, I felt a surge of hope and went out for a closer look.

The topography here is the legacy of a colossal slow-motion fender bender that's been going on for more than fifty million years. The Indian Plate smashed into and under the Eurasian Plate, forcing peaks five miles into the air to create the Himalayas, which include the Karakoram Mountains. As you observe when someone gets rear-ended in traffic, the wreckage juts up, folding into itself like an accordion. Fossils that formed in the primordial depths are now embedded in rock thousands of meters above sea level. Avalanches deposit snow into underground streams that gradually cut into the mountain, leaving deep crevasses and brittle ledges.

Mountains are never static, but the elderly ones that date back billions of years tend to be worn down and docile. In geological terms, the Himalayas are petulant adolescents. They talk back and misbehave, casting off rubble and debris without warning. Between the sharp peaks, frozen rivers and mountain waterfalls are constantly on the move, shifting three to six feet in a single day. A climber can easily slip into a deep crevasse and disappear into the icy abyss. They can get crushed by a tumbling serac or make some fatal mistake. They can succumb to sickness, edema, exhaustion, or hypoxia. They can fall, freeze, or simply fail to wake up.

At this writing, only 377 people have summited K2, and 84 climbers have died there, making it the second-deadliest mountain in the world, after Annapurna. For every twenty summits of Everest, there's only one summit of K2, and for every four summits of K2, one person dies, and the unpleasant reality is, very few dead bodies come off the mountain intact. Disembodied limbs, ghost gear, and frozen corpses appear and disappear in the shifting ice. The force of an avalanche tumbles the body like a stone in the ocean—bones breaking, joints separating, tendons snapping, cartilage crumbling. The body tends to come apart at its weakest junctures, starting with the neck. The pieces are likely to be found by birds before another human being comes along to shift a disembodied head into a crevasse or shuffle scree over a torso. At high altitude, expending energy to pile rocks on a corpse or attempt to retrieve it would endanger the life of the well-intentioned climber, so my goal was not to recover the father and son, only to identify them with DNA samples.

The Sherpa are spooked by death. Many of them won't visit the memorial cairn near K2 Base Camp. Some fear that even taking a picture of a dead body might interrupt the soul's journey. There was certainly no point in asking them to handle a dead man's ankle, so I'd invited my Ecuadorian teammate Benigno to hike up the glacier with me. He was still below the moraine when I saw a stretch of crystal blue ice and snow the color of whipped cream up ahead. The pale backdrop made it easy to spot the bold blue and neon orange boots. Different colors, same European brand. Maybe two climbers who'd shopped together for gear. Using my Garmin in-Reach, a satellite device that tracks movement and allows texting, I messaged Sequoia: "Were they wearing Koflach boots?"

While I waited for an answer, I made my way up the glacier to look for other signs of clothing, equipment, or remains. Climbing gear is as colorful as a circus act, specifically because we want to be easy to see against ice and rock. When I first started climbing, I hated this. I wanted to look like a ninja warrior, not a matching set of ketchup and mustard bottles on a grill, but La Sportiva Olympus Mons Evo boots were always going to be yellow. So it's like Henry Ford's Model T: you go with what gets you there. I hiked upward for a while, scanning the shadowed snowbanks. Nothing. It was overcast now, and I was pushing against a persistent wind that pushed back hard enough to engage a core of resistance between my ribs and breastbone. I went back to the boots.

I peered into the blue boot first and found that it contained a foot, an ankle, and a broken tibia with a good amount of flesh still on the bone. The quality of the tissue reminded me of the pickled pig's feet my mother used to love—whitish flesh marbled with jellied fat. I shuddered at the sight of her eating them when I was a kid. After this, I wasn't sure I'd be able to look at them at the neighborhood deli. On the positive, there was plenty of opportunity to obtain DNA. I'm no expert, but I understand the fundamentals and thought I could be fairly stoic about the sample collection, because I've been stoic about things like that since I was a kid.

I remember going to my first funeral when I was eight. My mother took me and my little brother, Ben, up to the casket to pay our respects. Ben was too small to see over the edge, but I stood on tiptoes and asked, "Can I touch it?" Mom nodded, so I reached in and stroked the tweedy sleeve of a starched bark-gray suit. I didn't know this person. He was an empty rack of clothes. His soul had gone to Heaven, everyone said, and I believed that with the un-questioning faith of a child. I still do. But when I pulled my sample collection kit from my pocket—surgical gloves, scissors, mask, sample container, and Swiss army knife—my hands were shaking. This was not some frog to be dissected in biology class. This was someone's brother, which made me think of my own little brother, and I felt my stoicism shrivel.

"Hey, Benigno," I called, and he clambered onto the icy rise and stood next to me, puffing white clouds of breath.

"I may be a bit out of my depth here," I said, offering him a mask and gloves. "I don't suppose you'd give me a hand? Or a foot, as it were."

He shrugged, grinning. Climbers are used to dark humor. I held the boot, instructed him what bits of flesh to saw away, and opened the container to receive the sample.

"Right. Perfect. Now can you snap off that bone fragment? Good. Same thing on this other one. I'll get another container."

We repeated the whole process with the other boot. When it was done, I removed my mask and gloves, labeled the containers, and bagged them with the knife.

"Hey, don't throw away the knife," said Benigno. "Give it to me. I'll clean and keep it."

Fair enough. I let him reach in the bag and take it. There was a deep crevasse a few yards away, so we gathered the rest of the remains and carefully placed them into the dark recess, marking the GPS coordinates.

"Let me say a prayer," I said.

Benigno stood respectfully, head bowed, hands behind his back.

"Our Father, who art in Heaven, hallowed be thy name. Thy kingdom come, thy will be done as Earth is in—on Earth in—in Heaven." My voice cracked. I'd recited the Lord's Prayer every day for forty years of living memory. Now I blinked my watery eyes, disturbed to find the familiar words out of reach while a host of unfamiliar emotions rushed in. "Lead us not into temptation. Deliver us from evil. Amen."

Farman, our cook and Base Camp manager, said he would keep the samples on ice. I sent another message to Sequoia, and this time the answer came back quickly. Neither her father nor her brother had been wearing that brand of boots.

Fuck. I was hoping it would be them. I had nothing else to offer this mother and daughter, who would linger on in pain, not knowing. Their unresolved grief sat in bitter counterpoint to the unidentified DNA samples in the icebox, meaningless if you can't connect them to a family member. I understood all too well. My mother died aching that same ache. My father could never talk about it, even before Parkinson's took away his ability to talk at all.

The scene stayed with me, threading nightmare themes into my restless high-altitude sleep over the following days, which played out like a bad dream anyway. An avalanche much like the one that took the father and son swept the contents of Camp 3 down the mountain, sparing lives but taking all our carefully cached equipment, tents, supplies, and oxygen. My second attempt to summit K2 ended in a witch's brew of shit weather and bad luck. I didn't know if it would be physically, financially, or emotionally possible for me to try a third time. At the moment, I felt like I'd been dragged under a door.

The more I climb, the more I see how climbing history repeats itself. The dynamics of the business world, my previous life, for better or worse, mirror the dynamics of mountain climbing: the way we learn; how we interact; what happens in times of ascendance and collapse; the cultures of teamwork, alliance, and lone-wolf-ism.

I truly thought I could MBA my way out of any problem that stood between me and the summit. The mountains corrected me.

Nonetheless, I received a hero's welcome from my friends, which is why I look forward to the celebration that follows every expedition. My husband of twenty years and counting means the world to me, and ever since I was a kid—from the time my own family fell apart—I've taken refuge in creating an ad hoc family wherever I go. My friends are the first sounding board for all my hopes, fears, and dreams. When I come home triumphant, they keep me grounded. When I come home defeated, they make me optimistic again. Jonathan takes a dim view of optimism until it's been supported by numbers.

When I met my husband, I was on top of the world, and I don't mean Everest. I was living in London with a fresh MBA and a thriving financial-sector career. Jonathan, a corporate accountant who survived the icy abyss of English public school from age seven, found all of the above compellingly sexy. He adored my "spirit of adventure," which entailed risky activities like twirling in sandals, jumping onto ski lifts—*carpe T-bar!*—and doing whatever it took to get back to the safari on time. I believe the technical term is *fun*: a three-letter word rendered foreign to little boys in draconian English public schools. What Jonathan didn't know then—what he's only come to know as I've come to know myself— is that some terrible things had happened in my life, and these things hadn't ceased to bother me. I was just very good at never talking about them.

I'm less good at that now. Every summit has changed me. My stiff upper lip has softened a bit. That said, I refuse to dish up the idea that climbing resulted in Jungian self-actualization or any such haggis as that. I subscribe to George Mallory's classic reason for wanting to climb Mount Everest: "Because it's there," he told a reporter in 1923. "Its very existence is a challenge." That much I agree with. But then Mallory went on to say, "The answer is instinctive, a part, I suppose, of man's desire to conquer the universe."

A man's desire, maybe. Not mine. I never wanted to conquer K2 or Everest or any other mountain. I see myself climbing into the lap of a mother mountain. Never would I consider myself stronger, grander, wiser, or more noble than she.

The first two men to summit K2 were Lino Lacedelli and Achille Compagnoni, part of a historic 1954 Italian expedition. The first two American men to climb K2 were Jim Wickwire and Louis Reichardt in 1978. The first woman to summit K2 was Polish climber Wanda Rutkiewicz in 1986, a year that saw thirteen climbers, including Rutkiewicz's climbing partners, lose their lives. In 2017, thirty-one years after Wanda, the first American woman to summit K2 was me. Because I have dual citizenship, I was also the first British woman to summit K2 and survive the descent. It was my third attempt. I was fifty-two years old and had been climbing seriously for less than eight years.

I'm as surprised as anyone to find that my business experience actually did prepare me for a life of adventure and exploration—and yes, there is a difference. *Adventure* is something you do for yourself; *exploration* is something you do for posterity and to give back. You don't always have to have *fun* to have fun. If fun happens along the way, that's great. I love the planning, research, and camaraderie of expeditions. I'm overwhelmed by the stunning vistas and the generosity of the local people in different countries. What a privilege it is to be embraced by the people of Pakistan and Nepal! But the actual climbing of a mountain is often a miserable experience while it's happening. Mentally, it's a grueling test of how many times you can sing "Ninety-Nine Bottles of Beer on the Wall." Physically, it's high mileage at best, and at worst, it's shattering. Frostbitten fingers and toes blister and blacken and sometimes get lopped off. Living outdoors for weeks or even months, there's no reprieve from the raw elements. Getting within shouting distance of the world's highest peaks requires travel through third world countries, where the drinking water is more dangerous than the jet stream winds, not to mention thugs whose cottage industry is holding climbers for ransom.

"I can't wait to never be here again," another climber once sighed, and this crookedly optimistic declaration comes back to me whenever I see cows eating cardboard on the banks of a sewage ditch or children working as field hands. I think of those words every time I enter a vermin-infested lodge with dirt floors or gag at the smell of a sludge-covered latrine. If I peel off a moist sock and find ground meat where the ball of my foot used to be, I remind myself that hope is backhanded; in order to experience it, you must be down on your luck. So it is in business and in life.

But sorting through some old family photos not long ago, I noticed something I'd never seen before. Almost every picture had mountains of some sort in the background. Here's a shot of me as a baby on a picnic blanket in some forgotten meadow. My handsome father leans in, resting on his elbow, the steep rake of a park bluff behind him. Here's me and my little brother, Ben, stuffed side by side into a kiddie ride, him grinning, me looking like I'm about to murder someone. Through the rickety rails, you can see the pyramid of a distant peak. Grand Canyon, Yosemite, Yellowstone—all the usual American family vacation goals plus a host of snowcapped hills and headlands I don't recognize. I see them now, great stoic sentinels, hulking in the shadows of a troubled time, lending their formidable mass to a world about to shatter. Long after my family disappeared, the mountains came back to claim me.

This is the story of how I climbed to the top of the world's highest peaks and navigated some dark valleys that are not easy for me to talk about. It's a story about resilience, the love child born to obstacles and avalanches, and about how the adventure of life evolves into exploration. Also, it's about how to pee while mountaineering, because for some reason, people always ask me about that. In order to tell the story in the most effective way possible, some characters and events have been composited, and conversations have been re-created to capture the spirit of the exchange to the best of my recollection. For a variety of reasons, many of the names have been changed. Events not relevant to the story at hand have been omitted. This memoir does not begin to cover the full scope of my life or career. I hope the people in my professional life and personal life will understand that their presence in this book does not directly measure their place in my heart. There are several versions of this story, and all of them are true in their own way, true as any memory shared with a friend in the shifting lamplight of perspective.

When it comes up in conversation with my friends, Stephanie is certain she's the one who said I should climb Mount Everest. Pippa says it started with a dare/double dare sort of email. Maya blames tequila, and I agree with her insofar as this is a story of unruly spirits. The foggy details no longer matter. I tend to fast-forward rather than rewind. Nostalgia is a waste of oxygen, and regret has a nasty tendency to avalanche. What matters is the mountain that stands before you.

PART I

GET YOUR AXE TOGETHER

1

I love when life points you in directions that you resist.
—MARTIN NWEEIA, MARINE BIOLOGIST

Hong Kong and I understood each other: both British by special dispensation rather than birth, two proud type A strivers who found ourselves in limbo. When Great Britain's ninety-nine-year lease expired in 1997, the Hong Kong colony was given to China. Margaret Thatcher negotiated a fifty-year grace period during which the residents of Hong Kong were allowed to cling to their British tearooms and free elections, but there was a palpable nervousness in the air. No one was quite sure what the future would look like. Likewise, in 2009, when a global economic meltdown rocked every corner of the financial world, everything I thought I knew about my future shifted. Through no fault or decision of our own, Hong Kong and I were ejected from a life of happy prosperity into a limbo of indecision, and Hong Kong handled it better than I did.

When I first moved to London in 1999, a woman with an MBA was like a unicorn walking in the door. I applied myself 140 percent, first as one of the youngest executive directors at Morgan Stanley, helping to build its European Consumer Division, then as finance director at Barclays, and finally as the commercial director of European Card Services at Bank of America. I earned awards and had more than two hundred people reporting to me. I sat on company boards and attended far too many management committees.

During the first decade of our marriage, Jonathan and I were equally committed to equally demanding careers, doing what we loved with unlimited upside. Most of the time I was in London, and the last couple of years he was in Tokyo. I would never ask him to forgo a career opportunity that took him to Asia, and he would never ask me to leave a job I loved in London, a quid pro quo key ingredient in the unique romantic glue that held us together. We were classic "chalk and cheese," living at times on separate continents, meeting up as often as possible at interesting places in between, comfortable enough with each other and ourselves that we never needed a joined-at-the-hip proximity that would force one of us to compromise. I never felt our long-distance relationship was a hassle or a drawback. It kept us from taking each other for granted and spurred us to visit a thousand off-the-beaten-path places in Southeast Asia we might have never seen otherwise. I saw my career as a hard-won chunk of territory that I'd gained a level of expertise in and could claim as my own as long as I worked hard enough to keep it.

It was devastating to learn that, in the best of circumstances, "job stability" is a fairy tale, a comforting bedtime story grown-ups tell themselves. As the London economy started to collapse, banks stopped lending and businesses went bankrupt. The UK followed the US into the worst recession since 1929, and expensive suits scurried for cover. The atmosphere in my posh office building in London thinned noticeably as the money drained out of it. Every time I called the number on someone's business card and found it disconnected, it felt like watching a colleague fall down an elevator shaft.

I'd been living in London long enough to become a dual citizen with both British and American passports, so not only was I between jobs, I was now between homelands. Because Jonathan was in Asia, his business was booming while mine was evaporating, so it made sense for the first time that we might find one place that suited us both. We had many long late-night discussions about logistics and possibilities, comparative tax rates, and all the ineffable factors that make a place feel like home. When we filtered all that through a map of the most appealing job opportunities, the choice came down to Hong Kong or Sydney.

"Hong Kong," I said. "No contest."

Really, think about it. Australia is home to 60 percent of the most dangerous creatures on land or sea, including spiders, snakes, and the duck-billed platypus. Hong Kong, on the other hand, is a six-star, high-tech, first world metroplex filled with shoe stores and opportunities. I loved the way the city moved me—literally. Hong Kong has the world's largest system of outdoor escalators and slide-walks so everyone can go about their business as quickly as possible. The Chinese place tremendous stock in efficiency, hard work, and the acquisition of wealth. I'm down with all of that. Hong Kong had everything I valued in a workplace. Everything except a job. The full impact of this didn't sink in until we'd been there for a while.

There was no pressure for me to get a job right away. I'd saved judiciously for this rainy day, and Jonathan's income kept us afloat, but it went against the very grain of me to be in a place I had no reason for being. Purpose, for me, was more than a point of honor; it was a source of self-worth. Not since I was fifteen had I spent a whole day not working. My entire adult life, I went wherever I needed to go for work. This was the first time I moved somewhere to *not* work, and the moving sidewalks of Hong Kong whisked me along, making sure I went nowhere as efficiently as possible.

There's a moment in *American Psycho* when a small group of executives compare business cards, sizing each other up by thickness of paper and quality of typeface, until one of them silences the rest by whipping out Paul Allen's card: a holy relic in tasteful off-white with Copperplate Gothic print. I no longer had a place in that sort of happy hour networking conversation, no embossed business card to proffer over lunch. If I'd offered my card, the receiver would have found the phone disconnected. Turns out, I was the one falling down the elevator shaft. When I stood at the Kee Club bar with the type of executives who used to be my peers, they did worse than judge me; they looked past me like I'd turned to cellophane. I ended up deep in conversation with the only other woman in the room: the bar manager, Stephanie, who introduced me to her fabulous expat friends, Pippa and Maya. The four of us quickly formed a tight little tribe. Despite coming from completely different backgrounds, we had the right chemistry for enlightened conversation, a good mix of wit and sympathy with sarcasm dished as needed.

Hong Kong was an easy segue from London. Almost everyone spoke English, and teatime was sacred. Red phone booths and double-decker buses were identical to the ones on the streets of Kensington. Chinese art and architecture wove seamlessly through the cityscape, but it was jarring to hear the Chinese national anthem at the start of the evening news, which was broadcast on state-run TV in Mandarin, not the Cantonese spoken by native Hong Kongers and certainly not English. It was clearly promoting Chinese nationalism, produced by the government-appointed Committee on the Promotion of Civic Education. On a corner across the street from a 7-Eleven in Kowloon, there used to be an open-air newsstand called Wong Fook Hing Book Store. People would joke that if you couldn't find what you were looking for, you must be in the Wong Fook Hing Book Store. I was starting to feel that on a cosmic level: Wong Fook Hing place, Wong Fook Hing time. There was plenty of activity in Hong Kong, but I longed for a purpose I could sink my teeth into.

I insisted on having an office in our apartment. Who would I be without an office? I didn't know and didn't want to find out. Before I knew how to drive, I understood how a person's work defines her, how it empowers her to carve out her place in the world. My first jobs were typical entry-level gigs for an American teenager: babysitting, flipping burgers, delivering newspapers, and waiting tables. I had no choice about working or not working back then. When I was in high school, I was an emancipated minor living on my own in the house that had been my family's: a two-story Colonial-style home in the suburbs of Detroit. My unsupervised crib was a natural hub for anyone who needed to escape their parents. A lot of people were constantly coming and going, but I had my tight little tribe—my friend Aspen, plus a few other people I could depend on to help me cook, clean, maintain the sprawling yard, and throw the drunks out when necessary.

After a full day of school and a full shift of work, we'd do our homework and post up on the sofa in front of the television like puppies in a crate. Looking back from the perspective of a jaded adult, I find it remarkable that, in the absence of adult supervision, we effectively created this nucleus of stability. We needed *family*, so we formed one and made it functional, each of us playing a necessary role, and my role was the Rock. I wanted to be like Dustin Hoffman in *Marathon Man*, able to stoically withstand pain and fear. "I am the rock!" became my mantra when I was exhausted, pushing through until closing time. *I am the rock. I am the rock.*

Via one of those work/school cross-pollination programs, I got a job in a busy real estate office. My boss was a fabulous accountant and super-cool mom whose son was in the Romantics, a Detroit new wave band who'd made it onto *Billboard*'s Hot 100 with their hit single "What I Like About You." Like that song, Romantic Mom was relentlessly straightforward, on beat, and going places. She fit right in with the leather-skirt crowd whenever the Romantics played in downtown Detroit, and sometimes, when I had performed above and beyond the call, she would take me with her.

This was 1983, a tipping point when electric typewriters were still standard office equipment, but computers were about to become a part of our lives. Romantic Mom's office was on the leading edge of all that, because the many-tentacled beast that is the multiple listing service (MLS) was such a natural point of entry for computers. Real estate is an elegantly binary business model—you need a house, I have a house, let's do business—and Realtors were the perfect early adopters, a highly motivated genus unto themselves, people who rock out of bed every morning ready to hit the pavement. Working in Romantic Mom's office, I was caught up in that resonant energy and learned a lot about the real estate business.

Long story short, that job and I transformed each other. The difference between a real estate office with a typewriter and a real estate office with a computer—that's the difference between me when I started that job and me when I went off to college. When I turned eighteen and my father sold our family home in Michigan, I was savvy enough to enter the property ladder, buying a place of my own in New York City, and I was all about that property ladder. I felt empowered by it. Like any kid from a dysfunctional home, I craved stability, but being born in the sign of Sagittarius, I also longed to shoot my arrow into the distance and explore new horizons. Real estate—investing in general, if you do it right—can be a delicious mix of the two.

In Hong Kong, the floor-to-ceiling windows next to my painfully clean desk offered a panoramic view of the city. I watched traffic pile up during morning rush hour, waiting for some kind of sign, my legs twitching to take me somewhere, my fingers tapping away, needing a list to cross things off. Paper napkin, spreadsheet, stone tablet—if I can list a thing, I can burn it down. I learned my first lists in Catechism: seven deadly sins, fourteen stations of the cross, Ten Commandments. I learned early and hard that the list is the high road to accountability. Later on, as a protégé of Jack Welch's leadership training at GE, I was exposed to his high-level brand of list making as a way of setting goals and clarifying strategy. I remember studying his penmanship on paper like it was the Dead Sea Scrolls.

My list—The List—evolved over a period of months; I didn't just scribble it down off the top of my head. I really thought about it, tasking myself with tough questions about intention and logistics. I inventoried my inner and outer assets. The easily defined resources included my savings, education, and a long-unused aesthetician's license. The slipperier, more esoteric gifts included things like tenacity, an eagerness to learn, intense concentration, and the patience of an egalitarian spouse. That was the easy part: clarifying what I had, the bird in hand. Then I started thinking about what I needed.

When the weather was mild, I walked around and thought about it. When rain or Hong Kong's typhoon signals kept me inside, I ran on a treadmill and thought about it. I thought about it while I watched Jonathan build a model clipper ship on the kitchen counter, turning the mast between his fingers, fitting the meticulous bits together. I kept my thoughts to myself until I was certain about five specific items that would define the parameters of my new purpose. I wrote them down, got them locked and loaded, but it took a few shots of tequila at the Kee Club before I felt ready to share The List with my girlfriends.

"The number one thing is a goal," I said. "A clearly defined end game."

"Go for that goal, darling." Stephanie raised a glass to it. "Be a goal digger."

"Two, it has to be quantifiable, something I can measure and say, '*Yes!* I did it. One hundred percent.'"

"Or, you know, *ninety-two* percent," said Pippa. "You get points for trying."

"One. Hundred. Percent," I clapped back. "Fuck that wobbly 'everybody's special' bullshit."

We drank to being special.

"Three: I see a two- to three-year timeline. Start now. Get 'er done. The financial sector will be back on track by 2012. I'll pick up my career and forget this happened." (Good thing my new purpose had nothing to do with economic forecasting, because I was spectacularly wrong about this.)

"Four," I said. "It has to be challenging. Audacious, even."

"To audacity!" Maya poured another round.

"Five. Last but not least. It has to be totally unrelated to financial services. Cough. Obvious reasons. No circular references."

"Darling, you've inspired me with this list-making activity," said Pippa. "You really have. We should all have a grand purpose burning within us like a peptic ulcer."

"To the purpose-driven life!" Stephanie poured the shots.

"So what does it all add up to?" Maya asked. "What's your new purpose?"

"It's a work in progress," I said, "but I was thinking I should cure malaria."

"Oh." She averted her eyes. "Not to be negative, but . . ."

"That's admirable, V," said Pippa, "but seriously, within two to three years? I'd leave that to the Gates Foundation. Why not create some lotion or potion? You're good at that."

"That's missing a defined end point. A project like that just lingers like the smell of durian fruit. Although—think of all those antioxidants."

"Get a black belt," said Maya. "You'd look fabulous in full judogi."

"Audacity factor."

"Rob a bank?"

"I said *unrelated* to the financial sector."

"Climb Mount Everest," said Stephanie.

At least, I think it was Stephanie. Or did Stephanie say that *she* was going to climb Mount Everest? The whole thing goes fuzzy after the third or fourth shot of tequila, but the suggestion never struck me as ridiculous. I was a climber. I had climbed out of a completely collapsed home life and created my own nicely functional take on a family unit with a revolving cast of satellite friends from the age of fifteen. I had climbed the stepladder of community college to a four-year degree and scrambled over a lot of logistical roadblocks to an internal MBA at GE and an external MBA at the NYU Stern School of Business. I had climbed the corporate ladder in an AAA-rated business that rang the century bell on Wall Street in an era that was notoriously cutthroat. And I had climbed Mount Kilimanjaro.

That expedition back in 2005 started much the same way this endeavor did: hyperbole. I always came up with over-the-top holiday plans while everyone else talked about going home to their Rockwellian family gathering. The difference between Kilimanjaro and Everest—one of many things I love about Kili—is that you can share Kilimanjaro with people who aren't necessarily hard-core climbers. Mount Kilimanjaro is a dormant volcano in Tanzania, the highest mountain on the African continent, with the summit at 19,340 feet. That's no walk in the park, but it's a pleasant two-week expedition you can do in regular hiking boots. Kili's been summited by a six-year-old American boy, an eighty-eight-year-old retired orthodontist, and hundreds of thousands of people in between. I was in good shape for a banker but not an athlete by nature or conditioning. I had turned forty only a few months earlier, so I was just starting to dip a toe into the Power Decades, that middle period of a woman's life where she realizes she is the world's foremost authority on herself. Jonathan had no interest in this grand adventure, so I recruited one of the few people I knew I could count on to be up for almost anything.

"Kilimanjaro?" Aspen said. "Hell yes!" This is why I keep Aspen on speed dial, even though we sometimes go years between phone calls.

We flew from Heathrow to Kenya on December 9, 2005, spent the night in Nairobi, and then took a puddle jumper to Tanzania. Rolling grasslands stretched out wide and dry between the villages and the snowcapped mountains on the horizon. The first day, we hiked for six hours up well-established trails through thick woods and lush vegetation. Sometimes there were steps cut into the hillside, reinforced with railroad ties. The second day, we climbed over boulders and rocky paths dotted with scrub and small gnarled trees draped with moss that reminded me of a haunted house. As the sun was going down, we reached Shira Camp at 12,300 feet, and we could see the summit in the distance, still four days away, protruding above the clouds like an island in the sky. On the third day, we swapped our shorts and T-shirts for sweats and hoodies and wool caps with earflaps. We labored up and over a sharp ridge called Shark's Tooth.

I was full of vim and vigor all this time, leaving the group to jog up a hill or nip off on a side trip, taking pictures, feeling a bit impatient with the plodding guides who kept telling me, "*Pole, pole*," which is Swahili for "slowly, slowly."

"I'm fine," I kept telling them. "I'm good!"

"*Pole, pole*, miss. You have to acclimatize."

Aspen wisely followed their advice, but I continued dashing here and there until I hit the wall. There's no way to truly understand what acclimatization is until you feel your entire body turning to wet cement. I couldn't run anymore. I could hardly keep up or catch my breath. The cheeky guide laughed and said, "That, my friend, is acclimatization."

People say "thin air," but the air at sea level is exactly the same as the air on top of Everest: 21 percent oxygen, 78 percent nitrogen, and a buffet of trace gases like argon, carbon dioxide, and random *what's that smell?* molecules. What changes with altitude is atmospheric pressure. As that pressure drops, oxygen molecules move farther apart. At sea level, you always have a dense selection of oxygen bubbles available in the immediate neighborhood of your face. Above the clouds, not so much. This is why oxygen masks drop down if an airplane loses pressure, and it's why climbers move slowly at altitude.

I still had a lot to learn, but Kili gave me my first taste of acclimatization, so if nothing else, I understood the mantra "Climb high, sleep low." Two steps forward, one step back. Up to a wall of hanging rocks, down to camp at 13,000 feet. Up to the edge of a crater, down to camp at 15,000 feet. Little by little, you coax your body to produce more oxygen-rich red blood cells.

We started at 11 PM walking up an endless series of switchbacks, beneath the full moon with thick cloud cover below. It was cold, and we wrapped ourselves in winter coats, guided by headlamps that lent an eerie glow to the ground around us. We reached Stella Point first, taking a short break, and proceeded forty-five minutes onward to Uhuru Peak, where we saw the glaciers for the first time. The rising sun revealed the bald summit and rocky ash pits and lit up our exhausted, elated faces.

I asked Aspen recently, "What do you remember most about Kili?"

"I recall you complaining about rationing toilet paper and running out and having to borrow my roll," said Aspen. "That last night climb, I flipped out when the heating pad in my glove went cold, and I thought I was going to get frostbite. The whole caravan had to stop so I could put a new warmer in my glove. I got a radiation burn on my forehead when we finally got to the top. They warned me not to take my hat off. I took it off. My forehead was purple for two days. We smelled like rot from sweating and farting all the time."

Ah, yes. No one tells you that passing gas is your body's way of letting you know that you're acclimatizing. You and everyone else. Climbing a mountain is something you should attempt with someone you know extremely well or not at all, because of all the strange ways your body reacts to high altitude. I also remember Aspen trudging along with toilet paper puffing out of both nostrils, persevering despite a series of horrific nosebleeds. Clearly, the takeaway here is: bring plenty of toilet paper. Climbers call it "mountain money."

I blessed and cursed the big camera that hung heavily around my neck, bouncing against my breastbone all the way up and back. I took hundreds of breathtaking photographs, but few of them are from the descent. While I was conducting research, preparing for my first attempt on Everest, I watched hundreds of hours of video—people ascending, summiting, celebrating—but there's rarely anything about the descent. It's as if a person climbs for days or weeks and then some magic funicular ferries them safely down. The truth is, once you've summited, you are faced with the reality that the summit is not the goal; it's only half the way to the real goal, which is getting home alive. The summit is only halfway.

Now you must reverse engineer the entire trek with gravity hammering your kneecaps and only a fraction of the adrenaline that drove you on your way up.

It's the same way in business. A spectacular crash and burn makes for a great story if it's the setup for a spectacular comeback, but there's little written about the type of reversal most people will experience in the long game of any career. The glacial decay of the typewriter industry doesn't make for a very energizing motivational seminar. They don't tell you how losing a career feels like losing a family and losing the World Series and losing your lunch all at the same time and that you have no way of knowing if you'll ever get back on your feet again.

I hadn't quite wrapped my head around it then, but that first year in Hong Kong was my descent from a twenty-year career high. That "two- to three-year timeline" stipulation was laughable. I can't imagine now why I ever thought it was possible for everything to go back to "normal" or why I would have ever wanted that. Clearly, I hadn't accepted the reality that the life I'd built for myself—the life I was proud of, the life I loved—was over. I never gave myself credit for the grieving such a thing demands. In the context of mountaineering, the descent is when the most deaths occur—and probably the most life as well. The most fear. The most loneliness. The most come-to-Jesus moments. But you don't let yourself go there. You keep putting one foot in front of the other.

Aspen and I hiked most of the way down Kili without speaking, focused on breathing and freshly humbled by the mountain.

"Mostly," Aspen says now, "I remember the utter silence and the views that went on forever. The rocks sounded like glass breaking when you walked across them."

The morning after the tequila shots with my girlfriends, I woke up before dawn, only slightly hungover, and lay there listening to Jonathan snore like a sea lion.

The Brits have a perfect expression: "The penny dropped." It refers to that moment when an idea slips into your head like a coin into a slot, and it fits so precisely, it sets everything in motion. A pay phone call connects. A player piano scrolls. A pinball begins its wild ricochet. I was suddenly crystal clear about my new purpose. Climbing Everest checked every box on The List:

1. Clearly defined goal. (Climbing Everest.)
2. Measurable success. (8,848 meters as a Brit, 29,035 feet American.)
3. Two- to three-year timeline. (Doable with determined optimism.)
4. Audacious/challenging. (Take your pick.)
5. Nothing to do with finance. (*Voilà*. Flag planted.)

I knew some people would see this new direction as random, but not the people who mattered to me.

"Spousey?" I said. "I'm going to climb Mount Everest."

Jonathan blinked sleep from his eyes and said, "How much will it cost?"

2

They may well ask why climb the highest mountain? . . .
We choose to go to the moon in this decade, and do the other
things, not because they are easy, but because they are hard.
—JOHN F. KENNEDY, RICE UNIVERSITY, 1962

Like any big endeavor, climbing Mount Everest takes a combination of opportunity and preparedness. Some ingredients are in the "got it or don't" category—focus, desire, a fire in the belly—but acts of God aside, the rest is within your control. A skill can be taught and therefore learned. Physical conditioning can be marshaled with commitment and hard work. Wherever you are right now, that's your starting point for whatever comes next, and the beginning of anything is information. My painfully clean desk quickly became cluttered with books, maps, DVDs, and hastily scribbled notes. Google was my new best friend.

SEARCH: climb Everest

48,700,000 results. The first few entries were paid ads for consultants and expeditions, and most of them asked the same question: *Do you have what it takes?* My kneejerk response was *Yes, I do!* but I was pragmatic enough to reality-check myself.

SEARCH: what it takes to climb Everest

If you type that in today, at the top of 21,800,000 results, you might see an article from the *New York Times* headlined "You Want to Climb Mount Everest? Here's What It Takes" or a blog post titled "7 Attributes Required to Climb Mount Everest." What I saw in 2010 was a less extensive motherlode of information. The takeaway: Everest demanded the same thing from contemporary climbers that it demanded from Tenzing and Hillary, the first to summit in 1953: mental strength, physical stamina, mad alpine mountaineering skills, lots of luck, and a deep, well-informed respect for the mountain herself. I would have to educate myself—from the ground up, if you'll pardon a pun.

SEARCH: Mount Everest

Mount Everest, the highest point on Earth, is called Sagarmatha on the Nepali side and Chomolungma from Tibet's perspective. It towers between Nepal and China with the international border running smack across the summit, where climbers sometimes face howling 200-mile-an-hour jet stream winds. It was named Mount Everest by the Royal Geographical Society in 1865 after Sir George Everest, the British surveyor general of India at the time, but I doubt this meant much to imperious Chomolungma.

There are two popular routes to the top of Everest: the South Col route, which starts in Nepal's Khumbu Valley, and the Northeast Ridge route via China. It's debatable which is the safer way up, and I quickly discovered that the climbing community will eagerly pile on to a bombastic debate of any topic from international politics to the thread count of your socks. Often the people who were most strident were armchair adventurers—"all hat and no cattle," as they say in America—but the mountaineering world is fiercely competitive. Battles rage over who was first or fastest and who had funding or oxygen or a single chewable children's aspirin to thin the blood. God forbid someone should take a vitamin C tablet and fail to make a full report.

This surprised me a little, because even though I'm a competitive person by nature, my initial impression of mountaineering was that it was not a competitive sport, and that's part of what appealed to me. Every 8,000-meter peak had already been summited by the time I was even born. I did not see climbing as a zero-sum game; my summiting Everest, for example, would not preclude anyone else from doing so. The only person I was competing with was myself, summoning the drive to push beyond my limit when I felt I couldn't go any farther. I had zero interest in arguing with anyone, so I lurked without commenting. "Seek first to understand" and all that.

As I went down the rabbit hole of climbing forums, blogs, and periodicals, I started compiling a shopping list, but "Things I'll Need to Climb Everest" ended up being more of a glossary, my introduction to the language of climbing.

Ascender: a latched clamp that slides up but doesn't pull down, helping you climb up a rope like a single-minded inchworm.
Carabiner: a metal shackle with a spring-loaded gate for connecting two things that might need to be unconnected in a terrifying hurry. Or stay connected in a way that might save your life.
Crampons: spiked traction devices that strap on to your boot and enable you to walk up an icy incline like a fiddler crab, invented in 1908 by British mountaineer Oscar Eckenstein, leader of the first expedition to make a credible attempt on K2.

Each item led to some fascinating side road into climbing science, history, and culture. I learned that a gully filled with ice and snow is called a *couloir* and that dexamethasone is used to treat severe altitude sickness, which is what happens when your brain or lungs are deprived of oxygen and swell up like a water balloon. There were endless anagrams: HAP, a high-altitude porter, not to be confused with HAPE, high-altitude pulmonary edema. A HAP with HAPE—more water balloon troubles.

I think Jonathan expected me to spend a few weeks steeped in research and come to the sensible conclusion that this was an insane whim we would laugh about someday, but the more time I spent with the idea, the deeper it went. It snagged me inside like a barbed hook, stirring a specific kind of excitement, hope, and curiosity.

To get a feel for the expedition experience, I ordered DVDs of a Discovery Channel series called *Everest: Beyond the Limit*, which follows New Zealand mountaineer Russell Brice and his wingman, Phurba Tashi Sherpa, as they lead expeditions to the summit of Mount Everest. I quickly watched the first two seasons, and by the time it was over, I felt well and truly chin-slapped by the visceral reality of what a climber experiences, especially in the "Death Zone" over 26,000 feet. The sight of feet blackened with frostbite made my own toes curl up like cashews. One guy moaned that the altitude had caused him to shit his pants at the moment of truth. Someone else complained that the expedition had cost him $40,000, and he wasn't even going to summit. It was definitely too early to mention that horrifying fact to Jonathan. Also best not to mention the dead bodies brazenly featured in the show's sizzle reel.

Everest has its ghosts. When George Mallory's body was discovered in 1999, he was facedown on the mountainside where he'd lain for seventy-five years, a snapped rope around his torso, arms outstretched, indicating a posture of "self-arrest," as if he was struggling to slow a swift descent gone out of control. The fabric of his tweed suit had crumbled away, leaving only the name tag, G. LEIGH MALLORY, but skin on his exposed back remained remarkably intact, like white marble sculpted by Michelangelo. The body of Hannelore Schmatz, the first woman to die on the upper slopes of Everest, remained for twenty years, reclining against an eroding backpack, eyes fixed on a distant ridge. As climbers passed by on their way up and down the Southeast Ridge, she kept her quiet vigil until high winds tumbled her down the Kangshung Face into some hidden resting place. Sleeping Beauty, Green Boots—enough stories to fill the long, dark nights at Base Camp. Images arose throughout my research, appearing and disappearing as the snow and ice shifted around them.

I couldn't help noting that, throughout most of the *Everest: Beyond the Limit* episodes, Monica, the expedition doctor, was the only woman in sight. The climbers were almost all men, hacking at the ice and slogging up the unforgiving glacier, fueled by testosterone and bravado, but I couldn't see how that was much different from the financial services industry.

"The Everest thing is happening," I told Jonathan. "In a commercial sense, I mean. People are doing it. A lot of the professional guides I've read about are offering expeditions every season. I can do this."

"I have no doubt," he said, "but at what cost? You spent an entire career up to your neck in finance. Suddenly it's as if you don't know how to balance a checkbook. You worked for decades to build this nest egg for your retirement. Now you're talking about investing a major portion of it in . . . in what?"

"Jonathan, what do you want me to say? I'm sitting like a kid in the naughty chair, trying to rationalize a choice most people will find completely irrational. It's easy to explain why I shouldn't go and impossible to explain why I should. I don't know what draws a bull to a red cape or a salmon up a stream. I only know I *need* this. I need to know if I have what it takes to summit. To survive."

Jonathan made as reasoned an argument as anyone is capable of making, but to his credit, he didn't throw down gauntlets or pose ultimatums. Looking ahead with the unflinching eye of an accountant, he measured what this meant for both of us. It would consume all my time and attention, not to mention a significant chunk of my savings, because I wasn't about to scrimp on anything safety-wise— the one thing on which we could wholeheartedly agree. Books, blogs, and documentaries don't spend a lot of time discussing what an upward slog it is to love someone who insists on climbing mountains, but it is a grueling test of will in itself, I now understand.

When I went to Pippa, hoping for a sympathetic ear, she said, "The whole thing strikes me as rather loopy-loop, V. In the most fabulous possible way, of course. But still."

"I'm as smart and fit and determined as any individual on these expeditions."

"I'm sure you are," said Pippa. "I just never saw you as the Captain Cook sort. Performing daily ablutions by the side of a stream. Beating your delicate laundry on a rock."

She raised some practical issues. Truth is, I wasn't a camper, but I'm a big believer in learning on the job. I'm an extreme personality, equally at home in a five-star hotel or a two-person tent.

"Climbing is a skill," I said. "A skill can be taught and therefore learned. You just have to dive in, feet first, accepting that the only thing you don't know is everything you don't know."

Training was my full-time job now. Building my daily schedule into a spreadsheet felt like a ceremony of sorts. It was a contract I made with myself. Keeping to the schedule, I rolled out of bed every morning, ate a big bowl of blueberries and granola for breakfast—a habit I picked up from my grandmother—and then set out running Rocky Balboa style up and down the hills of Hong Kong, sprinting up and down stairs instead of taking the public escalators. I worked out for two hours at the gym, ran home, wolfed down my lunch, and then ran back to the gym for the afternoon. I searched out a personal trainer who was up for the challenge of learning about high-altitude mountaineering, a New Zealander named Ross Eathorne, a holistic fitness specialist. He did a fine job hectoring me as I pumped free weights and kettlebells. My main focus was cardio, but I also wanted to make sure I was holding my own when it came time to shoulder my share of the climbing equipment and camping gear.

After six months of religious adherence to this schedule, my arms were like Gatling guns, my calves sculpted titanium. I generated a lot of laundry every day, but my confidence soared. Jonathan and I discussed the financial realities and decided the next logical step would be a practice run. Some things you have to learn by doing, and ice climbing is one of them. I comparison shopped, vetting all the available guide services. The idea was to familiarize myself with the mountaineering kit, get a feel for the equipment, and demystify the ice climbing technique.

I found a mountaineering course based in the tiny town of Wanaka on the west coast of New Zealand's South Island, which is reasonably close to Hong Kong. Jonathan was immediately supportive of my plan to go there. I suspect he was hoping I would scratch this itch and scotch the whole Everest component, but I knew even then this was just Mountaineering 101. I booked a week with an experienced guide who would take me up to Fox Glacier and optimistically invited a few friends to come along.

According to legend—and it's a legend I love, so I don't give a whit about its veracity or lack thereof—the great explorer Ernest Shackleton placed an ad in a London newspaper:

MEN WANTED for hazardous journey, small wages, bitter cold, long months of complete darkness, constant danger, safe return doubtful, honor and recognition in case of success.

—Ernest Shackleton, 4 Burlington St.

I sent a parody of this message around to a handful of friends, adding, "Anyone who wants in on learning to climb in New Zealand, opine now or forever hold back. Next stop: Everest!"

Replies trickled in. Some assumed it was a joke. Others thought I'd slipped a cog because the industry in which I'd built my life was now a dumpster fire. Even people who knew me well enough to take me at my word were skeptical. This didn't hurt my feelings at all. It's important to voice our intentions once we're certain of them, but it isn't necessary for everyone else to buy into them. I know the drill. I read *The Secret*. I would always attempt to draw positive energy, but I didn't need anyone's permission. All my best friends, including my husband, are creative and cerebral. Maya describes me as "an action figure waiting to happen."

Everyone assured me they'd be with me in spirit. Pippa and her boys planned to follow my progress up Fox Glacier with paper maps and smiley-face stickers. It seemed appropriate to gather at the Kee Club for a little send-off soiree, since that's where the whole thing had started six months earlier. In ceremonial fashion—lighthearted but not at all joking—each person there presented me with a talisman. Pippa gave me a small silver om symbol.

"It represents the world and everything in it," she said. "And it's a reminder to breathe."

Maya gave me an angel with wide-open wings, and my friend Bridie gave me an Irish claddagh ring. Jonathan placed a medal on my palm: Saint Christopher, patron saint of travelers. I added these to a long chain around my neck, along with my grandmother's delicate wedding ring, which didn't even fit my pinkie finger. I would wear this odd assortment of good luck charms on every expedition, big or small, for the next ten years. Always adding to it, never subtracting.

3

Fox Glacier is a river of ice fed by rain and snow that dumps into the mountains, riding on a wind pattern they call the "Roaring Forties." I smiled at that, being well into my own roaring forties, which some people might think is an odd time to start mountain climbing. Mark Sedon, the blue-eyed Kiwi who was my mountaineering instructor, was not of that opinion.

"Nah, that's choice, bro," he said, latching crampons to the soles of his boots. "You can't really know yourself till midlife."

I liked his laid-back Kiwi way of talking, but more than that, I appreciated how knowledgeable he was about the glacier and how willing he was to share his experience, educating me without making me feel stupid. Mark was an IFMGA (International Federated Mountain Guides Associations) guide, which meant he was certified in all three disciplines: rock, alpine, and ski. In the setting of corporate training or a visit from the IT tech, if someone feels the need to underline their expertise with arcane lingo, or if they advertise their know-how in the context of another person's don't-know-how, you can smell an insecurity that makes it hard to have faith in their actual skills. Not this guy.

My first day on the glacier, Mark and I started from scratch: on with the crampons, on with the harness, and once we were roped up, the glacier travel began. Over and over and over again, Mark would have me climb up and down the same wall of bluish ice. If he detected any attempt to shortcut a process, any lapse in attention, or a moment of bad form, he immediately called me on it and made me do it all over again.

At the end of the day, he rustled up a respectable camp-style dinner, something guides tend to be good at. Mark told me about his wife and his climbing life, and I told him about Jonathan, my old job, and my ambition to climb Everest. He was a climber, so in his mind, it was more surprising that anyone would *not* want to climb Everest. I stumbled off to our hut to sleep the untroubled sleep of someone who is physically wiped out but happy with their day's work. This was my first time sharing a hut with a stranger, but I quickly learned the etiquette: orderly stowing of gear, mutual respect for whatever modesty is possible, and a hall pass for any noises the body makes as it adjusts to its surroundings. Before the sun came up, I was jolted awake by the screeching of massive olive-green parrots that circled the hut, scouting for carrion and making an impressive racket.

"Kea birds," said Mark. "They're just curious, but if you see you with food in your hand, be careful. They're a determined lot."

"So we have that in common," I said.

"Rattle your dags. We'll break new trail up the gully there."

We hiked upward, onto the sweeping blue-and-white contours of the glacier. Waterfalls filled deep holes with cold, clean water that tasted vaguely of iron and fresh snow, like the snowbanks that lined Lake St. Clair in Michigan, where I grew up.

Every winter of my childhood was a steady gray parade of snow, sleet, hail, and ice storms, which I loved, because that meant my dad would take me ice fishing. He dragged his homemade ice shanty on a sled, and without giving it a second thought, I followed him out onto the frozen lake to his airboat, which roared to life, powered by a small airplane engine. When we found the right spot, I waited in the freezing cold while he drilled and drilled, down into the blue-white ice for what seemed like forever, crafting a perfect square. Then he positioned his shanty over the hole, and we sat on upturned buckets inside. Every once in a while, I saw the silver flash of a Northern pike or walleye beneath the surface, and I'd suck in a breath, but before I could squeal or say a word, my dad would hold up his hand.

"Shhhhhh . . ."

With the precision of a rattlesnake, he struck his spear into the water and dragged up a wounded walleye. I held a big bucket in place while he disengaged the bloody spear and settled next to the hole again. Sometimes I'd get up and wander around on the frozen lake, picking up dead eels and finding other cool stuff I could take to school for show-and-tell, but for the most part, we sat in silence for hours, my dad and I, staring into that hole. I could see how thick the frozen water was. The space heater that kept the shanty toasty warm didn't melt the surface one bit. The ice always held us up. It separated us from the dark water, where I could imagine shipwrecks and drowned sailors and the scuttled cars of old-time mobsters.

"Heels down," Mark reminded me. "Trust your feet."

Slamming my axe into a steep overhang and kicking in my crampons to create purchase gave me a sense of comfort. With my body pressed against the face of the glacier, I could smell the metallic tang of the ice screw I clipped in to.

Mark was methodical and technically well versed. He put safety first, pushing me just far enough to make sure I got a thrill without putting me in any real danger. He was also quite pleasant to look at, which didn't distract me from my task but didn't make the experience less enjoyable. Climbers in general have a certain wind-burned beauty that, if you want to be flowery about it, radiates from within. They share a healthy glow, robust energy, and lean conditioning, and let's face it, everyone looks great in an alpine sweater. It's not until we've spent ten hours mountaineering in the glacier and pulling ourselves up ten inches at a time that we look sweaty, gaunt, and exhausted, with cracked lips and raw, crusty nostrils. In terms of wear and tear, one week on the ice is equal to ten months on a tour bus with Kris Kristofferson, but by the end of it, I felt like an old hand. I was ready to take on the next challenge.

"Where can I put these new skills to use?" I asked.

"Lots of options in Asia," said Mark. "Top hundred tallest mountains in the world—literally, one through one hundred. Basically unlimited potential between here and Everest."

I'd come to the same conclusion after six months of studying maps and scanning the internet, but I kept coming back to Everest. Most of the commercial operators sold Everest in three packages: Base Camp (where expedition support staff stays with equipment, kitchen, and mess tents), Camp 2 (high enough on the mountain to crank up some red blood cells), and Summit (living the dream). I felt like Goldilocks. The summit was too hot. Base Camp was too cold. Camp 2 was just right.

When I called Jonathan to tell him I was on my way home, I pitched it to him.

"If Everest is the objective," I said, "why not go there and get some experience without actually trying for the summit?"

"Go on," he said warily.

"Don't worry, Spousey. I haven't completely lost the plot." I put it to him in the language he understands: numbers. "Everest Base Camp is at 17,300 feet, 2,000 feet lower than Kilimanjaro. I'd be using hiking boots, no climbing kit. If I go to Camp 2, I'm 2,000 feet higher than Kili, on actual snow and ice, using the alpine kit, and getting the Everest experience I'll need for later on."

"When you go back for the summit."

"Yes. But for now, I'm focused on Camp 2."

He couldn't argue with my logic, because he didn't know the same everything I didn't know—that my Everest research had missed the forest for the trees. I'd delved into the history of Everest, its geography, and Nepal's current events. With my eye on the summit, kit, and training, I overlooked the first obstacle that lay immediately beyond Everest Base Camp on the South Col route. The Khumbu Icefall would be a straight red card.

4

Success is a lousy teacher.
—BILL GATES, *THE ROAD AHEAD*

The guide service sent me a packing list: two duffel bags, a large backpack, passport with seven passport photos, trekking poles, sleeping bag rated to 0 degrees Fahrenheit, Therm-a-Rest pad to put under my sleeping bag, backpack cover for the rain, light shoes for Base Camp, gaiters to protect my pants from mud, five pairs of socks and underwear, hiking boots, climbing boots, base layers, mid layers, hiking pants, climbing pants, insulated pants, down jacket, upper and lower breathable rain gear, light gloves, heavy gloves, hat, helmet, headlamp and batteries, water bottles, camera, pocketknife, water treatment tablets, watch, sunglasses, goggles, sun protection, toiletries, medical kit, snack food, iPod, Kindle, ice axe, crampons, climbing harness, ascender, mitts, and a bowl/cup/spoon set.

I had to Google several items to find out what they were, but I was determined to follow the list to the letter. And then I had to fit this entire kit in two large duffel bags that each weighed no more than fifty-five pounds. Jonathan stood in the doorway, observing the whole lot laid out on the living room floor, clearly doubtful.

"Ye of little faith," I chided. "Who's the organizer of tasks, corrector of mistakes, and juggler of one thousand and one things?"

"Would you like some help?"

"If you insist."

Luckily, my husband is an excellent packer of bags, being extensively well traveled and having survived a decade of boarding school.

"Is all this mandated," he asked, "or are you puffing with extras not on the list?"

"If by 'extras' you mean sports bras, yes. Inexplicably, sports bras are not on the list."

"What about these?" He held up a plain cotton dress and flip-flops.

"That's obviously for the post-climb celebration."

He dropped the dress and shoes into a discard pile and held up a supply of Cadbury chocolate bars. "And these?"

"Now you're just jealous."

Jonathan and I had always collaborated on dieting, and now I could eat whatever I wanted, knowing I'd burn it off in the blast furnace of high-altitude metabolism. It wasn't fair. Following the chocolate, he tasked me item by item, showing no mercy, reducing the unmanageable heap to a neat pile of mission-critical necessities and puzzle-piecing everything into the duffels.

Toward the end of March, I took a Dragonair flight to Kathmandu and transferred to a small twin-engine aircraft for the flight into Tenzing-Hillary Airport in the little town of Lukla, Nepal, where the runway is so short, the pilot has to slam on the brakes and execute a spin-out maneuver we used to call "doing a doughnut" back in Michigan. I met up with my guide, David, and three other climbers—a sixty-five-year-old South African man, a young South African woman, and a British gent—all attempting to summit. I felt a bit envious when I realized I was the only person whose goal was Camp 2, but that was my plan, and I was sticking to it. David had a miserable cold, so it was understandable that he was a bit grumpy and subdued, but his lassitude didn't exactly inspire confidence.

"We're about sixty-two kilometers from Base Camp," he told us over dinner. "I expect it will take us eight or nine days to walk in." He added in my direction, "We go slower on the way in because our body will be acclimatizing."

All right, I told myself, *just smile and nod*. I wanted to assume he didn't mean to cast me as the underachiever in the group, but just in case he did, I was ready to prove myself.

The elevation of Lukla is just over 9,200 feet. The plan was to ascend at least a thousand feet per day until we reached Everest Base Camp at 17,300 feet. (Frame of reference: 13,000 feet is where you jump out of the airplane when you're skydiving.) I understood the challenges of acclimatization, having experienced it on Kilimanjaro, but because of the training I'd been doing, this initial trekking was a piece of cake. The other climbers were plodding slowly along, carrying as little as possible. To me, that made them seem lazy and not team players with the Sherpa. I felt so good the first few days, I volunteered to carry additional weight for "extra training."

The snail's pace the other climbers were keeping left me itching with impatience. It reminded me of the way my grandfather used to putt along in his appalling olive-green Dodge Coronet. Once when we visited him in Pennsylvania, my little brother and I came in contact with some poison ivy while we were playing outside. On the way home, Ben and I felt like we were coming out of our skin, dying to get some cold water on our burning, itching arms and legs. We sat in the back seat, scratching at the raised red blisters, saying, "Step on it!" but our grandfather couldn't hear us and just rambled along. When our grandfather died in 1981, I inherited the old Dodge, and as I drove it back to Michigan, I had that pedal to the metal. The engine roared as if to say, *Finally! Thank you!*

I felt the same pleasant rush every time I ran ahead, keeping pace with the Sherpa porters, who were wonderful company. Most Sherpa are about my height—roughly five feet, four inches—so I had no trouble matching their stride. Nepali is their first language, but most have learned English, so we exchanged jokes and stories as we trekked along. I asked a thousand questions, and they were glad to tell me about their culture, proud history, and climbing stories. Born and raised in the Himalayas, the Sherpa were accustomed to the high altitude, so there was less need for them to force their bodies through the rigors of acclimatization. They were singing and conversing long after everyone else was too breathless to talk. They knew every meter of the mountain trails by heart, and they loved Chomolungma with a zealous, protective reverence. The peaks are home to their gods, something to be approached with respect and humility.

In my experience, the Sherpa children are ridiculously ador-able, the women are striking and wise, the men are dedicated to their families, and family is everything. Their stone houses are often handed down from generation to generation, and that tight family dynamic extends to the close-knit agricultural community. Most Sherpa's names are derived from the day of the week when they were born: Pasang for Friday, Pemba for Saturday, and so on. Others are named for some particular virtue the parents hoped their child would embody. Kalpana invokes imagination and cre-ativity. Rupesh means handsome.

A day or two out of Lukla, I noticed that some people in our group had their faces covered with buffs—elastic bandannas worn around the neck so they can be pulled up over your mouth and nose. The buff wasn't on the packing list, so I didn't have one. I zipped along, inhaling every bit of dirt, dust, and dung being kicked up by climbers, Sherpa, and the great shaggy yaks that lum-bered along, loaded with gear and provisions.

I was fine until we hit about 5,200 meters, approaching the Kongma La pass. David strode up beside me and said, "You're wheezing, Vanessa. You need to control your breathing."

I nodded, unable to answer. With my iPod playing in my ears, I hadn't heard myself. Now that I was aware of it, I could feel my chest banging with every breath. I turned off the iPod and made a conscious effort to put a lid on the extra cardio workout. I was determined not to be singled out again. David and I hadn't exactly been getting along, so anything coming from him felt like criticism, and I was storing up a list of my own pointers to levy back at him, should I live long enough.

Every night, we stopped at one of the tiny towns that dotted the mountain trails. Large teahouses had been built to accommodate a steady parade of passing trekkers. Each teahouse had a big common room outfitted with long wooden tables and benches where everyone gathered to eat spaghetti, pizza, or the Nepalese equivalent of Tex-Mex food, like dal bhat (cooked lentils and steamed rice), momos (dumplings with vegetables or chicken), rice, and noodles. The big room was heated by cast-iron stoves fueled with yak dung, and the burning dung filled the air with acrid gray smoke that made our eyes water. I tried to breathe the steam from my noodle bowl, but my lungs rebelled, stiffening, telling me to cough. The Sherpa were used to it, but the climbers and trekkers all sat around barking like a pack of hyenas. The higher we climbed, the colder it was, and the colder it was, the more yak dung was shoveled into those cast-iron stoves. I quickly learned it was better to forgo the warmth, slurp down my noodles as quickly as possible, and hurry upstairs to my sleeping bag in the drafty hostel.

When I told my South African teammate about my smoke avoidance scheme, he said, "Good on ya. Next time, don't forget the buff."

"Noted. Any other tips or tricks? I'm all ears."

"Panty liners," he said. "That's my secret."

"Excuse me?" I coughed.

"You know, you put 'em in your knickers when you're on your cycle? No better way to keep a man's skivvies clean throughout the expedition. I prefer the Carefree."

"Good to know."

I noticed a familiar face across the smoky room, a climber I'd met at Fox Glacier.

"Felix! Hi!" I waved, and he waved back from the long table where he sat with a merry band of climbers who seemed to be having a lot more fun than I was.

"Vanessa! Come join us," he called, and he didn't have to ask me twice. With a smile and a shrug to the man in panty liners, I scooped up my meal kit and hustled over to the table, where Felix scooted sideways to make a space for me. "Everyone, this is Vanessa. We met on Fox Glacier."

"Hey," I said, nodding to folks around the table, trying to make a note of everyone's name. You don't offer your hand on the mountain. Everyone's either carrying some communicable malady or trying to avoid it. I felt like the loner who'd been invited to the cool kids' table in the cafeteria. Felix and his teammates were all accomplished mountaineers, so I was happy to sit and listen as they talked about their experiences, good and bad.

"Ice climbing practice must have gone well," Felix observed. "I can't believe you're here already."

"I'm just going for Camp 2," I said. "This is a dry run for me."

"It's a steep learning curve," he said tactfully.

"Is everyone on your team planning to summit?"

"That's the dream."

His team crowed and raised their tin cups to toast the dream, and I suddenly missed my girlfriends more than my watery eyes could bear.

Over the next several days, our teams crossed paths again at teahouses farther up the mountain trail. Felix and I always found an opportunity to chat, comparing notes about our respective climbing companies, teammates, and—most important—our guides, who wear a variety of hats on any expedition: safety patrol, nature ranger, camp cook, bartender, and route finder. As with any managerial role, tact and compassion are paramount. Meanwhile, it's important for climbers to remember that this fellow human being is just as exhausted and cold as anyone else. They've made this journey before, but that doesn't make the mountain any lower or the smoke any less acrid.

Felix liked his team's guide, Daniel, who was guiding with International Mountain Guides (IMG), a tall outdoorsman with a strong chin and healthy belly laugh, and the more he extolled Daniel's virtues, the more David's approach grated on my nerves. I wondered if this explained why my company had only three Everest climbers while every other expedition we'd met on the way—including Felix's—had a dozen or more.

"Seems like you have a great team," I said.

"Oh, I love my team! How's yours?"

"Small. And grumpy. Our guide showed up in Kathmandu with a bad cold, and he seems very disorganized. In my experience, if you want people to follow, you always need to have your own shit together. A certain amount of tough love is always involved, but you have to show people your leadership ability."

Felix nodded. "There's a certain amount of tough love involved."

I vampire-coughed into the bend of my elbow, and he looked at me with a mixture of sympathy and recoil.

"Khumbu cough," he said. "Cold, dry air and all that trail dust—it can seriously mess you up. Don't let it get out of control."

I nodded, unable to answer without coughing so hard my body

started to shudder. By the time we got to Dingboche, I had a split-ting headache. My sinuses were congested, and when I started coughing, I couldn't stop until I was wrung out, on the verge of vomiting. And I wasn't alone. The South Africans seemed fine, but the Brit on my team was throwing up every hundred yards or so. I started taking Diamox, a medication to treat acute mountain sickness (AMS), and the headache eased off a bit, but my cough continued as we ascended beyond 18,000 feet and traversed the Kongma La pass. This pass is a strain on even the best climbers in the best circumstances, so by the time we reached Lobuche on the other side, I was fighting for every breath.

When we finally made it to Everest Base Camp, I crawled into my tent like a wounded animal. At dinnertime, I forced myself to go to the mess tent, gasping, pausing to rest after ten or twelve steps. Not good. *So* not good. I felt as if my lungs were made of perforated paper. All night, I kept waking up, gripped by one rib-cracking paroxysm after another, coughing up reddish-pink froth and listening to the alternating gurgle and crackle inside my chest with every inhale and exhale. I lay there in my sleeping bag, will-ing myself to stop coughing. *Mind over matter. Mind over moun-tain. I will not cough. I will not think about drowning.*

The next day was a scheduled rest day, and I don't think I was upright for more than six consecutive minutes of it. I had never been so utterly knackered in my life. I felt like I was in one of those COPD commercials where the person has an elephant sitting on her chest. I vaguely recalled the rookie hubris I'd begun with eight days ago—or was it a decade ago? I would have given anything to recoup 1 percent of that energy I'd spent gallivanting back and forth on the low-altitude trail while the others lumbered along like a herd of woolly mammoths. I drifted in and out of uncomfortable sleeping-bag sleep, lulled by the far-off songs of the Sherpa on the other side of the camp as they performed the Puja ceremony for Felix's team before they crossed the icefall.

The Puja ceremony is a deal breaker for the Sherpa; they won't allow anyone to set foot beyond Base Camp without a lama conducting this ceremony on an auspicious day confirmed by the lama himself. A cairn is built at the center of the camp, and on the day of the Puja, climbers select climbing kits and personal items they want blessed and place them on the altar. Prayers and songs go on for ninety minutes or more and include asking the mountain deity for permission to climb, for a safe return, and for forgiveness for any damage done by our crampons or ice tools. In no particular order, the Sherpa throw rice, burn juniper, and smear *tsampa* (roasted barley or wheat flour) on each climber's face to symbolize the beard you'll grow as you live to a ripe old age. Lots of sweets, soda, and sometimes something stronger are passed around. Toward the end of the ceremony, prayer flags are raised above the altar in all four directions, strung together in a particular order: blue for sky, white for air, red for fire, green for water, and yellow for earth. A raven or crow almost always flies by and sits on top.

The next day, we practiced our alpine skills—ascenders, rappelling, crampon technique—up and down the slopes surrounding Base Camp. I was slightly annoyed that people who didn't intend to climb were practicing skills with the rest of us, so it took longer for every member to sequence through. We had planned to make our ascent up the icefall the following day, but in the mess tent at dinnertime, David said, "We're going to wait twenty-four hours. Give people a chance to shake off some health issues." He didn't refer to his own cold, but I didn't feel quite so singled out this time. The Brit who was vomiting previously now had a gastrointestinal bug, diarrhea that was just as impossible to hide as my frothy red cough—and given a choice between the two, I'd opt for the cough eight days a week.

The climbing company's doctor had no experience in high-altitude medicine, but he seemed kind and helpful in assisting people with their Khumbu cough. He had me cough into a Kleenex so he could see what came out, and his forehead wrinkled.

"That's an infection all right. See that green and yellow phlegm? This could lead to pulmonary edema," he said. "Water in the lungs. The pink foam—that's blood from bursting air sacs." He gave me antibiotics, which I started right away.

That evening, our Puja ceremony was somewhat less energized than the one for Felix's team, probably because they had twelve climbers heading for the summit and we had just three plus me, but I appreciated its spiritual meaning. I felt heartened by it when we set out across the Khumbu Icefall at three in the morning. Our goal was the Football Field, halfway between Base Camp and Camp 1, pitched just below the Western Cwm (pronounced "coom," indulging the Welsh aversion to vowels) in a sweeping saddle known as the Valley of Silence. The idea was to get there and then get back out before the midday sun warmed and destabilized the jagged seracs, massive columns of ice shoved upward by the shifting, city-size glacier.

I trudged along, knackered and hypoxic, following this guide I trusted little and liked even less. I was slow crossing the deep crevasses. Some were only an arm's length or so, and David shamed me into hopping across those, my heavy pack lurching against my neck. Others yawned several meters wide. Sherpa who served as "icefall doctors" had bridged the gaps with ladders. If one ladder wasn't long enough, two or more were lashed together in a way that looked quite sketchy to me the first time I saw one. Jerry-rigged. Skeletal. The lashed-together ladders are flanked by guide ropes to which the climber optimistically clips her harness. The temptation

is to go on hands and knees, but if you do that, you find yourself staring down into negative eternity. No, you must stay upright,
placing your crampons on the rungs of the ladder and your faith in
whatever god you cling to. My only advice is that you not fill your
bladder with as much black tea as I had that morning.

Each time I placed a tenuous foot onto one of those janky ladders, I tried to feel the Saint Christopher medal against my skin.
I kept thinking of a print that used to hang in my home when I
was little, *Heilige Schutzengel*, a familiar painting by Hans Zatzka
that shows two children crossing a terribly questionable wooden
bridge over a deep chasm. To me, they looked like Hansel and
Gretel. Or maybe like my little brother and me. The bridge is gap-
toothed and rotting. It's obviously a terrible idea, but the children
cross, gripping each other's hands. The big sister has a protective
arm around her little brother, and floating along behind them is
an angel, fair-haired and serene, looking very confident, like *I got
you*. I remember staring at that painting when I was little, taking
a great deal of comfort from it, but later, when I lived in the house
alone, it made me feel cheated and gullible. "Never run faster than
your guardian angel can fly," I always say. My guardian angel was
getting a lot of cardio.

It was pitch dark and bitter cold, the ambient temperature
hovering below 0 degrees Fahrenheit. A rising wind moaned between the seracs, a choir of aging baritones, making it even more
forlorn. My heart sank every time my headlamp found another
deep split in the glacier. "How much farther?" I asked a hundred
times, and every time, David harrumphed, "Not too far." Arguing
the subjective question of how far is too far would have been a
waste of oxygen. Better to trudge on in silence—one step, three
shallow sips of air, one step, three sips—jamming my crampons
into the snow. Turns out tottering across the ice with steel pasta

forks strapped to your boots is even trickier than running for the subway in stilettos.

After an hour or two, I felt myself becoming dehydrated. I was sweating, overheated by exertion. With each foot forward, I tried to force another breath in and out of my aching lungs. Each exhale formed a silver cloud in front of me, and I forced myself to walk into it. Step. Breathe. Step. Breathe.

The black sky turned silvery gray. I was losing my battle with the clock, and the longer we climbed, the more I slowed down. My team members disappeared into the icy dawn, weaving among the towering seracs well ahead of me. Fighting for balance and breath, I made my way along a steep ice cliff. Obligated to bring up the rear, David traipsed along a few paces away, haranguing, "Vanessa, you're falling back. Vanessa, pick up your pace. Vanessa, control your breathing."

The sun peeked over the distant ridge. It was well past breakfast time at Base Camp far below. The summit glowed like mother-of-pearl against a brilliant blue sky above. Sunlight spilled across the icefall, turning silver to gold. I paused, listening. I've been told that the child of a violent household develops a fine subconscious sensitivity, something always on alert just under the skin.

The "movement event" began with a fidgety stillness. There was a bit of a belly rumble from the restless mountain above us, then the shotgun *crack! crack! crack!*—one serac after another collapsing, creating new canyons, yawning apart, slamming together. Powdery snow billowed up and outward. Shrapnel from shattering ice and rock whistled through the clean air. The avalanche cascaded down the mountain, as swift and unstoppable as an armada of frozen ocean liners. I felt it reverberating from my frozen toes to my aching shoulders. My spine hummed like a tuning fork. My midsection contracted in a full-body flinch of cold panic. I had no sense of time or distance—how far away the avalanche was, how fast it was traveling, how long it would last—only the enormity of its presence, those cascading seracs, some as big as buildings, others mere bulldozers and minivans. It was impossible to take in all at once. My memory has selected images that shimmer for an instant: icy shrapnel, a serac exploding, the stunned puff of white breath hanging in the air in front of David's startled mouth.

"*Fuck!*" I rasped. "What should we do?"

One would like to imagine there's some set protocol for any predictable emergency, and an avalanche in the Khumbu Icefall is the definition of predictable, but there are no tools in the toolbox, no duck-and-cover mantra, no seat cushion that may be used as a flotation device. We stood there like two soft-boiled eggs on a railroad track. I closed my eyes, expecting blunt force trauma followed by the bright light that is supposed to shine before entering eternity. I remember feeling the spray of snow in the air, and the weirdly distant realization that I had stopped coughing. ("Hypoxic shock," the doctor told me later, examining my blue-gray fingernails and matching lips.) Instead, there was a sudden settling of gravity and noise. Followed by nothing.

Silence.

I didn't have enough air to ask, *What happened?* I don't know if it was blind luck or my guardian angels or Saint Christopher himself saying, *Hang on, luv, I've got this!* It seemed like the whole tumbling mass just lurched to a halt with a disgruntled *scrrrrrrrunch* a few hundred meters above us.

"Let's get out of here." David grabbed my carabiner, and I scrambled after him, down the way we came, descending as quickly as we could. I lost my ice axe in the chaos, which made things more difficult, but I was powered by pure adrenaline now. As the sun rose higher, we could hear the seracs cracking and shifting behind us.

It was after noon when we arrived back at Everest Base Camp. In the sick tent, the expedition doctor snapped a pulse oximeter on my finger to measure the oxygen level in my blood. Typically, more than 89 percent of your blood should be carrying oxygen, and a normal range is more like 95 percent for most healthy adults. This range changes while you're climbing, but we were still at Base Camp, and my pulse oxygen was hovering around 50 percent, indicating potential hypoxia, a critical deficiency in oxygen reaching tissues in my body. He gave me some medication, which I immediately threw up into a bucket. Reeling with nausea and shaking like a leaf, I didn't want to put anything else in my stomach, but I knew I had to drink water to rehydrate. Every beat of my heart felt like a sledgehammer to the back of my head, but it was two hours before I could keep Diamox down.

Diamox is formulated to treat glaucoma and epilepsy, but it aids altitude sickness and knocks down its most obvious symptom: a five-star, morning-after-Metallica-caliber headache. I've always taken it sparingly since that day, fearing the possibility of kidney stones, a potential side effect, but in that moment, all I cared about was being able to close my eyes and wake up without that headache. The avalanche scene played and replayed in my head along with a litany of annoyances I'd been cataloguing since I met David in Kathmandu. He showed up sick with a virus that could have easily spread; he took us out of our way over the Kongma La pass, putting on extra miles; he allowed the Everest Base Camp manager to practice skills with us, which meant it took longer for each climber to pass through the ropes course; and he brought a team doctor who had no high-altitude medical experience and was clearly along for a free trip. The list went on as I drifted into a restless sleep, along with a running dialogue between my better angels. *Keep it in perspective. Stay calm. Eyes on the prize.*

I awoke to the pressure of the pulse oximeter on my finger. The doctor looked down at me and asked, "How are you feeling?"

"Better," I said, pushing myself up on the infirmary cot.

"You're rehydrated, I see. Pulse ox is improving too." He looked over his shoulder at David, who was hanging back, arms folded in a body language I instantly recognized. I'd fired enough people during my career to know when someone is about to get canned.

"We've been having a chat about your situation," David said.

"Have we now." I knew the next words out of his mouth would be code for "GTFO," and he made little effort to sugarcoat it.

"We think it's best if you were to descend tomorrow."

"But my oxygen levels are starting to improve," I countered. They exchanged uncomfortable glances but didn't say anything, so I tried another tack, unwilling to accept defeat. "What if I pay to have a consultation with Dr. Monica at Russell Brice's camp?"

"I'm not sure that's a good idea," said David.

"I could try Viagra." (No, seriously. Setting aside the obvious punch lines, Cialis and Viagra are high-altitude medical tools that help blood flow more freely.) "Or maybe I could—"

"Vanessa, you're sick," said David. "Other people are trying to summit, and you could get them sick too."

"So could you! When we met up in Kathmandu, you sounded like you were about to hack up a lung." It felt like hitting below the belt, but he had to shrug and concede that point.

I didn't like them and they didn't like me. I was a liability, not a priority. David's company was in the business of getting climbers to the top of Everest, so I think they would have tried to fix me if I had been one of the summiting climbers, but they didn't give a shit about someone who was there for a Camp 2 Everest experience. It was fine to let me sign on and take my chances, but they weren't about to take any risks on my behalf.

David and Lowland Doc left the tent, and I lay there castigating myself for disregarding one of the fundamental principles of good business: Both parties need to have equal skin in the game. They have to want the same thing. Or they have to want two different things with equal enthusiasm, both of which can be accomplished by common effort. I was passionate about getting to Camp 2; they were passionate about getting people to the summit.

By dinnertime my oxygen had returned to normal, and I did my best to be animated, chatting with the other climbers as if my blood cells were fizzing with oxygen and congeniality, but later that evening the signs of pulmonary edema were still there. It was agreed that I should descend in the morning, accompanied by one of the less essential Sherpa. Starting at dawn, fueled by disappointment, anger, and shame, I trekked the whole sixty-two rugged kilometers back to Lukla in one day. This was no big deal for the Sherpa. He was glad to get it over with, and so was I.

"Are you sure you wouldn't like to rest awhile?" he kept asking.

"I'm good," I said with the static smile you get from too much Botox or a proper amount of new religion. Upset and humiliated, I tramped along, alternating between anger and tears, scrolling down the list of every little thing that irritated me. All the snappy comebacks that hadn't occurred to me in the moment played over and over in my head. *What I SHOULD have said was blah blah blah.* Worse than that, I saw every mistake I made, every intersection where I could have gone a different direction. *Two roads diverged in a wood, and I—I took the one . . .* that turned out to be dumbass.

The motivational playlist thrumming in my earbuds was an ironic soundtrack for my descent. Everything I'd seen on the way up, I saw again on the way down. The whole experience unspooled before me in a surrealistic rewind of the previous two weeks. Passing the place where we'd grabbed our last few hours of crampon practice, I saw myself struggling in the icefall with the team, and I had to admit that my mountaineering skills needed improvement. Passing the teahouse where I first coughed myself to sleep, I realized that my high-altitude health was 100 percent my responsibility. I knew I must seek out specialists who would help me master and understand AMS, HACE (high-altitude cerebral edema), and HAPE so I could carry and administer my own medicine. Passing the trail where I stupidly volunteered to carry additional weight, I saw all that muscle I'd built competing for oxygen that could be put to better use in my brain and lungs. It wasn't good enough to be fit; I had to be a particular *type* of fit. Strength was less important than stamina.

In *The Last Lecture*, Carnegie Mellon University professor Randy Pausch says, "Experience is what you get when you didn't get what you wanted." Back at the airport in Lukla, I reminded myself of the goal I started out with. This was never a summit bid; it was supposed to be a learning experience, and I had definitely learned a lot, so in that sense it was a success. I didn't get what I wanted on this expedition, but I got what I asked for, and in retrospect, I see that I got what I needed.

Learning on the job—in the best scenario—is synonymous with failure. When you push to the point of failure, you're cutting new trail, moving beyond the well-worn path of what you already know, so right out of the box, you accept failure as part of your game plan. Success pats you on the head and tells you to keep doing what you're doing; failure kicks your ass and tells you to shake things up, keep reaching, and explore new territory. Guess which one will get you closer to your long-term goals. Guess which one changes the world.

The mountain—whatever your mountain is—means something because it's hard. Because there's so much at stake. You risk failing, falling, and embarrassing yourself. You risk dying on that mountain. But if you stay home, you risk dying without ever hearing what the mountain wanted to tell you. You risk never knowing what you are capable of.

My inability to reach Camp 2 meant I had a huge slice of humble pie to digest, and I hated every bite, but flying out of Lukla, rising above the stunning Himalayan skyline, I felt surprisingly calm and grateful. I had plenty of time on my way home to evaluate what went wrong and plan how I was going to do things differently going forward. I had made some rookie mistakes, but I'd clocked them too. The confidence of a sage comes from experience, not pride. For me, gaining wisdom would mean climbing more mountains.

Taking stock of what *did* work for me, I realized that my business skills—leadership, risk management, teamwork, negotiation, allocation of resources—were quite relevant. When more-experienced climbers tried to make me feel ashamed of my background, they were simply incorrect. If I summoned my better angels at all the right moments, these skills—everything I had learned up until now—would serve me well. So would tenacity and focus. Over the preceding twenty years, succeeding and failing in male-dominated, ego-driven environments, I had developed a hide tougher than your average armadillo. If my pride was wounded, I would survive and move on. This I knew from experience and from all the *rah rah* lyrics on my motivational playlist. I was not giving up. Not this time. Not next time. Not ever.

I was determined. I would summit Everest.

5

In the Land of Mountains, there are 238 climbable peaks higher than 6,000 meters but only fourteen "Eight Thousanders"—peaks whose elevation exceeds 8,000 meters (26,247 feet). That's roughly five miles high, not to be confused with five miles *tall*. In the mountaineering world, *high* refers to the elevation above sea level; *tall* refers to the distance from the base of the mountain to the summit. By the high versus tall definition, Denali in Alaska is taller than Everest, rising roughly 5,500 meters from base to summit, which is greater than Everest's 3,700-meter rise, a difference of more than a mile. The world's tallest mountain is Mauna Kea in Hawaii; 10,204 meters from ocean floor to summit, but the base is about 6,000 meters below sea level, so you can't see it.

In the corporate and the climbing worlds, the playing field is about as level as the Land of Mountains. *Fortune* started compiling executive gender statistics in 1998, and I followed those numbers with interest as more and more women business leaders emerged. It was like watching the epic race between tortoise and hare. The *Fortune* 500 female CEO numbers rose—*so . . . so . . . slowly*—to 15 in 2009. And then began an agonizing decline to only 12 women

CEOs by 2011. Imagine my delight when the number rose to 24 in 2014. Yes, for a moment 24 women out of 500 CEOs actually seemed like a victory. But that's just 4.8 percent. By 2014, of the 3,696 total climbers (excluding Sherpa) who'd summited Everest, 415 were women. That's 11 percent. So the likelihood of a woman executive ascending to the rank of CEO is less than *half* the odds of a woman climber being able to summit the highest mountain on the planet. I'm only half joking when I suggest women executives need crampons to get to the top.

It didn't take long for me to discover female-unfriendly design flaws in climbing gear. Practicing on Fox Glacier and outside Everest Base Camp, climbing the steep terrain, and rappelling down in an exhilarating rush, instructors showed us how to clamp the ascender onto a fixed rope, slide the handle up, pull down until it was taut, and then summon every ounce of upper-body strength to pull ourselves up.

"Pretty straightforward," the instructor said. "Hold the ascender and use your thumb to flip it up so it grips the rope before pulling it down."

Simple enough in theory, but the ascender is designed to fit the hand of an average-size man, and my hand is considerably smaller than that. My thumb didn't even come close to that flipping thing. I have to grip the ascender with one hand and use my other hand to flip it, which means I don't have that other hand free to steady myself or grasp the rope. Instead of flipping my thumb with a small motor movement, I have to expend the effort to raise my whole arm, and at altitude, lifting your arm feels like bench-pressing an adolescent yak. Unless a male climber has one hand tied behind his back, I'm working twice as hard as he is for every vertical inch of progress. I suggested lobbying the CEO of the company that made the ascenders with the idea of a smaller size for female climbers, but that idea went over like caterpillar salad with my guiding company.

From the outset, I said I wanted to achieve something quantifiable, but I never thought beyond the traditional yardsticks, and it's never that simple. In my grandparents' generation, with no more than a high school diploma, you could climb the ladder of success simply by dint of wits and industry: show up, be smart, work hard. In my parents' generation, you had to show up with a bachelor's degree if you dreamed of moving up in a company you devoted your life to. In my generation, the goalpost moved farther away; an MBA is a good start, but you've also got to be willing to change jobs and move to a different city or even a different country. No matter how focused you are on a single goal, you have to adopt a broad view of how to get there. It comes down to Darwin. It's not enough to be the smartest or strongest; you must be willing to adapt.

I attended community college in Michigan and then made my way to New York to work toward my BA in economics at NYU. To support myself and pay for school, I worked as the office manager for a commercial real estate brokerage company, where I had carte blanche to run things the way I wanted. I introduced the firm to its very first computer, programmed all the sales letters, and databased all the lenders and sales leads. I went above and beyond at every opportunity, so the boss and team loved me and let me set my own schedule around my classes. This didn't leave much time for sleep or other nonessential activities, but I knew education was the key to moving up in the world.

One day, not long after I graduated with my BA, I spent my thirty-minute lunch at a Midtown job fair, talking with a representative from GE Capital, a division of General Electric back then. I knew nothing about GE other than that they made lightbulbs and refrigerators and could "bring good things to life." This woman seemed very knowledgeable and was impressed by the way I'd transformed the tiny real estate office while putting myself through school. Less than a week later, she offered me a place in GE's Financial Management Program. I wish I could say "dream job," but this was not even close. They expected me to take a pay cut, leave New York, and relocate every six months for two and a half years. This elite training program involved five rotating assignments spread out across GE Capital's twenty-five business units plus mandatory semiannual leadership stays at the GE Management Development Institute, a program designed and taught by Jack Welch, located in Crotonville, NY. That meant something to me. Welch's *Jack: Straight from the Gut* was legend in the business book world.

"I'll think about it," I said, and I did think, long and hard. Starting with my first job, I'd made steady upward progress. GE was asking me to take a step down in salary, but isn't that the nature of investment? You give something, hoping to get something better. The decision to invest is an exercise in optimism, especially when you're investing in yourself. You accept the risk, because the decision to *not* invest in yourself leaves you stuck where you are.

For me, then and now, the decision is the real issue, and my decision-making policy has only one rule: *Make one.* A decision must be made. Indecision is the plumbing leak of personal responsibility; it makes you look like a drip. Making the wrong choice is better than making no choice at all, because indecision is a choice to let the indifferent winds of fate dictate your circumstances. When you make a decision, you set a data point you can return to when it's time to reality-check quantifiable results a week, month, or year down the line, saying "Congrats, Self! Well played!" or "Wow, Self, that sucked, but I still believe in you." If you made the wrong choice, you still have the knowledge, skills, and experience you started with plus what you learned from the stumble. No one can take that away from you.

I accepted the GE Capital job offer, and with my data point established, I set out on my new, complex trajectory. Success is never a straight line. This voluntary baptism by fire was one of the smartest moves I ever made. Love him or hate him, no one could dispute the genius of Jack Welch. He had decided that every GE business should be number one or number two in its market. Nuanced choices had to be made in pricing and operating models to compete and gain that market share. Jack Welch reminds me of Robert Duvall—*Lonesome Dove* Duvall, not the Great Santini—with his inarguable common sense and laser focus. What I learned at GE—"Speed, simplicity, self-confidence"—stayed with me through everything that came after Crotonville.

Almost twenty years later, I left Everest feeling like I'd been sent to bed without my supper, but I made the decision to set a new data point and invest the time and effort it would take to return some-day and make it to the summit. Heading into the summer of 2010, I joined a local hiking group and started exploring Hong Kong–area trails, some of which were pretty advanced. Ross and I developed a game plan that focused on aerobic and anaerobic conditioning indoors, avoiding Hong Kong's summer heat and wringing 90 per-cent humidity. We talked about the effects of high altitude and how to make the most of every precious molecule of oxygen.

"I need to be strong," I said, "but I also need to be smart."

"Let's make it about the cardio," he agreed. "Let's do some high-intensity interval training alternating short periods of intense an-aerobic exercise with less-intense recovery periods."

"Sounds like fun," I said, all gung ho and positivity.

It was not fun. In fact, I think not having fun is the whole point of cardiovascular training. As soon as you're humming along, thinking you've nailed a certain maximum, you have to change it up, just to make sure your body never gets smug about itself or comfortable with a particular pace. I hated that lactic acid feeling, like Drano in my veins. I worked out hard five days a week, focusing on cardio, streamlining instead of bulking up. When I did carry a backpack for strength training, it was forty pounds or so—just enough for oxygen on summit day.

After a few weeks of forced self-discipline, almost anything will become a habit. You don't wake up wondering if you could skip the workout just for today; you simply get up and do it without issue. It ceases to be fun or not fun, painful or pleasant; it just is what it is, and you do it because it's the job that needs doing. True to Ross's plan, the increased agility and lung capacity kicked in. Every once in a while, I'd experience that "runner's high"—a rush of animal energy and euphoria. I liked the feeling of living in this body, and that's really something for me, because I never had a positive image of my body.

I was painfully self-conscious when I was a kid. My paternal grandmother used to shake her head with undisguised antipathy and say, "*Augh!* Those big boobs." I tried to dress in a way that squashed my chest and downplayed what I had been made to believe was a terrible deformity that automatically made me dumber and uglier than other girls. I hated buying size twelve tops with size ten bottoms. When nothing off the rack fits you, it sends the powerful message that *you* don't fit.

When I was still a teenager, my mother helped me lobby our health insurance company to justify breast reduction as a "medical necessity," saying the burden might give me back problems later in life. I welcomed the surgery. I wanted to get it done. I don't think I fully understood the "anchor scar" that would be left when they repositioned the nipples higher up and carved my chest with what still look like two broadly grimacing emojis. I certainly didn't understand that later on in my life, certain boys and men would display the same disgust—*Augh! What's wrong with you?*—and make me feel the same sting of shame my grandmother used to inflict. Another procedure five years later would fix the placement of the nipples and soften the scars, but this is the way women are judged, unfortunately. In your clothes or out of them, someone's not going to like what they see, and for some reason, they think it's okay to comment.

The English language is no more female-friendly than the average ascender. A man has "love handles" and "moobs"; a woman has "back fat" and "thunder thighs." Over the years, I had to change that vocabulary and learn to love my naked scarred self beyond the critical eyes of someone for whom intimacy was just another notch on the bedpost. I had to build my life with someone who loves me for all my scars, visible and invisible, and that turned out to be Jonathan.

By the end of June, almost three months after Everest, I was stronger and lighter, humble pie almost fully digested. I felt ready to climb again. I gingerly broached the topic with the Spouse, and his face automatically rearranged to stiff-upper-lip mode.

"I've been researching logistics for mountains other than Everest," I said, "especially those other thirteen Eight Thousanders in the Himalayas and Karakoram bordering Nepal, Pakistan, and China. It's a good height for someone trying to figure out how her body performs at altitude."

He folded his arms and said, "I'm listening."

"The best way to learn is to go to altitude. Statistically, Cho Oyu in Tibet is one of the most successfully climbed." I rattled out the specs like a teletype: "World's sixth-highest mountain, elevation 8,201 meters. Some say it's the easiest Eight Thousander. It has the lowest death rate—only forty-one climbers or 1.4 percent since the first ascent in 1954."

"*Only* forty-one dead climbers? This, in your mind, is a selling point?"

"Compare that to Everest," I said. "Just the right amount of daunting, I suppose."

He set that aside for the moment. "You've got it all sorted, then."

"I checked out the American guiding company Felix was so happy with when we bumped into each other on Everest. This guide he loved, Daniel, works for them. He's leading a Cho Oyu expedition in the fall. I'd like to go."

We both knew I wasn't asking permission, just hoping for his blessing. I respected his level of discomfort with the whole situation. Our alliance left him teetering on an exposed ladder between twin chasms of disaster: he watched my retirement savings disappear down one crevasse while my odds of surviving to retirement age disappeared down another. All I could do was take his hand and hope to be worth the trouble.

"You really think this other guide will make all the difference?"

"Proof is in the pudding. One team was happy and healthy. The other was miserable. I wasn't the only one who left there feeling like crap. I just missed the thrill of feeling like crap on the summit. Next time, I'll do without the drama."

"Even so," said Jonathan, "the best possible scenario calls for abject misery."

"The mountains are calling and I must go," I said.

"Oh, joy. We've moved on to the John Muir quotes." His expression was dead serious. "If you must do this, promise you won't take unnecessary chances."

I promised, and at least one of us probably believed it.

6

You mustn't confuse a single failure with a final defeat.
—F. SCOTT FITZGERALD, *TENDER IS THE NIGHT*

Experience is like the switchbacks that zigzag up the side of a mountain; you keep returning to the same parallel but with a higher point of view. Collecting my gear from the Dragonair carousel in Kathmandu, I felt like a regular returning to familiar stomping grounds. I'd packed smarter and lighter, having learned which listed items I could do without and which unlisted items I might be desperately glad for. Even before the 2015 earthquake, Nepal was burdened with poverty and pollution. This time I was prepared for the congested traffic and grimy air quality. I pulled my bird flu mask over my face to protect my lungs, determined to avoid the most devastating of my rookie mistakes, the irritation of my bronchial airways that paved the way for pulmonary edema.

When I met Daniel and my team at a restaurant in one of Kathmandu's touristy neighborhoods, the room was full of laughter and goodwill, just like the table in the modest teahouse where I'd first seen Daniel five months ago.

"Vanessa!" He swept me into a bear hug that smelled like pine needles and chai. "You look somewhat cheerier than last time I saw you."

"Congratulations on your Everest summit," I said.

With his strong jaw and Ray-Bans, Daniel was the best-looking guy at the table, and he seemed used to that. If David Beckham were a bit taller and going through a flannel phase—that's Daniel. I was relieved to find him every bit as organized and affable as Felix said he was. In the years to come, Daniel and I would climb a lot of mountains together, sharing many meals, stories, and tiny two-person tents. We didn't always agree. He's risk-averse, which I found frustrating now and then, but what can I say? Those guys live longer. I grew to appreciate his dry humor and shyly strategic way of thinking.

We were twelve: five Americans—three of them women—one Canadian, an Australian police officer, a Brit from a well-known family of explorers, a German, two Swiss, and one Italian. So net/net, compared to my first climbing experience, this was by far the more interesting team. This expedition opened my eyes to the diversity of the international climbing world, something I hadn't seen much of on my first trip to Everest. I like seeing a wide range of ages, cultures, languages, customs, and levels of experience. Climbers come from widely different socioeconomic backgrounds and educational levels. At the table are students, retirees, and every level of career in between. I'm fascinated by the difference in motivation—*why* people climb—and the differences in how they apply climbing dynamics to their everyday lives. Binding us all together is the common goal, the sacrifice each of us has made for it, and the understanding that most other people think we've completely taken leave of our senses.

Women are the minority, representing approximately 20 percent of all high-altitude climbers, so I always appreciate it when I'm not the only one. Over dinner, I fell into an easygoing conversation with the other women on the team: Kim, an experienced climber from Connecticut, and Lola, from Arkansas, who was less experienced but every bit as passionate. They both had school-age children, and like me, Kim was climbing Cho Oyu as a precursor to Everest.

"I plan to summit in 2011," she said. "Then I'll have my Seven Summits."

I'd heard of other climbers working toward the Seven Summits—the highest peak on every continent—and I'd skimmed the statistics, but my gaze was firmly fixed on Everest. I wasn't ready to think beyond that, and I certainly wasn't prepared to run the idea up Jonathan's flagpole, but I was interested in Kim's take on each of the mountains. Among the three of us, she was the voice of experience. My only summit so far was Kilimanjaro, and Lola's was Denali.

Early the next morning, a minibus picked us up at our guesthouse, and we jounced along for several hours on a rutted dirt road, hardly missing a pothole between Kathmandu and the border of Tibet. We left the bus in Nepal, had our passports stamped, and crossed the Sino-Nepal Friendship Bridge on foot to connect with our Chinese transportation.

"No pictures on the bridge," Daniel cautioned and reminded us of the long list of rules we were bound by: no Tibetan travel books, no pictures of the Dalai Lama, and so on. Other tourists were less prepared when armed guards along the bridge confiscated books and deleted photos from phones and cameras.

I couldn't help feeling that driving for acclimatization was not quite cricket, but *c'est la vie*. I figured I made up for it with all that extra work I did on the way to Everest Base Camp. We spent the first night in the town of Zhangmu and the second night in Nyalam. The third day, on our way to Tingri, we drove up to Lalung Leh, a high mountain pass where hundreds of prayer flags fluttered in the wind. We got out to take pictures, smiling in the clean mountain breeze. Other stops were less pleasant. On the road into Tingri, emaciated cows munched on cardboard and stray dogs rooted around the perimeter of a broad field of rotting garbage. Outhouses burdened the neighborhood with an indescribable stench. Lola nudged me with her elbow and opened her palm for a squirt of my hand sanitizer.

We were scheduled to stay in Tingri for two nights at a hotel with dirt floors and swarming flies. A couple of the Europeans, bless their hearts, trotted over a little bridge to do some reconnaissance while Lola, Kim, and I stayed well and truly outside the lodge, nervously imagining what it would mean to face the filthy outhouse in the falling darkness. Twenty minutes later, the Europeans returned with a noticeable spring in their step.

"There's a lodge up the road," said one of the Swiss climbers. "Fifteen dollars a night, and it has indoor toilets."

I felt a surge of hope. "Please tell me you're not hallucinating because of the altitude."

"The manager gave us a tour," he said. "Clean rooms, no dirt floors, running water, and en suite bathrooms."

"We're moving," I said without hesitation, and everyone agreed, but all sorts of hemming and hawing began when it came to the small matter of informing Daniel. I understood the etiquette involved, but it wasn't worth getting sick and missing our chance at summiting. Daniel's climbing assistant, Alex, was already suffering from severe diarrhea. Decisions, people, decisions! I made mine and went up to rap on Daniel's door. Alex answered and told me Daniel was on the satellite phone with his girlfriend. He'd met her on a previous climb on Cho Oyu. I could only assume that she was still living because she'd declined to spend the night in this hotel.

"It's important. I'll wait," I said, thinking, *Tick tock, Romeo.*

Daniel came out to find the mutinous team unified in our resolve. After a bit of point/counterpoint, it was decided that the team would shift to the other lodge, but because it was important in the Chinese culture to save face, Daniel and Alex would remain in situ. It's hard to say why the Chinese Mountaineering Association who'd arranged our lodging didn't go for the obviously healthier option to begin with.

"I need you all to come back for dinner and breakfast," Daniel said, and we all understood why that was necessary.

After two days, with a fresh rush of red blood cells working through our veins, we took the bus from Tingri, rolling across lowlands cut with reddish scrub, to the Cho Oyu interim camp. From there, we hiked a little over twenty miles up a series of zigzagging switchbacks to Advanced Base Camp (ABC) at about 18,700 feet, a little higher than Everest Base Camp. The mountain towered over us, but the summit was thickly shrouded in silver-lined clouds. Bright yellow tents dotted the rocky hillside. Beyond the camp, there was a sweeping snow-covered divide, and beyond that was Nepal. Cho Oyu is only eighteen miles from Everest, so the scenery is somewhat similar, but so far the two experiences were worlds apart.

I was feeling fine, eager to get on the mountain, but good sense told me to follow instructions and rest while my body adjusted to the new altitude. I had a Kindle full of books and an iPad full of movies, and if we felt social, there was gin rummy or poker in the mess tent. Mostly I slept and did everything I could to stay well, which felt like a near-impossible obstacle course. Gastrointestinal illnesses spread through a camp via contaminated food and water, causing diarrhea and dehydration. The cold, dry air promotes bronchitis, pneumonia, and pulmonary edema. Headaches are a natural part of acclimatizing but may also signal altitude sickness. One of the American men started feeling rough and decided to descend. I was determined not to follow.

Climb high, sleep low, you'll recall, is the golden rule of acclimatization, so after three days at ABC, we set out for Camp 1. We spent the next few weeks trekking up and down the mountain, setting up camps and working with our Sherpa to carry equipment from ABC to one of three higher camps. I grew to despise the hike through the rocky moraine that separated ABC from Camp 1. It started out fairly flat, but after a few miles, it pitched upward. The slick gray rocks started out the size of a cereal box, then grew to a jumble of icy, refrigerator-size boulders. When it becomes like a video game of *Frogger* where I'm hopping from log to log—*kerplunk*—sooner or later, I'm going down. Following a Sherpa who was about my height helped. With a matching stride and gait, I could make a good showing, but it rarely lasted more than fifteen minutes.

After several miles of slow incline, we came to a stretch I call Kitty Litter Hill: 1,500 vertical feet of precarious switchbacks covered with loose scree—tiny stones the size and consistency of kitty litter. It's steep and foot-unfriendly; even a mountain goat couldn't take the most direct route up. The only way to scale this slope is to go back and forth. The switchbacks never end, and there are at least three false summits before Camp 1. Every mountain plays this game, teasing the brain, tricking the eye with an optical illusion that makes you think the top is closer than it is. You lock your gaze on that point, and just when you think you're almost there, you crest a ridge or scramble over a boulder to find a whole ridge you couldn't see from a lower perspective. Setting your heart on that false summit saps your energy.

I trudged up Kitty Litter Hill, feeling like I was starting over again and again. And again. And again—as if the mountain gods were rolling dice and sending me back three spaces on a *Monopoly* board, after drawing a Chance card. It was soul-destroying, giving all my energy only to be disheartened again and again, but it taught me something I took with me to future climbs. I no longer fix my gaze on that duplicitous ridge. If you assume the mountain lasts forever, the true summit is a sweet surprise.

We cleared a 40-degree slope and saw the bright orange tents of Camp 1 at a little over 6,300 meters. Anchored to the rocks on a small, relatively flat area, they shivered in the wind, unnervingly close to a sheer vertical drop. After a brief rest, snacks, and hot tea, it was back down the switchbacks of Kitty Litter Hill and over the rocky moraine to ABC. It was cause for celebration when we actually got to stay overnight at Camp 1, but on the way down the next morning, I heard Lola scream. I ran over to where she stood, and it took me a moment to understand that I was looking at a human forearm.

The bones were bleached as white as quartz. Rags of flesh curled away from leathery muscle. The remaining skin was marbled blue and gray, but what struck me in the long moment I stood there staring was the specificity of the fingernails, which were surprisingly clean, the cuticles undamaged. The hand was closed, but not in a fist. More like when someone places something on your palm and you close your hand to keep it, like the Saint Christopher medal Jonathan pressed into my palm that night in Hong Kong. I couldn't bring myself to touch the gray marbled hand, but I wanted to believe it held something precious.

On day 38 of the expedition—though it felt like day 138—we returned to ABC, and a massive snowstorm howled in behind us. We were trapped in our tents for days, and our somber spirits dragged. We played cards, traded books, and told stories. Another American man developed a phlegmy cough and decided to descend along with the young Brit who had concluded that this was all just too bloody boring. The rest of us plodded on. With so many hours together in the mess tent, there was bound to be some proximity burn. Tensions sparked and subsided. Personalities clashed, and people sulked in separate corners. I remained as quietly neutral as I could, keeping my views to myself, particularly on volatile issues like politics and religion.

Finally—*finally*—the weather broke, and the nine remaining team members headed back up Kitty Litter Hill to Camp 1 at 20,600 feet, where we spent the night, dreaming of Camp 2 an enticing 2,300 feet above. The next morning, we headed back down to ABC while the Sherpa pushed upward, setting up Camp 2. The plan was for us to follow them the next day, and we were all motivated to get a strong start, but watching Daniel speed-walk over the rocks was like watching a video fast-forward. There was no way I could keep up with his long, lanky stride, so I fell back to the rear of the queue, trying to find my own rhythm. When we paused to take a break near the top of Kitty Litter Hill, I could see that the tents of Camp 1 were hung with ice, battered by freezing winds. Without crampons, we slipped and slid on the snow-covered rocks, but we made it to Camp 1.

Settling into our tents for the night, we heard anxious voices and radio chatter. The Sherpa were returning from Camp 2, carrying one man whose legs were badly injured and another with broken ribs. They'd been caught by an avalanche while fixing ropes. Over the next few hours, more Sherpa returned, wounded and shaken, one with goggles completely smashed. We did what we could to help them before Daniel sent them down to ABC. I watched them go, aching for the pain they were in and dreading what this meant for the expedition.

"Get in your tents," Daniel said. "Hydrate. Rest. We'll talk in the morning."

Inside our tent, Kim and I discussed the situation. I felt torn, worried about the Sherpa who were hurt, nervous about the conditions ahead, and trying to reconcile all that with how much it meant to me to be on this mountain, physically well and raring to go.

"In my experience," said Kim, "avalanches usually signal the end."

The next morning, Daniel told us the expedition was over. Furious and heartsick, I jammed my gear into my pack and stormed down the mountain, marking every heavy step: *Dammit! Dammit! Dammit!* There was no one to be angry at this time—not even myself. It was just rotten luck.

In the Tibetan language, Cho Oyu means "turquoise goddess." I looked up at the mountain as I descended, and I could see why. She towered over us, cloaked in snow and ice that reflected the blue sky. Since I'd first laid eyes on her, Cho Oyu had been trying to teach me two important lessons. At first, I was too busy to listen, and now I was too angry, but later the wind would whisper in my ear. The first lesson was patience. The second lesson was that the mountain is always in control. We crawl over her with our electronics and climbing gear, thinking, *Oh, yeah, I've got it all figured out this time,* but whatever control we think we have is an illusion. I resolved to focus on what I could control rather than what I could not.

This was a gift, really—this realization that I could control only what was mine to control. With it came the understanding that this applies to the rest of life as well. The burden of responsibility I'd taken on myself as a kid—everything I tried to grab on to as my family disintegrated around me—none of that was mine to carry. *Whatever is not yours,* said the Buddha, *you must abandon it.*

I'd been struggling all my life to control whatever I could in my small world. In my earliest memories, I'm huddled under the table, my arms around my little brother. I was determined to protect Ben from the storm of violence that blew in when our parents were drinking, screaming and punching, hurling things across the room, a howling, directionless blizzard of rage. My answer to this was to work, to grasp, to set my sights on something and calm myself with the illusion that if I was dogged and persistent enough, I could shape my world the way I wanted it. Every time I failed, I swallowed my wounded pride and worked through it.

Come back, said Cho Oyu, *when you have no pride left to swallow.*

7

The only place that success is before work is in the dictionary.
—JOHN WOODEN, BASKETBALL COACH

"Your climbing is pretty good," Daniel said as we were leaving Cho Oyu. "You should think about Everest."

Don't get excited. He wasn't talking to me.

I sat in a tepid stew of disappointment spiced with a few red pepper flakes of jealousy while Daniel and the Australian police-man launched into an animated conversation about making Everest happen. *Why him and not me?* I wondered, and not in a bitter rhetorical sense. I seriously wanted to know what it was that Daniel saw as the tipping point, the nuts-and-bolts difference between this guy's dream and my pipe dream.

Being brutally honest with myself, I wasn't ecstatic about my performance on Cho Oyu. I was stronger than ever before but still not as strong as the other climbers. I rolled into the high camps dead last, sucking wind, feeling like my legs were made of chicken aspic. I knew this meant my breath and cardio components were not in sync with my exertion levels. So clearly step one would be stepping up the cardio and focusing on VO_2 max (the maximum amount of oxygen my body utilized during intense exercise). Again. I dreaded the process with every last molecule in my quaking thighs. I'm exactly the wrong body type for high-altitude mountaineering: naturally muscular, short and strong rather than long and lean. Mother Nature was against me in this endeavor in more ways than one. I needed to get the science right and depend on the gifts Mother Nature did give me: good bones, tenacity, and 20/20 hindsight.

I went home determined to get this formula right. I spent the flight back to Hong Kong rewinding the past six months, filtering the experience through that part of my brain that still contained the MBA. Crotonville, GE's executive boot camp, focused on "soft skills" like inclusivity, awareness, and egalitarianism. Brainstorming went around the room like a cyclone: desire realized by method, method powered by logic, logic shored up by research, research sparked by desire. The experience left me with the tools that brought order to my ambition. I knew how to get a good idea on its feet, creating that story on the wall with scrap paper and Blu-Tack, building the foundation that makes you an intelligent risk taker instead of an impulsive shithead. On a mountain, the stakes are higher, but Jack Welch's voice was still there in the back of my brain, and everything he said still applied.

Create a vision, articulate the vision, passionately own the vision, and relentlessly drive it to completion.

As soon as I got home from Cho Oyu, I sent Daniel an email, thanking him for his efforts. I asked point-blank: "What would it take for me to climb Everest?"

His response was good-natured: "So you really want to climb Everest? All right, then. Here's what you need to do." He laid out a straightforward list of things he recommended to optimize my body and prepare my mind, an estimate of what I'd have to invest in the endeavor, plus a list of mountains I should consider climbing before I tried Everest again. I scanned the list, cross-referencing on

Google Earth. Interesting. He was sending me lower before going higher. Mount Washington in New Hampshire, Mount Rainier in Washington State, Cho Oyu or Shishapangma in the Himalayas.

My new training strategy was all about staying strong without overdoing the weights. I added Pilates for core strength, continued with high-intensity interval training for cardio, and included yoga for stretching. In many ways, training for an expedition is harder than the expedition itself. It requires patience, a quality I'm not naturally blessed with, and you have to keep up the training intensity over a longer period of time—no slacking allowed. There's no real or imagined finish line where you can say, "I'm done. That's enough." So in my mind, there's no such thing as enough. I always feel like I could have done more.

It was a bit of a body slam when Jonathan told me he'd been offered a job in Boston. He was asking me to leave my friends, the tight little tribe of supporters, and training resources I'd cultivated in Hong Kong. I hadn't lived in the United States for fifteen years. Jonathan had never lived there.

"I won't call it a nightmare," I said, "but this might take considerable sorting, starting with the electronics."

The segue from London to Hong Kong had been fairly smooth— both on 220 volts. The awkward switch to US outlets seemed symbolic. Would I fit in over there? On the other hand, I realized, Boston is a three-hour drive from Mount Washington, which now topped my "To Be Climbed" list, so . . .

"Off we go, Mr. O'Brien. I'll make it work."

A few months later, we were settled into our new home, making new friends and getting used to the food. (I'd almost forgotten the American penchant for serving lumberjack-size portions and how every supermarket floods its aisles with processed sugar.) I searched out new training facilities, and Daniel connected me with a guide named Craig John who would help me explore Mount Washington.

To be honest, I rolled my eyes when I first saw this molehill on Daniel's list. The elevation is a comparatively petite 6,288 feet, but it's the highest peak east of the Mississippi and has a reputation for insanely bad weather—a mix of screaming winds, blinding ice storms, and blizzards that bring everything to an inundated halt. At this writing, Mount Washington holds the record for the highest measured wind speed outside a tornado. At the summit, two jet streams intersect—compounded by upslope winds—and whip-crack the atmosphere, creating violent weather.

Speaking to how many climbers underestimate this "molehill," Nicholas Howe, author of *Not Without Peril*, tactfully observes that "poor judgment tends to multiply." In the past 170 years, almost 150 people have died climbing it, nearly half the death toll of Everest. Four years after I summited Mount Washington, a friend of a friend lost her life there, debilitated by extreme cold that was driven colder still by winds that outclocked Hurricane Sandy. This mountain was not to be taken lightly.

As Craig and I climbed in March, six months after returning from Cho Oyu, I began to understand why some indigenous people once called her Agiochook, the hidden summit, place of the Concealed One. We fought our way up in near-whiteout conditions—zero visibility, making it impossible to see my boots on the ground—with the wind howling like a stadium full of metalheads. My goggles froze against my face. My hands and feet turned to wooden clubs. I don't know how, but we summited.

Every mountain is a master class. Agiochook taught me that every mountain demands respect. She exacted a price for the lesson, but she brought me luck. I bounced back down the hill like Tigger. As soon as I had a decent signal, I called Jonathan.

"My nonsummiting days are over, Spousey. The winning streak is on!"

"Congratulations," he said, "though I'm not sure I'd quantify one summit as a streak."

"You're a numbers man. I get it. Think of it as a data point."

"Sure. Come home safely so we can argue the point. Did you get pictures?"

"Lots," I said, "but they all look like the inside of a blender."

The next item on Daniel's list was Ouray, a man-made ice park in the San Juan Mountains in southwestern Colorado. I spent four days there, working on my ice-climbing skills alongside Selki, a New Zealander who hadn't done much alpine mountaineering but was solid and outdoorsy. She took to the ice like a polar bear; I was more cautious, deliberate and mindful of good ice-climbing technique, positioning my body in a triangle with my legs apart, trying to relax my upper body, which tended to take over whenever I was in a hanging position on rock or ice. I noticed the huge difference between novice climbers, who slammed their ice axes in multiple times to get purchase, and the pros, who placed the blade with one steady, swift swing. I worked hard to perfect that purposeful swing and learned to keep my heels down, using my feet for support, rather than hanging on my axe for dear life.

On our way home, I told Selki about my plans to climb Mount Rainier, the next objective on Daniel's list.

"I signed up for Liberty Ridge," I told her. "They only take four climbers, but it's considered the most difficult of the four primary routes and my future Everest guide recommended it. Kautz Glacier is more mountaineering. Liberty Ridge is more ice climbing."

I guess my enthusiasm about it was a good sales pitch. A week later, the climbing company asked me to move over to the Kautz Glacier team so Selki could climb Liberty Ridge. She was eager to

sign on for the same reasons I was, and I am assuming the climbing company saw an opportunity to bring in two fees instead of
one. I'm not shy about trying to get what I want, so I get it. All's
fair, right? But up to this point, I'd experienced only friendly competition in the mountaineering world—nothing like this—so this
pissed me off. I drafted a smartly scathing note to the climbing
company to let them know I didn't appreciate this bait and switch
and that they should be investing in me, the one training and
spending money with them to climb Everest, not another client
who hadn't expressed long-term objectives, like climbing Everest
with them, as I had.

"Get it out of your system," Jonathan advised, "but don't send
that email if you hope to climb with them again. Seems like mountain climbing is a rather small world."

It felt like swallowing a domino, but I knew he was right. You
learn to choose your battles, and this was one I could let slide. I
let the frustration fuel my workouts for a few days and turned my
research to Kautz Glacier. Deep snow had made this a particularly
challenging year. So far in 2011, no one had been able to summit by that route. I was okay with that, shored up by my winning
streak of one. Bring on the challenge.

On my way to join the Kautz Glacier team, I passed by IMG's
camp where I found Selki getting ready for Liberty Ridge. We
greeted each other with guarded smiles and agreed to meet up for
dinner after our climbs. I also saw Craig, my Mount Washington
guide, who waved and loped over to me.

"Hey, O'Brien! Small world."

"So I hear." Score one for Spousey. The climbing world is indeed small, so climbers are constantly jockeying for position and
vying for sponsorship dollars, but at the end of the day, we're
out there together maintaining close quarters in a hostile envi-

ronment. Friction is inevitable, but it makes you work harder to cultivate supportive relationships and situations in which you feel connected.

"Are you leading the Kautz Glacier team?" I asked Craig.

"No, that's Jessica," he said, "but I'll be able to check in with you on the radio."

"Jessica?" Okay, it's not like a griffin flew over and landed on the picnic table next to us, but she was the first female guide I had encountered, and it felt awesome. Women make great leaders. End of story. And this woman was especially fierce, physically strong, and technically proficient. I would witness her in action later as she fixed ropes, balanced on the glare ice of the steep glacier. She and her three male assistants were facilitating eight climbers: five American men, an Italian guy, an American woman named Ruth, and me.

Protocol on Rainier is to divvy up group gear to transport food and accoutrements while keeping everyone's pack under fifty pounds. It's a double-edged sword, this group gear distribution, because at some point, the law of diminishing returns kicks in and the marginal weight of food or tents for one additional climber should be negligible, whereas the cost savings should be higher, because you've also got more people sharing that burden. I was hoping the climbing company knew what that number was and that it was within our team dynamics.

I know it sounds a bit colonial, but as a Himalayan climber, I had never carried group gear. Sherpa assist with group gear on longer expeditions, and in the Himalayas, pretty much all the expeditions are long because the mountains are enormous. Sherpa are more experienced with high-altitude mountaineering, and for many, it's both livelihood and tradition. As long as mutual respect and fair pay are standard, it's a good arrangement for everyone, particularly someone who's still working on the "travel light" concept. We joke about climbers shaving the stems off their toothbrushes to save weight. I'm the one with the family-size tube of toothpaste and a spare toothbrush at Base Camp in case someone else forgot theirs—and someone else always forgets theirs. Ruth arrived with no alpine gear, needing to rent everything, while the rest of us had arrived pretty kitted out.

I was strong after all my training and didn't mind toting the proverbial barge. Ruth showed up a little late, so there was only one piece of group gear left: a giant lobster pot filled with food. The others looked at me, and then looked at Ruth—who is also all of five foot four—and then side-eyed this enormous pot. What we didn't know was that Ruth was an army major, director of skull base surgery at Walter Reed Army Medical Center. She could build a tent and perform head and neck surgery inside it. That pot was probably half her body weight, but she picked it up like she didn't give a damn, and we set off for the park entrance.

We were looking at four and a half days to complete the climb. Jessica managed expectations from the start. "No one has summited from this route this season. We're likely to see deep snow and high winds."

I'd done my homework. According to National Park Service data, between 2006 and 2010, an average of 381 climbers attempted the Kautz Glacier route every year. The success rate as of 2010 was only 60 percent—and that was in an average year with moderate snow and wind. Now the heavy layer of snow disguised deep crevasses, and howling wind made it harder to hear rocks falling.

The first day, we crossed open alpine meadows of fragrant grass, but within a few hours, we were breaking trail through the snow fields and crossing the Nisqually Glacier, making slow but steady progress to our first campsite at 7,000 feet. Ruth and I were sharing a tent, and she had that thing upright and tight as a drumhead in minutes while I shoveled snow to level our campsite and stomped it flat. We crawled inside, and Ruth put on some mellow music. The climbing company had rented her a pair of double plastic boots, which are waterproof, warmer, and easy to attach crampons to, but imparted some vicious blisters. I noted she tended to them without whining.

"They can load me down physically, but they will never beat me mentally." She tapped her temple. "Everything I need to win is up here."

"Copy that, Major." I offered a fist bump, and we tucked ourselves into our sleeping bags.

The next day, we pushed through the drifts, step by laborious step, up to High Camp at 10,000 feet. The snow was over our knees now, and half the group was fairly knackered. After building our camp, we stood for a while, looking out at the distant vista. The spectacular view was worth the painful price. We were above a thick cotton-batting layer of clouds. The sinking sun created a prism of blue, yellow, and orange and ignited every ice particle on the mountain. The glacier sparked and glowed, lit from within, and eventually faded to silvery blue.

As we settled into High Camp, one of Jessica's assistant guides announced that he intended to stay behind with two climbers who were tapping out. I understood their decision, but I was feeling good about going on. Talking to Craig on the radio, I got an additional boost of confidence before I rejoined the hot tea huddle.

"Listen, everyone," Jessica said, "I have good news and bad news, and we have a decision to make. The weather is on our side, but the fact is, we're moving too slow to make the summit tomorrow. So I need a decision. Do you want to see how far we can make it as a group? Or do some of you want to stay here and allow others to go for a summit push?"

I looked around the circle. No one met my eyes. No one wanted to be the first to chime in. I heard Jack Welch in my ear: *Control your own destiny or someone else will.*

"I'd like to see someone summit," I said. "I'd like to see even a few of us get there—break this season of no summits—rather than have all of us climb a little higher, which doesn't buy any summits for anyone." I tried to laugh instead of cough. "Kind of an old-school Everest approach in the spirit of Tenzing and Hillary. Just get someone up there, right?"

I didn't try to sell the bitter gifts of not summiting to those who knew they weren't going to make it. I wouldn't be ready to hear that if I were in their position. For a moment, there was only the sound of the wind. A few others chimed in with a tepid "Hey, we're all in this together," but the majority of voices were aligned with my way of thinking.

"Okay." Jessica looked around the circle, not naming any names. Instead of asking for volunteers to stay behind, she asked, "Knowing tomorrow is the hardest day, who feels like you've got it in you to keep up the pace we have to maintain in order to summit?"

Ruth and I immediately raised our hands. The Italian raised his hand, followed by one of the Americans. That was it. Jessica waited, studying each face, meeting every eye. She wasn't making it easy.

"All right, then," she said. "You four will come with me and a guide to the summit tomorrow morning. The rest will stay here with a guide until we return, and we'll descend as a team."

This is the difference between typical male leadership and—that rarest of unicorns—a woman in charge of an endeavor traditionally dominated by men. In my experience, a male guide would have taken one of two approaches: A) cautious: "We're moving too slow to summit. We're all going down." Or B) authoritative: "You, you, and you are going too slow. You're staying behind. Everyone else, prepare to summit." If a woman said the same words in the same tone of voice, people would say she was A) weak or B) a bitch. Jessica's soft-skills approach—a two-way discussion that challenged us to be our best selves and come to an egalitarian decision as a group—was an example of how female leadership is often more collaborative and communicative.

That night, the wind was a relentless scold. We had to use our ice axes to secure our tents. After sleeping on it—what little sleep there was—the American guy had a change of heart. He swallowed his pride and stayed at the camp as Jessica and the last remnant of the team waded into the deep snow to access the Kautz Glacier and headed up, bracing ourselves against the "windy summit" dynamic that formed a shrieking vortex at the peak. Struggling to stay upright, Ruth and I clung to each other, grinning inside our buffs. The morning sun lit the silver sweep of ice below and the Cascade mountain range around us. Old volcanoes cast looming shadows that made the valleys look dark and wet. It was cold and quiet down there, the antithesis of all the fire and pandemonium that created this sacred place.

At camp that night, I recorded on my iPhone: *Mt. Rainier Kautz Glacier, 14,410 feet, summit at 11:30 AM June 16, 2011.*

My first active volcano. My first climb with group gear and a female guide. I didn't have the poetry to explain the ancientness and sacredness and grandeur of this mountain, Tacoma, the Mother of Waters, and I was too sleepy to force my stiff fingers to write down any more than the technical details. My mind was already on the Himalayas.

PART II

CLIMB AND PUNISHMENT

8

Whether you believe you can do a thing or not, you are right.
—HENRY FORD

"To be ready for Everest," I told Jonathan in July, "I need to get above 8,000 meters, and the only two seasons for reasonably sane attempts are spring and fall. If I don't move forward now, I'll miss the opportunity to experience high altitude before Everest."

"So what's the plan?" he asked. "Go back to Cho Oyu?"

"It's on the list, but—*ugh*, it's sort of demoralizing." My hammies clenched at the thought of all that up and down on Kitty Litter Hill. My quads groaned in unison. "There's another mountain climbers train on—Shishapangma, the only Eight Thousander entirely in Tibet. I was thinking I'd run it by Daniel to see if he'd consider it."

He nodded. "Shishapangma, then."

Yes. Another trip to the naughty chair successfully negotiated. When I pitched the Shishapangma idea to Daniel, he said, "I've never been there, but I've had several inquiries about it over the years from climbers who summit Cho Oyu and are looking for something else."

Gee, I wonder why.

"So theoretically," I said, "this could be like a reconnaissance trip to see if it's profitable for IMG to add Shishapangma to its roster."

"*Theoretically*. I know a Sherpa who's been there. Let me reach out to some people and see if I can get some climbers on board to make it feasible."

I ran with "feasible" and went on to researching the next step, pitching Daniel on a stretch goal. "Since we'd already be acclimatized, why not leverage our red blood cells and go straight over to Cho Oyu after we summit Shishapangma? According to my research, a lot of climbers have done this. There's this Swiss guy, Ueli Steck—"

Daniel barked a short clip of laughter. "Ueli Steck? Okay, then!"

I could tell I'd put my foot in my mouth, and a quick trip to Google informed me that mentioning Ueli Steck was like saying, "There's this British guy, Paul McCartney . . ."

Crap.

When I sent my second payment to IMG, I nudged the idea forward again. I knew I wasn't the only climber-of-a-certain-age gouging into retirement savings for these expeditions. The twofer would leverage more than the red blood cells; it would mean leveraging some of the travel expenses too, funding one eight- to ten-week expedition instead of two six- to eight-week expeditions. The answer came back: "No guarantee." But if I was willing to commit, they said, so was one other climber. The two of us would combine our resources and fund the $30,000 needed to maintain a base camp the company already had in place. If planets aligned, we might be able to complete back-to-back summits.

I flew to Hong Kong, caught up with friends during a brief layover, and went on to Kathmandu. I saw some familiar faces in town, including Craig, my lucky Mount Washington guide, who was now paired up with Alex, the assistant guide from my previous misadventure on Cho Oyu. The two of them were leading a team to Cho Oyu while Daniel, without an assistant guide, would lead our team to Shishapangma. The Cho Oyu team would be traveling with us as far as Tingri and included two women climbers, Heidi Sand from Germany and Emma from the United States, who both had climbing experience and were hoping to go for Everest someday.

In Kathmandu, most climbers end up at Hotel Tibet, a mountaineer-friendly place, or they bump up to the Yak & Yeti. I had found my secret hideaway called Dwarika's Hotel, which was presented with UNESCO's Cultural Heritage Conservation Award in 2006. The hotel walls are covered with intricate carvings and musical instruments. In the bar, there's a black-and-white photograph of the King with the King—Nepal's King Mahendra with Elvis—and that says it all. Great pains have been taken to respect and cherish the past while ensuring this building has a bright future. It was a good place to end any long expedition, a cozy bed to forgive the previous eight uncomfortable weeks.

The next morning, I met up with Daniel and the rest of the team: Charles, a teacher from California; Cliff, a seasoned Texas lawyer who'd already scaled several 8,000-meter peaks; and Norman, a Chicago pipe fitter. Initially, everyone was outgoing and friendly, and I was optimistic. This seemed like a mutually supportive team of cool climbers who could go the distance.

Charles hadn't been to Kathmandu before, so I gave him the grand tour. We checked out the architectural wonders in the old town. In Durbar Square, we caught a glimpse of the Kumari Devi, a young girl who serves as Nepal's incarnate goddess until she reaches the age of menstruation. We traveled to Boudhanath, a holy site rich in history and symbolism, where pilgrims spin prayer wheels and purchase yak butter and *tsampa*, the roasted barley flour used in the Puja ceremony. We sat in silence on the banks of the sacred river Bagmati, and watched as bodies were placed on wooden platforms for cremation. The monkeys in the Monkey Temple, Swayambhunath, rummaged in my pockets for peanuts and snatched my water bottle while I was distracted by the magnificent view of the sprawling, swarming city. As we sat on a street corner having our faces painted and blessed, I told Charles, "It doesn't matter if we're being snookered. We need all the blessings we can get today."

The next day, in Thamel, I stopped into Pilgrims, a bookstore where you can find every climbing book in the world—new, used, rare, and even some signed first editions—along with a lot of cool one-off climber novelties like playing cards with all the Eight Thousanders on them and knitted wool animal hats with long bits that hang down over your ears. I bought enough hats for all the climbers, guides, and Sherpa and distributed them that evening over dinner. Daniel was crowned with the rooster hat, and a lot of creative cock jokes ensued.

"Let's go around the table and get to know each other," said Daniel, and he got the ball rolling with a brief summary of his impressive climbing experience. Cliff donned his wolf hat and wowed everyone with his climbing résumé. This may have been the first time I heard the term *Explorers Grand Slam*.

"In addition to a few Eight Thousanders," he said, "I've done the Explorers Grand Slam, which includes the Seven Summits, and trekked to the North and South Poles."

"I haven't been over 20,000 feet," said Charles, who'd gone for the green frog hat, "but I've spent a lot of time in the mountains and ran safety in Yosemite."

"I'm Vanessa," I said. "I'm a relatively new climber too. Grateful to be here. I'll do my best not to hold things up." The consensus was that I should have the tiger hat.

"I've done a lot of climbing," said Norman, who'd opted for

the bear hat. "I just started consulting. I might hang out in Kathmandu for a while and make it my new home."

Climbers come from every stripe of the social sphere. Extraordinary things are seldom done by people who adhere to standards like "normal" (no such thing) and "how it's done" (time-honored battle cry of the status quo), so I'm all about people who are brave enough and free enough to be themselves. Still I found Norman vaguely unsettling; it was the implication that at the present he might be adrift with nothing to lose. In my experience, the greatest adventurers are tethered firmly to people or places they love. Imagine Odysseus without Penelope or Dorothy without Kansas. I'd given Pippa's boys a map so they could follow my adventure, and I was heartened every time I thought about those colorful lines connecting to my ipso facto family far away.

As Daniel talked us through the expedition, step by step, I revisited each milestone in my mind: the Friendship Bridge, the coffeehouses, even the "I can't wait to never be here again" town of Tingri. I was already looking forward to that fork in the road.

Early the next morning, we all crammed into a minibus with our duffels and bounced up the road. I'd forgotten about all those potholes, but my glutes remembered. I wriggled into my bus-sleeping position: slumped down, chin to chest, neck wedged with whatever kept it stationary, feet up on my pack, earbuds set to lullaby. About an hour later, I opened my eyes to find Daniel sitting next to me. He nodded toward the window and mouthed, "There's a spider."

I instantly turned into a writhing, slapping ball of adrenaline, but then I saw everyone laughing and realized he was pulling my leg.

"Asshole." I tried to chuckle as I collected myself.

The last mile of rutted road approaching the Friendship Bridge was cluttered with buses and transport vehicles. Just before we reached the border, the Sherpa facilitated passport stamps and we stopped for lunch. I was wearing an olive-green baseball cap—the iconic Chairman Mao cap—and Daniel looked at it pointedly before we went into the restaurant.

"Interesting choice."

"I bought it in Vietnam," I said.

"There are those who might see it as a political statement," said Cliff.

"I'm being ironic. The border guards aren't going to notice it like you do. Watch. It's like, 'Hey there. I see you, and I'm not scared.' We're all just people." I touched the bill of the faded cap. "We've all got the same sun in our eyes."

Of course, no one in China gave the hat a second glance as we crossed the border and went on to Zhangmu. Our hotel was a walk-up, and it seemed like three hundred stories up to my room. The walls smelled like mold, and the lights flickered and buzzed like a flea circus, but there was a bathroom, and the bedding seemed relatively clean. One of the other climbers discovered a fresh turd on his pillow. He brought it to the attention of the innkeeper, who said, "Oh, fine, fine. Just cat."

Our next stop was in Nyalam, where I bought as many bananas as my fellow climbers and I could possibly eat before we went off. I knew this was the last fresh produce we would see for two months, so I was happy to share. We stuffed ourselves with fruit and posed for a group picture wearing fancy Chinese robes stocked by the hotel, and then we made our way to Tingri, which hadn't changed a bit. The same little convenience store and restaurants were across the muddy road where cardboard-munching cows and nocturnal dogs roamed. The same smell of sewage hung over the ditches. I could practically hear the mycobacteria teeming on every surface, including the dank cement floor of my room.

"Touch nothing," I advised Heidi and Emma. "Disinfect every-thing."

I had no way to call Jonathan. No matter what I tried—SIM cards, international coverage, Wi-Fi—service was comparable with the cell reception you'd get in Dante's seventh circle of hell, unless you had a satellite phone, which I never did.

It was time to part company with the Cho Oyu team. With bear hugs all around, I said goodbye and wished them well for their summit. I felt a pang of sympathy, knowing they were facing all those acclimatizing hikes up and down Kitty Litter Hill. This was my opportunity to outsmart Cho Oyu and show up ready to rock with a fresh cache of red blood cells. On the other hand, Cho Oyu had been summited over 3,000 times, while Shishapangma had been summited just 302 times, and there were plenty of reasons why. The only way to fully understand the rationale for this mul-tiple of ten was to go there.

I loved being part of this off-the-beaten-path reconnaissance mission. Only Ang Chhiring (Kami) Sherpa had climbed this mountain before. It was new territory for the rest of us, including Daniel. He was a different person when he wasn't on autopilot, when he didn't know what was ahead and really had to pay atten-tion and rely on his experience. It kept him fresh and on his toes.

We set up our Base Camp next to a lovely little glacial stream, positioning all the tents on grass with a view of the mountain twenty miles away. As we worked, a magnificent thunderstorm rolled in, and Shishapangma disappeared into the greenish-gray clouds. I chose a tent close to the water, wondering as I crawled in if there were spiders this high. We were now at 16,500 feet and planned to acclimatize here for at least three days while we sorted our gear. The Sherpa went ahead with a few yaks to set up camp while we made day hikes to the nearby hills, climbing above

20,000 feet and coming back down. Then it was climb high, sleep low, climb high, sleep low, until it was time to move on to Advanced Base Camp (ABC).

"Keep some flip-flops handy," Daniel advised. "There's at least one stream to cross."

When we came to the icy water, I took off my boots and socks and stepped in. Within minutes my feet were numb with cold, but I managed to cross the rotting logs and slick stones. We followed the river for a while, then crossed the plains to the hills.

At Shishapangma ABC (18,375 feet), our home for the next four weeks, I chose a tent, put on music, and organized my gear: sleeping bag, snacks, layers of clothing, Kindle, climbing kit, and the all-important device that made it comfortable and hygienic to pee into a bottle at night, kneeling in a corner of the tent instead of weathering the frigid darkness. ABC was a small world in itself, a busy little village of teams coming and going, climbers representing every continent, race, and religion. Two Norwegian climbers—a schoolteacher and a policeman—had long hair and beards and wore black fishnet shirts. I reckon only Norwegians could get away with a look like that. Or maybe ABBA. Various climbers would come to visit us, congregating in our mess tent, laughing, telling stories, and sharing strategies for acclimatization.

"I'm looking forward to getting above 20,000 feet again," I said. "No spiders. The little bastards can live as high as 17,500 feet, so until I get to Camp 1, I never say never. I do a thorough inspection of my tent before I turn out the light."

I can pinpoint the moment my arachnophobia kicked in. I was seven years old. It was summertime. My mother fired up the barbecue, and armed with a squirt gun, I was supposed to watch the fire to make sure it didn't go anywhere. I was just hanging out, squirting whatever happened to be in reach—a black carpenter ant, a low-hanging leaf—and I felt a strange little tickle on my shoulder. A large wood spider had dropped down onto my arm and was making its way up toward my neck, and because it was so close to my face, it looked as big as a walnut. I flailed, screaming the raw, guttural scream of someone who's being burned alive. That's how it sounded to my mother, as she hobbled down the stairs to help me. It took her forever, because she was on crutches.

My mother was on crutches.

This is the first moment I recall being really aware of that, being aware that she was not the same and never would be again. The story, to the extent that I understood it, was that she and my father were out hunting, and Mom inexplicably rested a loaded gun on her foot, and somehow the gun went off, and then her foot was gone. Seeing that story in my mind, repeating it by way of explanation over the years, the foot just disappeared. I never had a clear vision of the messy horror that must have been. Maybe the mental self-defense mechanism that refused entry to that image is the same one that protects me from imagining the messy horror of a body being tumbled by a glacier.

I never gave much thought to what led up to the maiming of my mother, only what remained: a bluish-white stump over which she used to fit a hard, fake flesh-colored prosthetic. I never saw her display any emotion about this missing part of herself or any of the other physical damage she sustained in the years I knew her. She was not a stoic when it came to grief—she took her later bereavement like a body slam—but physical pain she knew how to handle. She toughed it out, dressing accordingly without compromising her well-comported suburban style other than a grudging farewell to high heels. Ben and I enjoyed the silver lining of her handicapped parking access, which we saw as the equivalent of valet parking, because we didn't really think of her as handicapped and were too young to know better. There were very few moments that triggered any real memories about it, and for me, that spider moment was the first.

My nightly spider check is a little ritual that allows me to sleep nights, and my finely honed Spider-Woman sixth sense makes me hyperaware of any movement in the dark corners of a tent lit by a dangling headlamp. At Shishapangma ABC, there were no roaches or centipedes, but one night I was visited by a little mountain vole. Hearing me shuffling around my tent talking to myself, Charles came to the rescue and grabbed the little bugger with a plastic bag, trying to save it from being murdered by me. He seemed a bit hurt when the vole rewarded him with a needle-sharp bite.

The first day of blood-building acclimatization day hikes from ABC was a scramble, leaping *Frogger* style from the top of one boulder to the top of the next. I envied Daniel's mountain goat agility; I kept slipping and sliding, narrowly averting disaster. About midday, we reached the *nieves penitentes*, sculpted snow and ice formations up to fifty feet high. They're called "the penitent snows" because to some early explorer, they looked like parishioners on their way to mass, but to me, the area looked like an inverted version of the Khumbu Icefall, with huge white blades jutting up toward the blue sky instead of blue crevasses slicing down into the white snow. Even from a distance, I was blown away by the scope of the legion of steep ice towers that stood, high and silent, robed in blue, as if to guard the mountain from intruders.

I put my crampons on and quickly realized how rusty my ice-climbing skills had become. Crampon technique is "use it or lose it." The steeper the mountain, the more horizontal your feet splay, unless you're using the French technique, in which case both feet are horizontal to the mountain, sidestepping one foot over the other, facing the same direction. When the mountain is nearly vertical, you may opt to do something called front pointing—slamming the metal teeth on the front of the crampon into the ice or snow—but you do it sparingly, because it doesn't take long to burn out your calves and shins. Staggered by how hard it was initially, I tried to calm myself down as everyone else zipped off into the sunset. After struggling through for a while, I looked up and felt an unpleasant bolt of panic. I was alone. The ghostly white penitents thronged around me, serrated heads bowed to pray, dripping and whispering.

"Hey!" I called. "Hey, where are you guys?"

For a terrifying moment, there was no answer but the Gregorian chant of the wind. Then Daniel appeared. He waved from the top of a formation that seemed miles away.

"Hey!" I waved back and tried to keep my voice level. "Wait up!"

He gave me a thumbs-up and disappeared again.

"Keep calm. Keep up." My own take on British climbing motivation. My mind raced through a number of mini mantras. "I am Scylla the rock—Marathon Man—I can endure any pain."

We did this again the next day and the day after that. Over the boulders and through the *penitentes*, back through the *penitentes* and over the boulders. By the end of the third day, I had my mojo back and was keeping up with the team, but I wasn't overconfident. That first day kept me humble. I was probably praying harder than the *penitentes* were.

A local lama came to perform the Puja ceremony, and once the ritual was completed, the Sherpa were ready to climb. However, the next morning there was a 6.9 magnitude earthquake in India near the Nepalese border, and it was strong enough that we felt it in Tibet. Daniel made a reconnaissance climb up to Camp 1 at 21,000 feet and found that landscape significantly changed. He called the other expedition leaders together for a meeting so that everyone could share the geological and weather information they were getting from forecasters around the world. Each team had their own take on this inexact science, but Daniel rallied everyone around the common desire to summit. They compared notes, inventoried climbing resources, and tried to determine the overall readiness for summit of each team. The goal was to understand who was willing to pitch in and with what, manpower or equipment, in order to make the summit.

We climbed to Camp 1, just to acclimatize for a couple days, but the weather got steadily worse.

"I need to head back," said Charles, my Camp 1 tentmate and by far the most chilled out of the bunch. "This is taking too long."

I was disappointed, but not surprised. An expedition is sometimes like the dwindling cast of an Agatha Christie mystery. You turn the pages, wondering who'll be the next one knocked off. Back at ABC, a lot of people were packing it in. Those who remained combined resources. We'd been there for five weeks of tremors, high winds, and bouts of blowing snow, and the fatigue was beginning to show. This was not Nepal. We were in Tibet. The Chinese didn't have the same reciprocal relationships with the United States that Nepal did, so if a problem arose, there would be no rescue resources, no access to medical consultation, and no medevac.

Alone in my tent, I read about Alex Lowe, a renowned climber who died on Shishapangma in 1999. He'd set out with two friends—Conrad Anker and David Bridges—planning to become the first Americans to ski down the summit of an 8,000-meter peak. A serac broke loose several thousand feet above them, creating a 500-foot-wide avalanche. They stood watching. They even took pictures. My trusty self-defense mechanism kept me from imagining that moment when they realized the true size and speed of the avalanche. Anker was found, broken but alive. The bodies of Lowe and Bridges were missing for sixteen years, until Ueli Steck and David Goettler spotted yellow Koflach boots. It was them.

I lay in my sleeping bag, willing my mind to slow down, focused on the weather. There's always a lot of gossip and networking, especially on mountains where teams have to work together, so data is constantly being shared and compared. Sherpa weigh in with the canny voice of experience, which is sometimes more on point than the faraway meteorologists, who know about weather systems and the behavior of the atmosphere but don't always get the timing right. Each team tends to be biased toward the weather service to which they subscribe, and ours was warning us about strong winds and frostbite danger on the exposed ridge leading up to the summit. Wind speed determines whether you'll be able to stand up or be forced to crawl the ridge on your hands and knees. I was in the mess tent with Pertemba Sherpa and Norman when Daniel radioed down from Camp 1.

"ABC, what's the wind forecast looking like? Over."

I said, "Hey, Daniel, Vanessa here. We're good to go. Over."

"Uh, not quite, Daniel." Norman wedged between me and the radio. "The winds are forecast to be forty miles per hour. I don't think we want to be climbing in that."

I hesitated. As a relatively new climber, I was unsure of myself, but as a team member, I still carried the core of self-confidence I'd developed during my years at GE. I knew what I heard.

"No . . . I don't think that's right," I said. "The winds are forecast to be forty *kilometers* per hour. Repeat, Camp 1—forty *kilometers* per hour. That's only twenty-five miles per hour. Over."

"ABC, which is it?" asked Daniel. "Forty miles per hour or forty kilometers per hour?"

Norman glared at me like I'd just spit in his Wheaties. He said,

"She doesn't know what she's talking about, Camp 1. Wind speed is forty miles per hour. It's a no-go."

"No, the weather is usually reported in kilometers per—"

Norman started to bluster, red faced, zero to livid in three seconds flat.

"Okay, hang on, Camp 1," I said. "Just hang on a sec. Here comes Pertemba. He listened to the report with us."

Avoiding Norman's glare, Pertemba Sherpa said, "Boss, we go tomorrow. Forty-kilometer-per-hour winds. It's okay."

Norman fixed his angry gaze on me, arms locked across his rib cage, as we wrapped up the call, agreeing to leave at 5 AM. Pertemba Sherpa ducked out of the tent, and I moved to follow him, but Norman blocked the door, looming over me, standing close enough that I could smell his stale coffee breath.

"You fucking bitch," he said. "You'd better watch your back." And he walked out, leaving me standing there, frozen, stunned. I didn't dare move or breathe for several seconds. My heart was pounding. My hands were shaking.

"What . . . what the hell?"

My core reaction was anger, followed by confusion and then a shiver of apprehension. I'd read about people losing the plot at high altitude—guns brandished on K2 in 1902, crampons stolen from K2's Camp 4 in 2007. Throughout mountaineering history, there are examples of climbers cracking under the extreme stress of this extreme environment. What did I really know about this guy? Only what I'd witnessed, and what I witnessed a moment earlier scared me.

I lay in my tent that night, the brief episode replaying in my head. *You fucking bitch. You'd better watch your back.* What is it with control freaks? And what could he actually do? If he was in charge of boiling water, he could contaminate mine. He could tamper with my crampons or hide my safety gear. *What else? What else?* I was jolted awake by my watch alarm. I pulled on my clothes and headed over to the mess tent for breakfast, where I experienced a rude second awakening.

"Where's Norman?" asked Cliff.

"Gone," said the cook. "He took off on his own. Left for Camp 1 about an hour ago."

I couldn't believe it! That bastard had gotten up early and split. Now I was in a right state of panic. All I could think of was the climbing equipment that we had stashed—crampons, harnesses, helmets, ascenders—sitting in an unlocked storage tent near the *penitentes* on the far side of the vast rock scramble. He would have to stop there to collect his gear before continuing to Camp 1, and it would be so easy for him to sabotage my gear. All he had to do was damage or hide my crampons and I wouldn't be able to summit Shishapangma or Cho Oyu. I shoveled a few bites of scrambled egg into my mouth and downed my hot tea, trying not to burn my tongue but doing my best to hustle everyone out the door without letting on that I was freaking out a little. Norman was a more experienced climber than I was, but I was in survival mode, endorphins coursing through my veins. He was alone. I was with Dasonam Sherpa.

"Let's try to catch up with Norman," I said, pretending to make a game of it.

"Sure, *didi*," he said. (*Didi* is the Nepali word for "older sister.")

The two of us were about the same height, so we fell into a coordinated gait as we crossed the treacherous rock scramble. Dasonam Sherpa is always swift and sure-footed, and I bounced along behind him, trying to land my feet exactly where he landed his. I thought of Sun Tzu's words in *The Art of War*: "Move swift as the wind and closely formed as the wood. Attack like the fire and be still as the mountain." After an hour or so, we spotted Norman off in the distance. As if on cue, I slipped on a rock traverse, sending a shower of small rocks down the slope. Norman turned, startled.

"Hello up there," Dasonam Sherpa called with a friendly wave.

I felt Norman's eyes on me as I picked myself up, shaking off the stumble, and watched him as he headed upward again, picking up his pace. We trailed him for another hour. Dasonam pointed to a notch between the boulders.

"It's not easy," he said to me, "but I know a shortcut."

"Let's do it." I nodded.

When Norman arrived at the equipment tent, Dasonam and I were already there enjoying a cup of tea. Cliff arrived soon after, asking, "What's the rush? Everyone's in such a damn hurry today."

We stored our hiking boots and other nonessential gear and ventured into the *penitentes*. My heart sank when Norman took off at a gallop. Maybe he didn't want a woman to beat him to Camp 1. Or maybe he wanted to get there first so he could taint my water supply. Or maybe he would try to talk shit about me to Daniel and make it seem like I was a liability when it came time to summit.

Believe me, I know how paranoid this sounds. Still, in my experience, "paranoid" is often what women are taught to call ourselves when men do shady, shitty, inappropriate-but-maybe-not-overtly-abusive things that make us uncomfortable, starting on the playground with "he only shoved you into that snowbank because he likes you." Norman had told me to watch my back, and I took him at his word. My childhood experience had been that if a man is capable of threatening violence, he's capable of effecting violence. If my father said, "You better watch it, bitch," it was an utter certainty that my mother would be scraping herself off the floor approximately seventy seconds later.

I made my way through the *penitentes*, forcing myself to focus on the task at hand. It was hard work. I knew that if I fell behind Norman, I would not be able to make up for any lost time on the ice. Topping one of the frozen peaks, I saw him heading up the gentle snow slope, a 20-degree incline no more challenging than a ski run on the far side of the icefall. I stood panting, shaking with nerves and exertion.

"Dasonam, we've gotta catch up. We need to hurry."

He shrugged. "Okay, *didi*."

We both knew I was the one slowing us down. I swung my arms for circulation, stomped some warmth into my feet, and when we finally got through the *penitentes*, I took off like a bat out of hell up that ski slope. Every once in a while, I can count on my "wrong" body type for the kind of motor power that isn't great for high altitude but allows me to muscle my way up slopes. *Don't fail me now, hammies.* I passed Norman as the angles steepened and we approached the top of a small ridge. The bright orange peaks of the Camp 1 tents appeared in the distance. Getting closer, I saw Daniel shoveling a path between them like he was mowing a front yard in the suburbs. I picked up my pace, hustling along at a trot. By the time I got to him, I didn't even have the lung capacity to say his name.

"Wow. You made record time getting up here," he said, offering me a high five. "Take a load off. You're in that tent over there with me."

I nodded, elongating my exhale to slow down my heart and regulate my breath. In all those horror story scenarios that had played through my mind all day, it hadn't even occurred to me that I could have been bunking with Norman, a thought that made me physically ill. I climbed into the tent, searched out a morsel of critical comfort food—a frosted raspberry Pop-Tart, not too crumbled—and started hydrating.

About fifteen minutes later, I heard Daniel congratulating Nor-

man and Cliff as they came into Camp 1. There was an easy camaraderie between the three men. As there should be. Infighting is the
kiss of death to any climb. If I were to go to Daniel and tell him that
I felt threatened, Norman would have to defend himself by saying I
was just being a bitch, and Daniel would likely call off the summit
bid, which would also scrap our chance for Cho Oyu. Net-net: all
this work, all this planning, all this money, for zero summits instead
of the chance of two—a risk I wasn't willing to take.

"Conditions look good," Daniel said over dinner. "Looks like
we'll get our shot at the summit."

"What about Cho Oyu?" I asked.

"I'm not quite ready to commit. Let's stay focused on Shishapangma."

"Right." I forced a smile. "Wouldn't want to jinx it."

We secured the tents against high winds that might kick up,
said good night, and crawled inside. Daniel started boiling water
for tea. I trusted him, as a guide and, increasingly, as a friend, but
I couldn't see any upside to telling him what was happening. He
wouldn't take that kind of information and just park it. I certainly
wouldn't if I were team leader. I'd force a resolution then and there,
and if it couldn't be sorted out, I'd send both parties packing. So
I said nothing. We drank our tea, chatted, listened to music, and
quizzed each other.

"Name all fourteen 8,000-meter peaks," I said, hiding the map
with my hand. "Left to right. No—in order of elevation."

"Everest, obviously, then K2, Kangchenjunga, Lhotse, Makalu,
Cho Oyu . . ."

I was reading mountaineer Anatoli Boukreev's *Above the Clouds*,
and it was filled with my margin notes and highlights. I'm a collec-
tor of wise words that come back to me when I'm hunkered down
in my sleeping bag with only a sheath of tent fabric separating me

from the endless night sky. My half-sleeping mind becomes a cork-board of pithy adages I've stored up to apply as needed.

The next day we pushed through a gathering wind to Camp 2. Daniel met with the Sherpa to get their advice on a summit attempt, and they settled on a slightly new approach. The Sherpa's rope-fixing team started out ahead that night. The rest of us were to follow at 4 AM. I was testing a new pair of heated footpads called Hotronics in advance of Everest, and it took a few minutes to get them turned on and situated in my boots. Kami Sherpa, who would take me to the summit, waited patiently as I figured out my new gear, and we were on our way well before Norman, so I was happy.

Slowly, slowly we made our way up the sloping terrain to the steeper bits, then a rockier patch that was just what I imagined the Hillary Step on Everest would be like. We could use our jumars or ascenders to pull ourselves up a few places that had fixed ropes until we finally caught up with the rope-fixing team on the summit ridge. They were working so quickly, we had only a few minutes to rest, and then we were moving again. Daniel snapped a picture of Kami and me as we came around a rocky outcropping, and in that photograph, we're grinning ear to ear with miles and miles of endless mountaintops as a backdrop.

I was counting the steps now, with the summit in sight. Someone—a stranger from another team—extended a hand to offer me a final pull-up, and I was there, standing atop my first 8,000-meter summit. Kami, Daniel, and I group-hugged and took pictures, gusting great sighs of relief that formed clouds over our heads. The breathtaking view went on forever. The actual summit was tiny. Only a few climbers could position themselves on it at any one time. I surveyed the full 360-degree view. All around me were the world's tallest peaks. They looked like enormous meringue tips created by a master baker, a phenomenal mountain cake, iced white against the cloudless sky.

We stayed for fifteen minutes or so on the central summit, taking pictures, pointing out the other peaks, and drinking water. Not a single climber was interested in going to the true summit, another five meters higher, because of the snow conditions.

Anatoli Bookreev sums this up in *Above the Clouds.* He too summits Shishapangma central, writing, "Those who hunger for blood will maintain the summit is the summit and not a meter less. Each of us is physically capable of making that traverse under sane circumstances. Despite that, each of us was satisfied he had honestly climbed Shisha Pangma."

Then it was time to descend and make room for other climbers, the way others had stepped off to make room for us. Free climbing and mostly arm rappelling down to Camp 1, I felt downright ecstatic about this first summit bid and optimistic about the possibility of a second. Hiking down to ABC the following day, Daniel loped over to me and said, "It'll take a few days to arrange yaks to take the supplies back to base camp."

"Does this mean you're ready to commit?" I asked.

"Maybe," he said, which I took as slightly less of a noncommitment than I was used to. "I made a sat call to Craig and the Cho Oyu team last night."

"Did they summit?"

"Nope." He squinted up at the blue sky. "Avalanche risk. A couple of teams are giving it a try today—Koreans, Swedes—but people are saying it's another year with no summits."

"After so many great seasons, how is that possible?"

I felt bad for Heidi and Emma especially. All that buoyant anticipation. Women climbers work a step and a half harder than our male counterparts, and we get a fraction of the opportunities.

They deserved their moment, and I knew they'd feel the same way I did about attempting Cho Oyu twice.

"So the climbers and guides are going home?" I asked. "What about the Cho Oyu Sherpa? And the Cho Oyu cooking team—are they willing to stay?"

"I don't know," said Daniel, "but our Shishapangma Sherpa team is definitely going home."

"So let's ask their team. I mean, they depend on the season to last to the bitter end, right? They might be grateful for the opportunity. And if two other teams are attempting to summit, maybe they know something we don't. We're looking at weather reports. They're looking at actual weather."

Daniel laughed. "I figured I could count on you for a sales pitch. Either that or some wise saying."

"If at first you don't succeed, maybe Russian roulette is not for you."

Daniel rolled his eyes. "Ha, ha. Very funny."

Climbing is a long game. We'd parted ways with the Cho Oyu team in Tingri the last week of August, almost five weeks ago. It was early October now. Resources were running out. People needed to get back to their families, jobs, and lives. Opportunities do a drive-by, and if you're not patiently waiting on the curb, you're left behind.

"Still think you've got a twofer in you?" Daniel asked.

"I feel totally invigorated. Shishapangma's been amazing, especially the reconnaissance aspect. I loved every minute . . . almost." I tried to sound casual when I asked, "What's Norman's take on Cho Oyu?"

"Fifty percent. You both paid for Cho Oyu, and the money's not refundable. Other than that, he doesn't seem to care one way or the other."

Annoying, I thought, but out loud I said, "In for a penny, in for a pound. I still want to maximize my time and training. One hundred percent. Five hundred."

That evening at Base Camp, we said goodbye to Cliff and met up for dinner with a team that was doing the same thing we were doing, but in reverse. They'd just come from Cho Oyu without a summit and were as keen to hear about our experience as we were to hear about theirs. We peppered each other with questions about wind, snow depth, and camp conditions. My heart sank as they spoke wearily about snow on snow on snow and the constant rumble of avalanches. The satellite phone rang, and I perched on the edge of my seat.

"Yep . . . Uh-huh . . . Wow . . . Okay." Daniel's side of the conversation was cryptic, and he gave nothing away with his expression or body language.

When he hung up, I nudged his arm. "And?"

"We're in," he said. "Danuru and Karma Rita Sherpa of the Cho Oyu climbing team are willing to stay, as is Kaji Sherpa, the cook, to support our summit bid."

"Yes!" I jumped up and hugged him.

"How about it, Norman?" said Daniel.

In the corner, Norman gave a thumbs-up, but, to me, his smile was more grimace than grin.

9

If you're not about the namaste, *get the hell out of my way.*
—TERESA GIUDICE, REAL HOUSEWIFE OF NEW JERSEY

Cho Oyu's ABC was situated at the foot of the Nangpa La pass, a traditional trade route between Tibet and Nepal, a few kilometers west of Cho Oyu, and thirty kilometers northwest of Everest at an elevation of 5,700 meters. In 2006, a group of unarmed Tibetan pilgrims attempted to use the pass to leave Tibet, and Chinese border guards gunned them down as they moved through chest-deep snow.

I knew our camp cook, Kaji Sherpa, from the previous Cho Oyu expedition. He waved when he saw me, and I ran over to embrace him. It felt good to see a familiar face.

"I'm so chuffed that you're here," I said. "Thank you for giving us a chance to summit."

The previous team, bless their hearts and souls, had left three tents erected for us, along with a shower of sorts—a bucket with a ladle set up in a tent that allowed you to stand and dump water over your head, which was a luxury. There was no need to acclimatize because we'd already climbed the other mountain, so our strategy was simple: Take advantage of every possible break in the weather. Just go. Camp 1, Camp 2, summit. So far, I'd managed to stick close to Daniel and Kami Sherpa, successfully avoiding any interaction with Norman, but now Kami Sherpa wasn't here, and as we were sorting through our gear at Cho Oyu ABC, Norman said to Daniel, "I just hope you don't spend all your time with Vanessa, like you did on Shishapangma."

Daniel looked up with a startled half smile. "What do you mean?"

"You and I ought to be sharing a tent," Norman told Daniel. "Vanessa can share a tent with the Sherpa."

"What are you talking about? He was leading the expedition," I said. "We were all—"

"This is bullshit!" Norman lumbered to his feet, and I took a step back.

"Hey! Hey!" Daniel cut in. "Dial it down, both of you." He looked at Norman, then at me, sensing something else. "What's going on here?"

I pushed my hands farther down in my hip pockets and said nothing. Norman mumbled something about how group gear got divided.

Daniel sighed. "We've got a lot of ground to cover tomorrow. Let's get some sleep."

After one rest-day to re-pack our summit gear, we loaded up and headed for Camp 1 at 6,400 meters, but on the way, I made a rookie mistake. I set my Nalgene water bottle on the ground for less than a nanosecond at Camp 1, and it took a nice spin over a cliff into the valley.

"Bloody hell," I moaned as I watched it bounce off the boulders and disappear into the twisted underbrush. "Unbelievable."

Daniel radioed back to Base Camp, and after an hour or so, as if by magic, Kaji had sent up one of his own water bottles for me. It was bright pink and needed a bit of a clean, but it made me laugh. "That was so sweet of him!"

Norman brushed past me and muttered, "Shut the fuck up, you stupid bitch."

When we arrived at Camp 1, Daniel said, "Vanessa, go ahead and tent with Danuru Sherpa from here on. Norman, you're with me."

I told myself not to read anything into that, reminded myself to focus on what I could control. Hydration. Spicy noodles. A decent night's sleep. I would need a calm disposition and unwavering concentration to follow the snow and ice ridge before tackling a short but demanding ice cliff leading to Camp 2, at 7,040 meters. The next day we reached Camp 2 and decided to make our summit bid from here as we felt strong, healthy, and properly pre-acclimatized. I hoped for a bit of shuteye before our scheduled departure at 12 AM, but it was impossible to quiet my mind.

No one ever gets into full-blown REM sleep the night before a summit. Too much anxiety and anticipation. It didn't help that I could hear Daniel and Norman bro-ing down and laughing in a way that made me want to go out there and pitch a rock at their tent. I lay in my sleeping bag, reading *Songs of Blood and Sword: A Daughter's Memoir* by Fatima Bhutto, a moving portrait of political life in Pakistan. I eventually dozed off with Bhutto's rich story in my head.

My morning ritual began at 11 PM: hot water for oatmeal, summit kit, Hotronics, crampons, mitts, oxygen. As I left my tent, I saw Norman's and Daniel's headlamps like two fireflies already well off in the distance and thought, *Oh, for fuck's sake.* They could take their chortling, testosterone-fueled brotherhood and shove it up their asses.

I love the German expression *Sturm und Drang.* It literally translates to "storm and drive"—a perfect expression of how conflict behaves on a chemical level within the bloodstream: a maelstrom of all-over-the-place cortisol and a straight bolt of fight-or-flight adrenaline. Playground, board room, bedroom, battlefield—it's all the same to your bloodstream. You have a choice: get distracted by it or let it hang a motor on your ass. I chose the motor.

Danuru and I made good time climbing the notorious Yellow Band, a short section of exposed limestone leading to where Camp 3 would have been. As the route continued to get steeper, I used the "rest step" technique, placing a bit of extra weight on my back leg to give my front leg a break. Dawn was breaking, so I could see for some distance now. Daniel and Norman had widened the gap between us. The energizing burst of anger had dulled to a frustrated headache. I was getting tired and a bit sloppy, which is dangerous.

"What do you say we take a break?" Danuru Sherpa suggested.

"No, I'm good," I insisted, but then I tripped over my crampon and dropped my ice axe. Danuru made a grab for it, but the handle slipped through his fingers and the axe slid as quick as an eel down the trail, and luckily—*Thank you, God*—it got hung up on some loose rocks. Danuru dashed down to retrieve it and handed it up to me.

I clutched it against my chest and said, "Holy shit. That was close."

"Too close, *didi*. We should take a break."

"Okay. Maybe just for a sec."

I shook my head and slapped my face, trying to clear the cobwebs. What was going on? My brain felt like an owl's nest. I sat for a few minutes, resting my head in my hands. Sunrise was flirting with the horizon now, and daylight made everything a little easier. I took a drink of water and ate an energy gel, and then we continued up the ridge. We came to a large plateau at about 26,000 feet. Danuru must have seen the elation take over my face, because he raised his hand and said, "Not yet. False summit."

"I hate when mountains do this," I said, "and they all seem to do it."

"Almost there. See?"

He pointed to an ascending hill leading to the real summit, and there went Daniel and Norman, just starting their ascent, plodding along. I leaned forward, hands on my aching hips, struggling to breathe evenly while we waited for another Sherpa to bring us a fresh oxygen bottle. I was so knackered, I didn't even know if I could move another step.

"Of course you can."

I turned toward the person who just a moment before had been Danuru but was now a beautiful Pakistani woman, just like those I envisioned in the memoir. I watched as Karma Rita Sherpa similarly transformed as he approached, and the two ladies greeted each other with musical laughter. Danuru's oxygen mask was now a chador, a softly draped veil that covered most of her face below her luminous brown eyes. She blinked her long, lush lashes and said, "Come. Follow me."

I stared at her quizzically. "I think . . . my oxyjuhzhun . . ."

"Come, *didi*." The women held out their elegant hands. Their voices shimmered like wind chimes. "Follow us. We'll take you to the summit."

I let them take my hands. I felt nothing but love. My love for them. Their love for me. Clouds below. Heaven above. Love, trust, eternal blue eternity . . . or something . . . and I walked in unison with them, my boot on a rock and my other boot on another rock, one boot, other boot . . . and suddenly, up on a hill, I saw the most beautiful terrain that shimmered in the sun, colors ranging from frosty silver to dove gray. Dazzling. Sparkling. Like moon rocks. Or an amazing eyeshadow palette. We continued to the top of the mountain and traversed a spiny path to a string of prayer flags that fluttered in the wind like a great flock of multicolored birds lifted by the pristine breeze, whistling and chirping *summit, summit, summit*.

I stood in stillness on the top of Cho Oyu. The Land of Mountains rippled out around me, opening its great arms. There were strangers—Lhotse, Nuptse, Makalu—and my recent acquaintance, Shishapangma. But of all the mountains before me, the one I fixed my sights on was Everest. Chomolungma. The object of my desire.

My every waking moment. There she stood, not forbidding or aloof. She was patient, having already known all the time in the world. I made her a promise I could articulate only on a cellular level.

French poet and surrealist René Daumal left his novel *Mount Analogue* unfinished when he died of tuberculosis at thirty-six, but in it, he wrote: "What is above knows what is below, but what is below does not know what is above. One climbs, one sees. One descends, one sees no more. But one has seen."

This was the not-so-gentle lesson of Cho Oyu: For better or worse, perspective reveals the big picture.

Daniel strode over and raised his hand for a high five. I smacked his glove and felt the tang of contact all the way up my arm. He said some gibberish that ended with "twofer!" and raised his water bottle to the rising sun. We sat for a moment, quickly eating and drinking. I still had the sense that my skull had separated from my neck and was hovering over my shoulders like a bobblehead, but hydrating helped. Daniel and Norman headed down, and I watched them leave, feeling detached, blessedly indifferent. A little while later, I started down with my Pakistani lady friends, who transformed back into their Sherpa selves as the air grew thicker and my hallucinations dissipated. I was a little sad to see them go.

When we reached Camp 2, Danuru and Karma Rita set to work packing up the tents and gear, and rather than wait for them, I decided to head down on my own. I've always been quick on the descent, so it didn't take me long to catch up with Daniel and Norman, who were preparing to rappel down the headwall to Camp 1.

"Hey, Daniel!" I called, and he waved.

"Hey there! Come on down with us."

I was grateful to have him there to lead and check my rappel. I was still feeling a little unsteady after my hallucinations, heady from this awesome back-to-back twofer.

"I'll go first," said Daniel, "then Vanessa, and we'll meet you down on the ledge, Norman."

This was a long rappel down, and the ledge was standing room only. Once on the ledge, you would have to position yourself sideways on a cliff, your back flattened against the sheer rock face. Daniel rappelled down, and after a moment called out for me to follow. Checking my rappel setup, I shouted down to Daniel.

"On rappel!"

I lifted the brake rope briefly with my right hand to allow the rope to pull through my ATC and started walking backward off the edge of the cliff, letting my weight sink into the harness. Taking that first step always requires a big sense of trust—in God, in life, in whether it is your time—and that's the best-case scenario, when you feel good about the people around you. But now Norman stood in front of me with the rope, my lifeline, between his feet.

You better watch your back, you fucking bitch.

His words echoed in my head yet again. I knew he had a knife in his pocket. Every climber does. I gripped the rope and pulled it taut, trying to avoid making eye contact with him. I tipped my head down, checking for obstacles to avoid as I lowered myself over the edge. I used my feet to guide myself down the mountain as I rappelled slowly, mindfully, hopping nice and easy against the rock face, lower, lower, but as I looked down, I realized my pacing was off. I was too far to the left. Below me, Daniel was perched on that tiny ledge, way off to my right. Above me, the high end of the rope ground against the edge of the cliff. I couldn't see Norman, and I knew I had only so many bounces left before either I undershot the target or the rope ran out—or both. I didn't know if I could make it over that far.

"Vanessa!" Daniel hollered. "Vanessa, swerve to the right!"

"I know! I'm trying!"

"Okay, hold tight and keep swerving. That's it. You got it, Vanessa. One more kick and you're here."

I'd rappelled or abseiled many times. Normally, I could gauge this inconsistency and work my way over, but at this altitude, two summits' worth of stress in my bloodstream, and my brain still full of cobwebs, now potentially out of rope, with that psychopath overhead, I started to panic. I felt a warm rush running down my leg, a sudden automatic response over which I had no control.

Fuck. Not now. Please, don't let me pee on him.

The implications flashed through my mind: mild humiliation if I privately wet my pants, extreme humiliation if I peed on Daniel's head. Both were only midlist between certain death and the discomfort of wet fabric chafing my thighs. Meanwhile, I struggled to keep my feet on the rock face, trying everything I could to swing my body over toward the ledge, and give it that one final kick Daniel had asked for.

Finally, like Jane meeting Tarzan, I landed on the ledge, horrified, freaked out, and trembling but trying to shake it off, pretending everything was fine. Nothing to see, folks. Everything under control, including my bladder.

"Well done. Fucking close call." Daniel gave my arm a brotherly nudge and called up, "Okay, Norman! You're up."

We waited for him, backs pressed to the rock wall. I focused on my breathing and tried to biofeedback myself into some semblance of a happy place. I kept my feet wide apart, hoping the extreme dryness that always turned my lips to Pringles would do me a favor now, and the wind did not disappoint. It could have been worse. I'd heard many appalling stories about HAFE (high-altitude flatus expulsion, which is as bad as it sounds), gastrointestinal bugs, digestion problems, and climbers who shat themselves in abject terror—

literally scared shitless. Apparently the sympathetic nervous system takes over during moments of great duress, and the rest is history.

By the time Norman landed on the ledge, my pants had pretty much aired out, and I was feeling calm and strong. We continued down to Camp 1 and took a break to hydrate and eat noodles for lunch, and as we sat there, Danuru and Karma Rita, who'd been breaking down camps, caught up to us. They were making good time. Having been on the mountain for two expeditions now, they were keen to get back to their families.

"You think we might make it down to ABC?" Danuru asked.

Daniel shrugged and said, "Think you can make it, Vanessa?"

I was a little annoyed to be asked. On the way to Camp 1, I had been moving right along while Norman struggled and fell behind. But whatever.

"You know me," I said. "I always cruise on the downhill. What's a twofer if you don't make it all the way down to Base Camp from the second summit?"

"That's my girl." Daniel slapped my knee and got up to pack up the rest of the camp. Norman slurped his noodles and said nothing. He sat with his elbows on his knees, shoulders slumped, much of the air gone out of him.

The Sherpa were very appreciative, and when we got down to ABC, Kaji Sherpa had made a chocolate cake that said CONGRATU-LATIONS ON SUMMITING CHO OYU on it. As we hiked out the next morning, the Sherpa told me that they had not received any tips from Norman yet. I dug through my gear and came up with all the cash I could, just to make sure everyone was covered. I was enor-mously grateful to the Sherpa who'd stayed and made our second summit possible.

We had summited Shishapangma on October 4, 2011, and Cho Oyu on October 12, 2011, back-to-back summits eight days apart.

I called Spousey as soon as cell service was available. He laughed when I told him about the beautiful Pakistani women and winced on my behalf when I related the whole peeing myself episode, and then a tumbled version of the whole Norman conflict came out.

"It was a shit show," I said. "I was well and truly terrified."

"Sounds like he was scared as well."

"Scared of what?"

"Of being embarrassed by you."

"*Embarrassed?*" I flared. "I can overlook someone calling me a bitch, but 'watch your back'—that's a threat that implies something worse than *embarrassment*. If he's embarrassed, he should handle it with a bit less enthusiasm. Can't you be on my side for a minute? For fuck's sake!"

"I am, and always have been, on your side," Jonathan said crisply, and then there was an awkward silence. I looked at my phone and saw a single thin bar of signal.

"Jonathan? Are you still there?"

"Yes, but I'm sensing there's no correct thing for me to say, so I'm just listening."

"I don't want to talk about it. It was fucked up. That's all. I felt like I was alone out there. I've never been so terrified in my life."

We both knew that was untrue. I certainly had been that terrified. Many times. Terror was a staple of my emotional diet as a child. I was fed terror on a regular basis until my brain was habituated to it. That's why Norman got to the very marrow of me without lifting a finger. To my ear, he had the perfect pitch of a talented bully, shutting down principled disagreement the way bullies do.

One climbs, one sees.

Emotional scarring, PTSD—whatever you call it, I carried the legacy of those hours spent huddled under the bed with my brother. By the time we were too big to fit under the bed, we were so thoroughly acclimated to the terror that we could play a board game while our alcohol-fueled parents physically attacked each other. Ben was my only ally in that particular trench, so when I saw the pulsing blue lights of the police cars in front of our house, I naturally thought, *Mom.* I figured my father had finally killed her and would go to jail. Or maybe she'd killed him and would plead self-defense. It didn't cross my mind that this had anything to do with Ben. Perhaps at sixteen—perhaps even now—it was impossible for me to process the loss of him.

"Feel like getting dinner at Dwarika's tonight?" I asked Daniel on the bus to Kathmandu. "Or . . . if you and Norman have plans, that's cool. We can do it another time."

"No, let's do it," he said, and sitting across the table from me that evening, he asked, "So what happened between you and Norman?"

As I told him, he listened, crestfallen, his fork paused halfway between his plate and his stubbled chin.

"I had no idea. Vanessa, you should have said something."

"No way. You would have called off the summit—and Cho Oyu."

"Probably."

"And that would have been on me," I said, and waved it off when he started sputtering. "It's not about what I *should* have done. It's about what he *shouldn't* have done. And until everybody wraps their head around that simple equation, nothing will change. Anyway—setting all that aside—this is a celebration. We did something very few people have done."

"Cheers to that." Daniel raised his glass, and I clinked mine against it.

"Now," I said, "let's talk about Everest."

10

In Kathmandu you have car traffic.
On the mountain you have people traffic.
—ARJUN ADHIKARI, NEPALESE GUIDE, *MEDIUM*
"13 DAYS IN THE KHUMBU VALLEY" BY SIGNI LIVINGSTONE-PETERS

Back home in Boston, I studied my cadaverous reflection in the bathroom mirror, trying to connect it to the person I was when I left for Shishapangma eight weeks earlier. Usually, I'm about 140 pounds, a solid size ten or twelve with broad shoulders and a long-shoreman's musculature. Now I weighed 120 pounds, which is fine for Hollywood but looked wasted and gaunt on me. My collar-bones jutted forward under a favorite little black dress that now fit me like a pup tent, and when I took the dress off, I was confronted with the bony rib cage of a malnourished Tingri hound dog. I'll admit to a frisson of former-fat-kid glee; I'd proven beyond a reasonable doubt that my basic bone structure required some weight on it. I would never again buy into the fashion magazine ideal that tries to tell us skinny means beautiful.

Now that I was back at sea level, my high-altitude biochemistry was in a tailspin. The thick, oxygen-rich red blood cells would be pumping through my veins for another thirty days or so, turbo-charging my metabolism, and I didn't hate the idea of being able to eat whatever I wanted for a while. Training for Everest would start with restoring some meat to my bones. More troubling was the tangled mass of hair on the floor of the shower every morning after I shampooed. I have an underactive thyroid, so even in the best of climates my body struggles to regulate temperature, energy, and metabolism. That becomes problematic in high-altitude cold, so I thought the hair loss might have something to do with that, but after a battery of blood, urine, and saliva tests, the doctor tersely concluded, "You're stressed." Never mind how stressful it is to be told that you're so stressed your hair is falling out. Can we say "circular reference" together?

My inner General Patton told me, *If everyone is thinking alike, then someone isn't thinking.* I focused on the future. I felt ready for Everest, and when I reality-checked that with Daniel, he agreed. Next step: naughty chair. I pitched Jonathan on Everest for May 2012.

"That gives me seven months to train," I said. "The only problem is, it's a substantial financial commitment."

"Your gift for understatement never ceases to amaze. Continue."

There was no use trying to charm or finesse him, so I laid out the numbers. "I'm estimating eighty thousand dollars minimum to do it right. I'm running out of banked bonuses and savings, and if I take another job, I can't train full-time, let alone take two months off for the expedition. I've been pursuing this bloody mountain for two years. I've read every book, consumed every documentary, worked my ass off to get this far—literally! I have the ass of a scarecrow. If I don't see this through, what was it all for?"

"You tell me," he said dryly.

"Like Mallory said. *Because it's there.*"

"So is *Mallory*," said Jonathan. "Not too fine a point, but he's still there, along with Christ knows how many others who've been killed or maimed or pauperized."

"We won't be pauperized."

"That is the least terrifying possibility on a very long list."

"Spousey, money is a resource that can be replaced. Time is the resource I can't afford to waste."

He drummed his fingers lightly on the kitchen table. "In for a penny, I guess."

"Exactly!"

"And if you don't summit—?"

"I will," I said, and I believed it. I was ready to bet my bony ass.

I called the guiding company to let them know I was a definite maybe for spring. "Great!" they said. "We'll look for your payment before the end of the year."

"Yes, yes. No problem," I said with my spleen in my throat.

Now that I was committed to this expedition, my game plan was training my body to prioritize, transport, and utilize oxygen. It was all about the VO_2 max. I met with Dr. Aaron Baggish at Massachusetts General Hospital's Cardiovascular Performance Program, who specialized in improving athletic performance. I also consulted Dr. Peter Hackett, who runs the Institute for Altitude Medicine in Colorado. Together, we designed my Everest medical kit—everything I would need should something go wrong on the mountain. My biggest fears were pulmonary edema (water in the lungs) and cerebral edema (inflammation of the brain). I didn't know if my thyroid meds would work above 8,000 meters. Scar tissue from past surgeries, any area where blood supply had been disrupted, was vulnerable to frostbite and hypothermia. My mountain-specific kit included dexamethasone for inflammation and cerebral edema; nifedipine, a calcium channel blocker for high blood pressure and chest pain; sildenafil (aka Viagra or Cialis) for pulmonary arterial hypertension; and acetazolamide for acute mountain sickness. Along with all this, I assembled the basics of any good medical kit: antibiotics, prescription and nonprescription painkillers, antihistamines, Band-Aids, eye rinse, Imodium—a pessimist's cornucopia.

The last key member of Team VOB was Peter, a marathon coach who tasked me to my very limit for one hour twice a week. Wielding his stopwatch like an electric cattle prod, he pushed me through the lactic acid buildup to my last shred. I ran a ten-minute mile around the Charles River, which is nothing in marathon terms, but on the mountain at 8,000 meters it's not about speed, it's about endurance, crafting each breath in, controlling each breath out. I did weight training designed to keep my muscles strong but not overly built and Pilates for that iron core. I couldn't get my head around a massage not seeming like a luxury, but at the insistence of Team VOB, I endured the bread-kneading ordeal of deep tissue massage twice a month. When Peter recommended an ice bath, I gave it a go, but not with much enthusiasm and not as often as he would have liked. Jonathan set a timer for me and tried to ignore the string of profanities coming from behind the bathroom door.

I approached the management of the two tallest buildings in Boston, the Prudential Center and the John Hancock Tower, asking if they'd allow me to run up and down their stairs for training. They both replied with a flat, skeptical no, but Meredith Waites, general manager at the Boston College Club on Federal Street negotiated on my behalf to use their building—966 steps up, 966 steps down—after I provided a letter from my cardiologist promising I would not drop dead on their property.

With two duffel bags for an eight-week expedition, I debated the cost and benefit of each item. Clothing had to layer. Snacks had to appeal to a lost appetite. Tech gadgets had to multitask. Hotronics required a solar charger, but nothing is more dangerous than bone-deep cold that jeopardizes feet that must not fail.

The statistics were never far from my mind, or from Jonathan's. By 2011, the death-to-summit ratio on Everest was 1.18 percent, an artificially low number because expeditions (and summits) were doubling every decade.

"But to put it in perspective," I said, "it's not like I'm climbing Annapurna, which has a death rate of thirty-two percent, or K2, which has a death rate of twenty-three percent—for every four or five summits, a climber dies. The death rate on Everest is marginally lower than Cho Oyu, which is a relatively safe 1.4 percent."

Jonathan wasn't particularly swayed by all this, but to my mind, Everest, though it's the highest, was far from the most dangerous of the fourteen Himalayan Eight Thousanders. These ginormous, breathtaking beauties are the deadliest peaks on the planet. They command respect, on the way up and the way down. Drilled into my head was the reality that 85 percent of deaths on any mountain occur on the descent, where climbers battle exhaustion, dehydration, headaches, nausea, and the possibility of running out of oxygen.

Everest is almost always climbed in the spring, when climbers meet the least resistance from hurricane-strength jet stream winds that whip through the lower layers of the troposphere above 23,000 feet, west to east, scouring the summit bald and sending up plumes of crystallized snow and ice. In early May, monsoon rains push the jet stream north over Tibet, providing a summit window. The same thing happens in the fall, but the extreme cold keeps most climbers away. The winter summit is a beast I don't even want to imagine.

Even in May, under the kindest possible circumstances, everything above 8,000 meters (26,000 feet) is referred to as the Death Zone: the altitude where the human body begins to deteriorate, no matter how many millions of red blood cells have been produced, no matter how many layers of warmth are piled on or how much money is spent on technology. Those thick, juicy red blood cells are twice as likely to cause a heart attack or stroke. The brain goes fuzzy in the dispersed-oxygen environment, so cognitive ability is impaired. Digestion shuts down. The body turns to its fat reserves, and when it's consumed what it can find there, it starts to burn muscle for energy. A single summit bid burns up to fifteen thousand calories—ten times the daily average, the equivalent of forty cheeseburgers—putting the body at a serious energy deficit. The kidneys struggle to unload bicarbonate to compensate for alkalosis (the excessive alkaline condition of the body fluids or tissue), working overtime thanks to the Diamox and other diuretics one takes to combat AMS, and dehydration only makes things worse. Every day, every hour in the Death Zone comes at a terrible bodily cost. The one and only imperative is to get in and get out as quickly as possible.

As a sport, high-altitude mountaineering doesn't exactly attract shrinking violets. You're more likely to see type A, competitive people who are real-life decision makers. Trouble is, you're not in real life. You're in the middle of the Himalayas, as far from real life as anyone could imagine. No matter how proficient a climber you are—or think you are—the mountain calls the shots. The four critical factors for summiting can't be bought: physical ability, willpower, decent weather, and an esoteric blend of good luck and God's impulse to pull your name out of a hat.

Weather forecasting for Everest has greatly improved in recent years, but ironically, that created a whole new problem. With reliable, easily distributed weather forecasts, there's no guessing game. Everyone knows exactly when the summit window is about to open, and the mad dash is on. If the forecast reveals the first bluebird day of the season, eager climbers stampede for the summit. Bottlenecks form on single lanes that have to accommodate traffic going up and coming down.

The most notorious gridlock happens well inside the Death Zone at the Hillary Step. This iconic feature collapsed after a 2015 earthquake, but you still have to climb plenty of vertical rock face. With hundreds of people attempting to summit between midnight and daybreak, potentially lethal chaos ensues. Climbing that last 3,000 feet from the South Col (Camp 4) to the summit of Everest, people run out of oxygen as they face crowded slopes and bottlenecks while battling fatigue, dehydration, extreme weather, brutally low temperatures, and mountain sickness. They risk losing fingers and toes that go numb as they stand there, waiting for their turn to pass. As I write this, in the spring of 2019, my news feed is full of startling images from a recent tragedy: a bluebird day, nothing but azure skies above, but eleven climbers are dead as hundreds reportedly jockey for position in the Khumbu Icefall and on a single rope near the summit.

None of these risks were ever in the hypothetical for me or for Jonathan, but just to drive it home, Jonathan was required to sign a standard Body Disposal Election Form (BDEF) agreeing to leave my body on the mountain should I meet an untimely end. If I were lucky enough to perish lower on the mountain slopes or even on the trek heading into Base Camp, he could, for a (cough) nominal fee, opt for either repatriation (shipment of remains) or cremation. The BDEF doesn't mince words, encouraging the signer to be practical and reminding them of the traditional mountaineering code of conduct. The higher you are when you perish, the more likely it is that you will remain there for eternity. Above a certain altitude, the danger of trying to transport dead weight is not worth risking another life. Sherpa and guides routinely get requests and offers of big money, but for most climbers, it's a hard no.

Jonathan studied the form, brow furrowed. "Good God. They want another eighty thousand dollars for repatriation. Is this a Dolce & Gabbana crate they're shipping you home in?"

"In a perfect world."

"I'm ticking the box for you to be kicked into a crevasse, just so we are clear."

"I love you too, darling," I said. "I'll obviously have to come home alive, then."

"Indeed." His stiff upper lip twitched slightly. "Maybe if I bump you up to business class on your way to Kathmandu, you'll have a better start. Get as much sleep as possible."

"Thank you, Spousey." I gave him a hug. I'd have gone in for a snog too, but I suspected he was using air miles.

"I've also weighed your bags," he said, ever the pragmatist. "If you sit in economy, you'll end up with excess baggage fees."

Before I left Boston, I sent out an email to my friends, letting them know where I was going, and an unexpected show of support came back to me. Kindest wishes filled with genuine love, good luck, and positive energy. I'm not always sentimental about such things, but all these notes touched me greatly.

In Hong Kong, I breezed through customs with a thumbprint ID that still worked and swiftly switched terminals to board my Dragonair flight to Kathmandu. It was almost midnight when I arrived, too dark to catch a glimpse of the Himalayas as we landed. On the way to baggage claim, I was conscious of my confident stride, on familiar turf. I was tempted to stay up revisiting maps and lists but took advantage of the opportunity to sleep. I sent myself to bed and got up early to meet my Everest team at breakfast.

In the business world, you assemble a team based on need, experience, and general good fit. It seemed strange at first to apply these principles to a random group of strangers who happened to sign up with the same expedition, but in my experience, there's no better equalizer, no stronger bond than a common goal. High-altitude mountaineering seems like something you do alone, at your own pace. While you do spend a lot of time inside your head, we need other people to get there, and a large part of the satisfaction comes from sharing the experience with your companions. It goes beyond splitting costs and pooling resources. Everest was first summited in the 1950s with a militaristic team approach. In modern times, maybe the best word to describe it is *coopetition*, or cooperative competition.

I was climbing with IMG and Daniel. We had twenty-two classic climbers with Western guides and shared Sherpa support and ten hybrid climbers with one Western guide and one-to-one Sherpa support. Overall, that meant twenty tons of gear, food, fuel, and oxygen and four miles of rope would be brought to Everest Base Camp. Over the course of the eight-week expedition we would consume more than 2,500 eggs.

Climbing is big business for a relatively poor country like Nepal. In addition to millions of dollars spent locally by expedition teams, there's revenue from permits and tourism. Teams aren't allowed to register for summit certificates; the Nepal Department of Tourism issues a summit certificate to an individual only if and when they provide summit photos and descriptions proving they actually made it to the top. It's fantastic for the Nepalese economy overall, but this money can be a political hot potato when it comes to mountaineering safety, Sherpa life insurance, and licensing local operators. The average Sherpa earns the equivalent of US $5,000 a year—seven times the national average—but risks their life doing it. I'm adamant about proper pay and fair treatment for these people I've come to love and admire.

I was part of the hybrid team guided by Daniel and his assistant

Sam: eight men and two women, including seven Americans, a Finn, a Middle Eastern prince, and a German. Our youngest was in his late twenties; our eldest was sixty. Many were completing the Seven Summits, having saved the highest, Everest, for last. Highest doesn't mean hardest in the 8,000-meter game, but it certainly does in the Seven Summits game.

At breakfast I was happy to see Emma, the teacher I'd traveled with when I was on my way to Shishapangma and she was going to Cho Oyu. Emma is a tough cookie—sweet with a crisp edge—and very passionate about the things she believes in. Heidi was there too, as part of the classic team, and the three of us met up now and again on the trail. Everest was the last of Emma's Seven Summits, so she was übermotivated to get there. Faisal, our Middle Eastern prince, had been educated in Boston and ran a popular Western fast food franchise in his home country. This was his seventh summit as well, and if he succeeded, he'd be the first, the fastest, and the youngest person from his country to climb the Seven Summits. He was funny and playful but serious about the task at hand. When a Sherpa from another expedition was injured by falling rocks, Faisal personally paid for helmets for all the Sherpa on our expedition and had them delivered from Namche Bazaar, the largest market town between Lukla and Everest Base Camp.

Jim was our bird spotter, and there would be birds to spot. The University of British Columbia asked us to record any sightings of bar-headed geese flying over the Himalayas. Apparently, bar-headed goose migration patterns and altitudes have been a source of wonder for decades. How does a bird this size, four to seven pounds, achieve such aerodynamic lift at altitudes of 18,000 to 20,000 feet? Why do that at all when they could be sunning themselves in Bangladesh? And what does it say about the climate and water tables in the lowlands where they lay their eggs? This would be my first encounter with how science and expeditions interacted, and we took the task seriously.

Bill was a lawyer from Virginia—a judge by the time we returned—and also very funny. Perry was a grandfather and an ultramarathon runner, arguably the fittest among us. Hence his nickname: Perilous. Johannes, the Finn, turned everything into a musical, adapting popular song lyrics to whatever was going on, especially if there was tension. He worked technological miracles whenever our computers failed us, and he downed massive bottles of orange Fanta, so we all joked about his drinking problem. Austin from the Golden State managed money, so he and I spoke a common language. He was an Ironman competitor and read three books for every one that I read. I caught him reading *Fifty Shades of Grey* on the expedition and never let him hear the end of it.

And then there was me. I came aboard feeling fit, confident, serious about summiting, and first in the line to be on Daniel's ass if something wasn't right. I was the Martha Stewart of the expedition, organizing birthday celebrations, holidays, acclimatization hikes, postclimb dinners, and side trips. I was also the go-to medicine woman for stomach problems and blistered feet.

Every one of us was there for his or her own reason. As we bonded, however, we were painfully aware that not everyone would make it to the summit. Only Daniel and I had climbed above the Death Zone, and though I hadn't climbed as many mountains as some of the others, I'd climbed more Eight Thousanders and knew what high altitude felt like.

We flew to Lukla, and this time I was prepared for the triple axel stop on the short runway. I knew to pull up my buff as I hiked up the dirt path, avoiding the cloud of pungent dirt kicked up by the Yaks. In Pheriche at 4,258 meters, we climbed a hill to take in the panoramic view of Dingboche, and Jim spotted a single bar-headed goose flying with its wings spread wide, cruising the valley. He was elated to add it to his bird report, and I took it as a good omen.

My spirits rose with the familiar sight of prayer flags lifting on the breeze, carrying their blessings across the countryside. Passing through the little mountain villages, I put out my hand to spin each prayer wheel and walked clockwise around the stupas three times to show respect, as these ancient domed structures often contain Buddhist relics. We stopped to visit Lama Geshe, the highest-ranking Buddhist lama in Tengboche—a must-do for every climber heading to Everest (including me when I was hoping to reach Everest Camp 2 two years earlier) so he could bless us for our climb. Faisal waited respectfully outside, but the rest of us queued to meet Lama Geshe and make an offering.

Lama Geshe was small, about my height, with closely cropped hair and intensely kind eyes. He sat, robed in cardinal red, surrounded by gifts and relics. Summit photos—the many climbers who'd come for his blessing summited and returned safely—papered the walls as if they were photos of his grandchildren. When it was my turn, I clasped my hands and bowed. Lama Geshe asked for my name and wrote on a notepad. He took another red cord from his collection and motioned for me to lean forward so he could place it around my neck. He tied the red string with a loose knot, speaking a blessing. I couldn't understand the words, but the meaning was clear. *Go in peace. All is well.*

When I offered him my *khata* prayer scarf stuffed with Nepalese rupees, Lama Geshe immediately recognized the elaborate red string he'd given me prior. He smiled broadly and gestured to it.

"Yes." I nodded. "Yes, this is yours. We've met before."

He laughed an affectionate belly laugh. This small recognition in tandem with the ancient tradition meant more to me than

I could fully understand in that moment. This wasn't a silly red string; it was blessed and meant to be worn as a form of protection and to ease any suffering. I was told that a blessing string on a person or animal, even if they are long deceased, can purify the negative karma. It's still potent, even without the presence of consciousness. A hard lump formed in my throat. When he touched his forehead to mine, hot tears spilled from my eyes.

"*Namaste*," I said, and he smiled his infectiously joyful smile.

As we were leaving, I brusquely wiped my face on my sleeve and said, "Oh, great. Of course, people were taking pictures." I'm not one to cry in front of strangers, but my heart felt light and open. If it wasn't the bar-headed goose, it was holding court with the lama that gave me my first premonition that a summit was possible.

11

No climber would go through
the icefall if Everest wasn't waiting at the end of it.
—DAVID BREASHEARS, MOUNTAINEER AND DIRECTOR OF *EVEREST*

Hiking through the foothills, we fell into our personal rhythms. I'd learned the hard way that no good came from sprinting on ahead. I took in the sights: the prayer flags lining the suspension bridges we crossed, the yaks carrying colorful North Face duffel bags, and young porters carrying a tremendous amount of equipment. Climbers, trekkers, yaks, porters, and Sherpa all lined the narrow paths through the Khumbu Valley. How fast or slow you hike tends to foreshadow how fast or slow you'll climb, so it's natural while hiking to find out who your potential summit buddy will be. Typically, this is not something you can plan, because you never know another person's rhythm until you're out there.

The plan was to summit Lobuche, a nearby peak at 20,075 feet, in an attempt to avoid one acclimatization pass through the Khumbu Icefall. As we set up our tents at the base of Lobuche, I recognized the telltale hacking of the Khumbu cough coming from elsewhere in the camp. I also heard wetter, more rattling coughs that indicated viral bronchitis. I was depending on Daniel's take-no-prisoners policy to separate those and stop the spread of infection, but unlike the first Cho Oyu, where he'd had the quarantine tent familiar to yours truly, he now seemed indifferent.

I sat as far as I could from anyone who was visibly or audibly sick and made some rather obvious references to "some loud coughing going on." Someone would have to have been pretty daft not to catch my drift. The unspoken mountaineering code of conduct calls on each of us to be self-honest and separate ourselves as needed so as not to get everyone sick, but to my dismay, the coughing—and the daftness—continued unabated.

The weather turned against us, and our mood synchronized with the cloud cover. Nonetheless, we set out the next morning to go up halfway and back down Lobuche, and because it was getting chilly, I did something I had never done: I put on two pairs of socks. Halfway up the hill, my feet were going numb from too much compression. Trying to shake circulation to life, I must have looked like I was tap dancing. Luckily, Kurt Wedberg, founder of Sierra Mountaineering International, joined us with a private client and became members of our hybrid team. He saw this funny dance of mine and said, "Whoa. Stop. Take off your shoes and socks."

"What—here?" I said. "In the snow?"

He nodded, stripping off his coat and opening his shirt. Thirty seconds later, I was on my backside with my bare foot against his bare chest, trying not to yelp at the burning sting of the reawakened blood flow. The numbness gave way to indescribable pain. Not a lactic acid feeling. This was like screamin' meanies, burning from the inside out, like flushing antifreeze through your veins. Kurt briskly rubbed my feet and ankles, ignoring my distress and everyone else's laughter and catcalls—"Caliente!"—and the paparazzi camera shots capturing lots of embarrassing, um, footage.

At dinner, we were still laughing about it. Johannes entertained us with new foot-related lyrics to an old Barry Manilow tune, adding insult to injury. It was almost enough to distract from the noticeable increase in coughing. I finally nudged Daniel and said, "Remember how on Cho Oyu, you practically ostracized me for a single sneeze?"

He shrugged and said, "Oh, c'mon. There's only two people coughing."

"It only takes one person to infect the entire team. That's what you drilled into me when you banished me to that purgatory we call the sick tent."

"Just worry about your own health. I'll see to the rest."

On Lobuche the next day, we climbed a fair bit and then built tents to rest in before our summit bid. I spotted two other climbers across a small lake, and Daniel said, "I think that's Ueli Steck."

I peered over the top of my sunglasses. "No way."

Way. It was the legend himself. I grabbed Emma for moral support, and bearing a gift of candy bars, we headed over to meet the Swiss Machine. I happened to be wearing one of his personally designed jackets.

"I love it," I told him, "but seriously, did you have to make the women's jacket pink?"

"Marketing decision," he said with a sheepish grin. "What can I do?"

We chatted and laughed and parted with mutual well wishes, and I felt another pleasant rush of kismet. I love it when life does its Spirograph design, crossing paths and interconnecting, just to let you know you're in the right place at the right time.

At three in the morning, we got up, ate a light breakfast, and began our Lobuche summit bid. It was hard going in the cold darkness. The terrain was steep with soft areas of knee-deep snow and hard bald patches where the loose rocks shifted under our feet. When the sun rose on the mountains, showing us the tipped wing of the summit and the jagged mountains all around, I felt a second wind. Johannes and I reached the top just before 11 AM and waited for the others to join us. We gathered for group photos with the breathtaking Khumbu Valley below us and then headed down, walking mostly, rappelling when necessary.

All but one of our team made it to the summit of Lobuche. At dinner, everyone sang a concessionary tune, encouraging the straggler and saying it didn't mean anything, but I could see the Sherpa watching and assessing each of us, calculating who was most likely to summit Everest and who might not. (As it turned out, the straggler would not summit, but neither would some of the Sherpa.)

Back at Everest Base Camp (EBC), the tents were organized by groups: classic climbers, hybrid climbers, and those aiming for Lhotse, the fourth-highest mountain in the world. We shared a communications tent for charging phones, iPads, and camera batteries, but each team had a separate dining tent, shower, and loo. Some optimistic soul put a fuzzy cover on the seat in the hybrid toilet, but considering the digestive distress it was up against, I predicted it wouldn't last the day, and I was right.

Our shower tent, on the other hand, was a work of art. Somehow Kaji—the cook who made the cake for us on Cho Oyu and had sacrificed his own water bottle for me—rigged a water system with a square of teak flooring and a hosepipe at the top for a showerhead that actually allowed for a small amount of hot water. The only downside was that you couldn't anticipate if the water coming out would be burning hot or ice cold, but it was still an improvement from the bucket-and-cup routine. Kaji arranged an attractive display of plastic flowers and lined up all our snacks and condiments in the dining tent. Some of the competitors' dining tents had space heaters, but ours had Kaji's warm heart, and that made it feel like home for six weeks.

Each climbing company's camp was small, but when you add up all the teams at EBC, it was home base for more than seven hundred climbers spread out over thirty-two expeditions every year—and this number would grow. From a bird's eye view, you would see large mess tents with hundreds of little tents scattered around them. Rusty reds and oranges seeped through the predominantly brown and gray landscape, until snow fell, refreshing the worn campsite with a blanket of fluorescent white.

Expeditions usually kept to themselves to prevent the spread of infection; at this altitude whatever went around, gastrointestinal or pulmonary, was not going to go away easily. Even within our group, the classic and hybrid teams tended not to mingle. I had to get group permission for Heidi from the classic team to join us for dinner, even though she was with the same company.

Our weekly routine involved acclimatization hikes, showers, meals in the mess tent, the never-ending piling up of laundry, and a lot of hanging out and downtime while our muscles recovered and our blood cells increased. I kept my personal tent swept and tidy, read ebooks on my Kindle, and watched movies on my iPad. I'd purchased a local SIM card, but it was useless, so I paid for just enough satellite time to check my email now and then. Whenever I felt a bit lethargic, messages from my friends brought me a burst of fresh energy.

No climbing could take place before the Puja ceremony, and each team had its own. Once we'd had ours, Sherpa from multiple teams headed up to Camp 1. Large expeditions on Everest team up to supply rope, money, and manpower to fix up to 9,000 feet of rope above Camp 1, with smaller companies chipping in to whatever extent they can. The icefall doctors, a separate team of highly skilled Sherpa, take responsibility for the Khumbu Icefall all season, fixing ropes and installing ladders across the deep crevasses.

At dinner, Daniel updated our schedule, and I was dismayed to find he'd added another rotation through the Khumbu Icefall. That previous icefall avalanche played on a loop in my head. I didn't want to say anything in front of the group, but I confronted Daniel privately after the meeting. I thought this was the wrong move, and I let him know it.

"Why are we doing this? What was the point of climbing Lobuche if we're not avoiding that added risk?"

"Vanessa, I have the right to change the schedule," said Daniel. "I'll do whatever I think is necessary to get this team to the summit."

"This team? You know, not everyone—" I bit back the rest. "Fine."

I stomped to my tent and spent the night tossing and turning, trying to push down my rising anxiety. I wasn't the same person who stood in the path of that icefall avalanche two years ago, in mind or in body. Since my Camp 2 failure, I'd climbed all of Hong Kong, Mount Washington, Mount Rainier, Shishapangma, and Cho Oyu twice (almost), not to mention a mountain range's worth of the same 966 stairs, up and down, over and over. My marathon coach, cardiologist, high-altitude doctor, and personal trainer had kicked my arse from one end of Boston to the other. I hadn't sat still one single day. But I couldn't see any of that making a difference now. All I could remember from the icefall was the avalanche, and all I could hear now was fear. In the background of my fitful dreams, the icefall was shifting. It sounded like bones breaking.

Preparing to leave camp at 3 AM, I met my climbing Sherpa, Phinjo Dorjee Sherpa.

"You climbed Shishapangma with my father," he said. "Kami Sherpa."

"You're Kami's son?" I was over the moon. Phinjo Dorjee had climbed Everest six times. Then, and now, I trusted Kami with my life. It felt like he'd sent me a guardian angel.

We crept through Base Camp in silence, trying not to wake the other expeditions. At the edge of the icefall, we stopped and put on our crampons, and then we started our climb. Right away, the icefall felt different. The pathways and ladders felt completely changed from the terrifying precursor to the place where the avalanche ended everything. Phinjo Dorjee and I were going only to the Football Field—that halfway point I hadn't quite reached in 2010. The icefall doctors had lashed the same janky ladders in place over each crevasse, but somehow the chasms below seemed less pitch-black and fathomless. The icefall itself was the same three-dimensional maze, but it made more sense to me now, no more intimidating than the London subway system.

As Phinjo Dorjee and I made our way through it, I tried to reconcile the ice-white reality in front of me with the overwhelming fear that had dogged me since the moment I saw that avalanche coming at me. I couldn't identify a moment when my experience put it into perspective, but somewhere along the line, it had become less threatening, just another thing a mountaineer must carefully manage. We reached the Football Field with relative ease, took a break to rehydrate and have a snack, and then made our way back to EBC. All that anxiety and fear was a waste of energy. It's amazing how we let that sort of monster grow in our imagination. When I saw Daniel at dinner, I said, "It was the right move. I apologize for second-guessing you." When I'm wrong, I'm willing to admit it.

That night, as if to remind us not to get overconfident, strong winds swept in and shook our tents like we were in a cement mixer. The next day, as Phinjo Dorjee and I passed through the icefall again, a Sherpa crossing a ladder slipped and fell into a crevasse just ahead of us. In a fraction of a second, he was gone. Word spread quickly, and when we crossed the ladder a little while later, I couldn't drag my eyes away from the splattered red blood on the pale blue ice below the ladder.

Acclimatization continued, and weeks went by. Russell Brice announced Himex would call off their expedition because of conditions in the Khumbu Icefall where a massive chunk of glacial ice on Everest's West Shoulder extended over the climbers' path. This left others second-guessing their own decisions to stay on. Some of the departing team members were gutted; others, I suspected, were secretly delighted to get the hell out of Base Camp. At the time, some people criticized Russell, but two years later, he was proven right. That same serac collapsed, killing sixteen Sherpa, doubling any single-season death toll on record.

Our team decided to continue on. We made our way up to Camp 1, nervously eyeing Nuptse's jagged ridge, watching for falling rocks, staring at the seracs as if our steady gaze could keep them from toppling. The next morning, we started up the Western Cwm, a rising glacial valley between Camps 1 and 2. The valley is beautiful, a shining sea of swooping snow and ice, and relatively flat, but it's an awful place during daylight hours with blinding glare and temperatures soaring to 100 degrees Fahrenheit, which turns a heavy summit suit into a convection oven.

Layering is more art than science. If you get too hot, mountain sickness brings dizzy spells, nausea, and headaches. Dehydration is an all-consuming physical and mental thirst that makes it impossible to focus on whatever it is you should be focused on. If you sweat and then layer down, cold wind slices through your wet body like a machete.

This part of the route had a few ladders to climb—vertically up one or two snow walls and horizontally over crevasses—but for the most part, it was a relatively straight march. Phinjo Dorjee and I found a rhythm and pushed through, which meant we were the first to arrive at Camp 2, which meant I had first choice of tents. I picked one with a nice view of the Lhotse Face I thought Emma might appreciate. I'd heard on the radio that she was nauseous, so I swept the bottom of our tent, organized her things and mine, and blew up both of our air mattresses, so she could rest when she arrived.

"You'll feel better after you throw up," I told her, and that proved true.

She'd had one hell of a tough journey. I offered her some anti-nausea medicine and propped up extra "pillows" I made, stuffing our clothing into baby pillowcases. Knackered beyond belief, we lay there with barely enough energy to stare at the grandeur of the Lhotse Face—1,125 vertical meters of ice that would require front pointing and technical climbing. At the moment, we could not even contemplate that endeavor. Pulling back the flap of our tent for fresh air, I offered Emma an imaginary remote control and said, "Here. Enjoy some Mountain TV."

"Gee, I wonder what's on." She pointed the pretend clicker toward the open flap. "Oh, look. Mountains."

Across the way, one of our teammates appeared in the vestibule of his tent with his shirt off. He whipped out his penis and filled his pee bottle.

"Uh-oh," said Emma. "We've gone Nat Geo."

We kept silent, not wanting to embarrass him, but after he zipped up and disappeared into his tent, we burst out laughing like schoolgirls.

"Shame it wasn't you-know-who," I said, and yes, we both knew who I was talking about. Apologies to male readers, but the powder room is every bit as earthy as the locker room. We lay there comparing the guys on the team—who was not bad-looking, who was handsome but maybe not the sharpest tool in the box, and who we suspected was strongest in the pee-bottle department.

We rummaged through our snacks. The higher you climb, the less appetite you have, and Kaji was a Cordon Bleu chef compared to the sullen cook above the icefall, who routinely served what we called "four quadrants of crap": a plate divided into equal portions of canned tuna or sardines, congealed noodles, tinned beans, and clumpy rice. If we were lucky, it came with a slice of Spam. It was that or military MREs (meals ready to eat) that might or might not be within the expiration date.

The next day, when the Sherpa went out to fix ropes up to Camp 3, they found the Lhotse Face dry and brittle. Falling rocks rained down on them, and one of them sustained a fairly serious head injury. While many climbers have evacuation insurance, many Sherpa do not. After some back-and-forth, the guiding company that employed the injured Sherpa finally agreed to pick up the $10,000 tab for his flight to the hospital in Kathmandu. We watched them fly off, not knowing what would happen next.

The existing route was now deemed unsafe. Combined teams of Sherpa and guides investigated alternatives to the right of the Lhotse Face and chose a route that was longer and would take more time but would (hopefully) avoid the rockfall and be safer. The more experienced members remembered it from the late 1990s, and it purportedly mirrored the journey of the 1953 Everest expedition. I was up for this on principle, but logistically, it meant that we would miss our overnight stop at Camp 3 at 7,200 meters—a semicritical part of our acclimatization schedule. Ideally, we'd spend at least one night each in Camps 1, 2, and 3 before attempting the summit, but the summit window is all about the weather. The next time we climbed up to this height, it would be for our summit bid.

We headed down to EBC to rest and repack our summit gear, and I spent an uncomfortable night alternately wishing I could sleep and longing for the simple comfort of being able to move my bowels. I was, at the risk of being indelicate, stopped up like a cork in a beer keg, trying to assure myself *this poo shall pass*. Constipation is the 180-degree antithesis of everyone's worst summit-day fear—diarrhea—but I was miserable. For better or worse, the wake-up call came at 3:30 AM. I chugged mugs of hot tea, hoping a little caffeine would help, but it wasn't going to happen.

In my tent, I slipped into my summit suit and sorted my climbing kit. Outside the air was fragrant with juniper the Sherpa were burning with their last-minute prayers. At the edge of the icefall, Phinjo Dorjee and I donned our crampons and headed into the maze. Everything was dark and quiet. We made record time to the Football Field and, after a quick break, carried on toward Camp 1. I saw the tents at Camp 1 as dawn broke, but this wasn't our destination. We paused just long enough to rehydrate and down a bowl of noodle soup. One of the Sherpa had some hot tea on hand, and it was like a gift from the gods. We pushed on to Camp 2 and stopped for the night. I stayed up, organizing and reorganizing my gear like a jigsaw puzzle, deciding what would stay and what would go up, double-checking to make sure I had everything I wanted to take to the summit, my Hotronics and decent flavors of energy gels. Because we'd skipped our acclimatization overnight at Camp 3, oxygen was available at the base of the Lhotse Face.

I hesitated, telling Phinjo Dorjee, "I don't want to use oxygen below the Death Zone."

In my experience, a three-liter bottle of oxygen should last six hours, but the six pounds of weight wasn't worth the benefit until you hit 8,000 meters. But we'd missed the Camp 3 rotation, and going up, with extra exertion, it might be worth it. All the other climbers were taking it except Daniel.

"*Didi*, it's better," said Phinjo Dorjee, handing me the bottle.

I decided to give it a go, turning the cylinder on two liters per minute, and we started climbing the Lhotse Face. For an hour or so, everything seemed fine, but then I looked down to check a foot placement when I was front pointing, and my oxygen cut out. In the instant between exhale and inhale, it was as if someone had clamped their hand over my mouth and pinched my nose.

I can't breathe I can't breathe I can't breathe

When your lungs send that urgent message to your brain—*WTF! We got nothing! Death imminent!*—nothing else gets through. The fight-or-flight impulse sparks and adrenaline jacks up, wrenching you into a state of panic, and—*Dammit dammit dammit!* There goes the bladder control. The same bloody thing that happened on Cho Oyu. *Fuck!* I lifted my face toward heaven, gasping in anguish. Then, suddenly, like divine mouth-to-mouth resuscitation, I could breathe again. What happened? I looked down at my feet, and it was like getting kidnapped again. *Shit! What the—?*

Ah. I get it, says the brain.

Looking down bent my air hose and cut off my oxygen. Looking up allowed it to flow again. Bloody inconvenient. I knew I shouldn't have taken this oxygen tank so low on the mountain. I needed to see where to place my feet, so now I had to waste energy developing a pattern: inhale, hold my breath, look down, exhale, look up, inhale, hold my breath, look down. One more thing to contend with besides hanging on to a behemoth block of ice for dear life as Phinjo Dorjee and I ascended to Camp 3.

We were shocked at what we found there. It looked like a war zone, bleak and frightening. Sections of tents were scattered about the abandoned camp, poles mangled beneath huge ice boulders and drifts of snow.

"Avalanche?" I asked.

Phinjo Dorjee nodded. "What a mess."

I recalled a story I'd heard about an avalanche in the wee hours on Manaslu in west central Nepal. Boots and crampons stored outside the tents were lost forever. Can you imagine? How would you get out? How would you survive without boots? From that day forward, I kept my boots inside my tent and carried a pocketknife to cut myself out of a tent if I had to.

At Camp 3, Emma and I crawled into our sleeping bags and shared a bottle of oxygen at the lowest flow rate. Happy hour at high altitude. Our tent faced Johannes and Faisal's, so we snapped pictures of each other to document how dreadful we all looked with our pale faces, skinny necks, and tangled hair. Congested breathing underscored our hoarse, dehydrated voices and the occasional music of the Khumbu coughs. Johannes was down to his last orange Fanta and struggling to even muster a parody John Denver song. I was surprised to see Daniel arrive last to Camp 3. Daniel was never last. Last was simply not his style.

"That's why you always have an assistant guide," I used to tease him. "To keep up the rear."

Emma and I eavesdropped as best we could through the rising wind, trying to pick up any gossip from the other tents. We caught something about climbers in rough shape. Nothing we could get a handle on. Daniel and Sam started to discuss strategy, but their voices were too faint, the winds too high, and their tents too far away. Daniel came by about an hour later.

"Hey, guys. How's everyone feeling?"

We all shrugged with noncommittal nods that said, *Surviving, but just.*

"Listen, there's something I need to tell you," said Daniel. "First, all of you are really strong. I've been watching every one of you from the beginning, and I know you're going to do well tomorrow. But a couple guys are going to head down."

"No—" I protested, but he wasn't finished.

"Not just them. I'm going down too. I've been fighting an intestinal bug since Camp 2. There is no way I'll be able to join you in the summit bid. I'm going to take the guys down in the morning."

We sat there with our mouths open. This was our guide. This was our Everest.

"I'm really sorry," he said. "I've been to the top of Everest more times than I can count. I know what it takes to summit, and I don't have it. You guys have a great Sherpa team, and Sam will be with you."

It broke my heart to see Daniel so defeated. I was here because of him. He'd trained, motivated, and inspired me. We did the twofer on Shishapangma and Cho Oyu together, and we should be doing Everest together. He had spent five weeks acclimatizing for the next forty-eight hours. Now all that was for nothing. I knew what that felt like. It sucked for him and the two teammates going down with him, one with signs of pulmonary edema and one with frozen corneas and the onset of snow blindness.

"I'll see you guys in the morning," said Daniel. "Try to get some sleep. You have a big day ahead of you."

We murmured good nights and regrets and crawled into our sleeping bags. No one said it out loud, but we were all wondering the same thing: How were we supposed to summit if Daniel didn't? Sam had never climbed Everest.

The game plan was to get an early start, climbing toward the Yellow Band, a famous and fairly steep bit of limestone, assisted by fixed lines. This would take us up to the Geneva Spur, a large rock buttress named after the 1952 Swiss Everest expedition. But when we opened the tent flap well before dawn, we found an enormous queue—more than a hundred people—stretched out like a knotted cord between us and Camp 4.

Everest certainly wasn't a lonely place during summit season, but this was the first year climbers had to contend with this queue phenomenon that continues to cause difficulty and death on Everest. No one was ready for the endless anaconda of climbers from Camp 3 to the summit. Remember the end of the movie *Field of Dreams*?

A long, long line of winking headlights snakes across the dark farm-land, because "If you build it, they will come." What got built on Everest, for better or worse, is an industry that buttresses the economy of an entire nation. With advances in weather-predicting technology, state-of-the-art climbing equipment, upscale (it's so hard to avoid the puns) commercial expeditions, and better training for guides from the Khumbu Climbing Center, Everest has evolved like no other.

Closely monitored statistics are kept by the Himalayan Database. Between 2000 and 2009, 3,372 individuals reached the summit, a 47 percent success rate, and 49 people died in the attempt, a death-to-summit ratio of 1.4 percent. Even in a year like 2019, when deaths on Everest have received a lot of coverage in the media and online, when you consider the exploding population up there, that ratio is extremely low.

These numbers include some of the greatest climbers in the world, but they also include those who, like me, had to learn along the way. And sadly, it includes a lot of people who should not be there at all. I personally believe no one should be trying for an Everest summit until they've been above 26,000 feet elsewhere and experienced extreme Death Zone conditions. This is hard for me to say, because my initial attempt at Everest Camp 2 wasn't the best idea, even though it was only slightly higher than Kilimanjaro, and also because this would have excluded some members of my Everest team—one of the best teams I've had the pleasure of climbing with. However, making an 8,000-meter peak a prerequisite for climbing Everest would relieve congestion and reduce environmental impact of humans on Everest. Incentivizing climbers to go elsewhere in the Himalayas for that 8,000-meter certification would spread the Everest wealth to broader regions and develop more communities where climbers (and their tourism dollars) would be warmly welcomed. What we saw in the wee hours of our summit day in 2012 was only the first rude awakening.

"What in the hell—?" Daniel took in a sharp breath that set off a paroxysm of dry coughing. "Hurry! Everyone, get out! Get in line!"

I'd prepped to the nth degree before I laid down to nap, so I was into my boots and out of the tent in a flash. This was happening. I was going, and Daniel was not going with me.

"Daniel . . ." I didn't know what to say, so I gave him a big bear hug.

"I'll be on the radio," he said. "I'll listen in on your summit from Camp 2."

By the time we joined the queue, it felt like the line had doubled. More than 250 climbers jostled and trudged, plodding along, not yielding an inch. I was freezing my ass off while people seemed to have their feet stuck in glue. At every rock step, a bottleneck of people set by the slowest pace brought groups to a halt. Bollixed by a large group of people who were being totally useless, making no attempts to move forward, I couldn't take it anymore. I motioned for Phinjo Dorjee to use a short rope, which meant we could rope up together and step outside the line to walk alongside the queue of people. This was dangerous—impossible at times— because we were breaking trail through deep snow, occasionally coming closer to a crevasse than he or I would normally dare, but the danger of standing there with my blood pressure dropping and my feet going numb seemed like a far worse option. We used the short rope option twice for about an hour each time. We were able to move up the lines, but the lines were not moving. It took three extra hours to get to Camp 4, which meant less time to rest.

Daniel's plan called for us to arrive at Camp 4 well before noon. Well, that was a laugh. With the queue, we weren't even close. I was getting tired, and I knew myself well enough to know that meant I was getting sloppy. Heading up toward the Geneva Spur, standing in line for what seemed an eternity, I made a stupid rookie move. I took off my helmet and set it on the ground, which seemed relatively flat, but of course was not. I rested the helmet between my feet for a nanosecond, and off it went, tumbling down the hill like a bright red bowling ball destined for the gutter, taking my GoPro video camera with it.

"Shit! Phinjo Dorjee, my Everest film! Do you think—I mean, would anyone—seriously, that's a thousand dollars if . . . *dammit.* Never mind."

Phinjo Dorjee just looked at me with a bemused expression like, *Say b'bye, GoPro.* We both knew the drill. This was Everest. Cameras, kit, bodies, and anything else that fell along the way was destined to remain there forever. By the time we arrived at Camp 4, I was too frazzled and spent to care. It was 3 PM, and given the long queues, Sam was pushing for an 8 PM departure for the summit bid, leaving only five hours to hydrate, rest, and get some oxygen. So much for our carefully laid plan to get in at noon and leave at midnight. This wasn't a matter of early bird gets the worm; this was about not getting trapped behind a bunch of slow climbers in a bottleneck of one-way traffic.

I set about preparing my summit kit. Without my GoPro, my camera and extra batteries were paramount. No summit certificate without summit photos. I had four summit banners, though none were for sponsors per se, just thanks. SuperCarClub for my friend Iain McKenzie; First Republic Bank, from my friend Patricia MacDonald; Boston College Club for the stairs, the stairs, the stairs; and my alma mater, NYU/Stern. The first and only summit suit I'd invested in was holding up beautifully. I placed gels, candy bars, and medicine in specific pockets where I could find them easily. Oxygen. Liquid. Hotronics. I laid everything out on my sleeping bag and went over it again.

As aggravating as our ascent to Camp 4 was, Phinjo Dorjee and I had made better time than a lot of people. Emma had struggled along with the rest of us, but when she arrived at Camp 4 she was in for a surprise. As she unpacked her kit, she found that the Sherpa had left her summit bag at Camp 3, and Daniel had already descended to Camp 2.

"Okay. Calm down. Let's focus on damage control," I said, instantly in crisis management mode. "It's easy to find spare gloves. We can both use my camera for summit photos. If I go first, I'll give you the camera on my way down. Do you have your headlamp? What else was in the bag?"

"Just . . . an important picture, that's all."

"Of what?"

Emma evaded the question, but her cheeks flushed deep red.

"Do you think they can send a Sherpa to get the summit bag?" she said. "I'll pay. Whatever."

"We can ask, but Emma, they're going to ask the same questions. So just tell me. What are you missing?"

"A picture of my parents. Okay? My *dead* parents. This whole goddamn climb is for them. Symbolically, emotionally, spiritually—this is about them. They *are* my sponsors."

"Okay. Got it. *Fuck*. This might be a challenge. The Base Camp manager doesn't have a sentimental bone in his body. In his mind, a sponsor obligation is all about cash. He'll want something with a logo. But it's worth a try."

Sam brought over a sat phone, and the Base Camp manager came on the line. When he asked Emma if anything in the bag was irreplaceably "summit critical," she got tight-lipped and quiet. He asked the wrong questions, and she gave the wrong answers. They talked at cross-purposes the way people do when one is angry, the other is clueless, and they both become defensive. He never asked her what she was upset about, and rather than volunteer it, she tried to negotiate the price of having a Sherpa bring the bag up, and that made no sense to him. It probably sounded as ludicrous as someone trying to throw a thousand dollars down the mountain after a hundred-dollar GoPro.

"Wait, wait," I cut in. "Aren't your Hotronics in the summit bag? There you go. Summit critical."

The Base Camp manager was unmoved. "C'mon, Vanessa, plenty of people summit without Hotronics."

I tried to make the case, but his solution was for Sam to give his own Hotronics to Emma.

"Hey, now, wait a minute." Sam's eyes went wide. "I don't know what I'm about to encounter up there, and Daniel isn't here. Do you really think that's a good idea? This is my first summit as well, so . . ."

"Forget it," Emma said. "It's too late."

We were already an hour into our scant five-hour rest period. There was no way the bag was coming up. We lay in our sleeping bags. I stared at the tent ceiling. Emma was mad. I prayed her anger would carry her to the summit and not turn to sadness.

A few hours later, we got up and dressed, pulling on moisture-wicking everything, from bras and underwear to long underwear, top and bottom. And then, for reasons I can't even fathom now— maybe I was feeling chilly, or maybe the very idea of –40 degrees got in my head, or maybe because it was Everest and I'd been programmed to worry that the summit was fierce—whatever the reason, I second-guessed myself and put on an additional long-sleeved midweight zip-neck base layer for added warmth, breathability, and wicking before I climbed into my summit suit. As we were getting ready to head out, Sam came round and offered Emma his Hotronics, which surprised me, and she gratefully accepted them, which surprised me even more.

"The queue is already forming," he said. "We need to get going."

Phinjo Dorjee and I joined the queue and quickly lost track of everyone but each other in the darkness. We climbed for about an hour, working hard. Temperatures dropped, but I was sweating inside my summit suit, wondering what the hell made me put on that additional midweight layer. I always run hot when I'm exerting myself. Why would I go against my own carefully considered plan? We were early in the climb, and I was already miserable. I forged on, trying to ignore it, but the path was steep, and I couldn't stop focusing on the hydration factor. Every drop of sweat was a drop of water I couldn't afford to lose.

After another hour, I pulled off the fixed line and motioned to Phinjo Dorjee that I had to take a layer off. Ridiculous. Again I could see that bemused look on his face as I struggled with my backpack, oxygen tank, face mask, goggles, and headlamp. Undressing was a reinvention of awkward, given the steepness of the pitch, the darkness of the night, and the bulk of the down suit, which basically turns you into a gingerbread man. When I finally fought myself free of the ill-conceived extra layer, I stood there half-dressed in the subzero cold with the wind whipping razor blades of powdered ice against my skin. I cussed a blue streak, but I got it resolved. We rejoined the queue, which was growing fast.

I'm fascinated by economic game theory, the study of human behavior as it relates to conflict and cooperation, how we tend to flock with and fight each other at the same time. This is how it is on Everest. Guides cooperate with each other, even if it appears not to be in their best interests to do so. Expedition leaders share weather predictions and compare notes with one another, even fix ropes to the summit, but they all hold back their exact summit plans as if they each have some unique strategy no one knows about. Ultimately every expedition does the same thing: they make a beeline for the summit on the first forecast bluebird day, as if Mother Nature will never provide a second weather window. Even though they know this will create bottlenecks, crowding, and queues. Even though they know those things will increase deaths and danger.

Still below the Balcony, probably close to 27,000 feet, Phinjo Dorjee and I resumed our short rope strategy that had worked so well earlier from Camp 3, and we quickly bypassed a few people and made up for the lost time I'd spent on my costume change. I looked around for Emma, but she was somewhere behind me, one of the faceless many who trudged upward through the darkness.

Stay angry, I wished upon her again. *Use that energy to get to the summit.*

Rage is a better fuel than frustration, and tears would leave her weak. *Mothers die. They let you down. You don't need her.* I don't know if I was talking to Emma or the child within myself. The sentiment played on a subconscious loop from the time I was a kid until I was in my midforties.

Stay angry. Stay angry.

I was still living in London when my mother died. She had just retired from nursing. She was fit. She did her hair and makeup every morning and maintained a dependably sardonic view of the world. Her favorite expression was *I don't give a rat's ass*, which I hated. She'd been divorced from my dad almost as long as she'd been married to him. She was dating someone I didn't even know and renovating a seven-acre farm in the middle of nowhere, where she lived with her dogs, cats, and a potbellied pig, which I believe was there only to irritate the neighbor. When she was hospitalized for pneumonia, she assured me it was nothing.

"I'll fly over to the States if you need me," I said.

She didn't give a rat's ass. Two days later, her friend Dottie called to tell me my mother was on a respirator, couldn't speak, and had been offered last rites by the priest. Feeling utterly blindsided, I jumped on the first flight from London to Detroit. I'd been living outside the United States for twelve years and had no idea how the US health care system worked. I didn't know my mother's views on anything except mercy killing and euthanasia (for and for), so I didn't know how she felt about double-blind placebo drug trials and do not resuscitate (DNR) alerts. I certainly didn't know about her banking, safety deposit box, wills, or PIN codes.

Jonathan arrived, a calming presence as my mother lingered, septic and unresponsive, for twenty-one days. Complicating matters was the growing agony in my foot. I'd had bunion surgery six months earlier, thanks to decades in fabulous shoes, so I had steel staples and two titanium screws in each foot where the broken bones were reset. Now one of those bloody screws had worked itself loose. Every step sent up a sharp sliver of pain. I could actually see the head of the screw under my skin. Obviously, I was compelled to text a photo to one of my friends. "If someone doesn't take this thing out, I'm going to the hardware store for a Phillips-head screwdriver."

I sat beside my mother's bed reading Elisabeth Kübler-Ross's book on the inevitable stages of grief: denial, anger, bargaining, depression, acceptance. I was able to tick every box as her brain activity ebbed and her body shut down. Tracheotomy. Pneumonia. Acute respiratory distress syndrome. Sepsis. The kidneys went, and I decided dialysis was okay. The liver went, and I figured liver transplants happen, right? But her circulation wasn't right with her amputated leg, and when they talked about amputating it higher, I hesitated.

"Oh God, no. If she wakes up without a kidney or a liver, that's one thing. If she wakes up without her leg, she'll kill me."

The next day, an ultrasound of her intestines confirmed that there was no longer a choice. The surgeon detected no brain activity. Jonathan and I agreed to increase the pain medication and turn off the machines. She wasn't afraid to die. I was the one who didn't want to let her go. Wiping away tears, I agreed to add DO NOT RESUSCITATE to her chart to ensure that there would be no CPR intervention if her heart or breathing stopped, but only after the doctor assured me she would have plenty of pain medication. The priest arrived and administered her last rites, and she died a few minutes later. Jonathan and I went to find nonhospital food for dinner and a drink. He sat across the table from me, a calm eye at the center of a terrible storm that had swirled around me since I was a little girl.

Stay angry. Stay angry.

We'd started up the mountain as a team of ten. Now we were six. Even our guide was gone. An echo of my family of four, reduced to three, dwindled to two. Now it was just my father and me, and even if I had the right questions to ask him, Parkinson's and dementia made it impossible for him to answer. I was on my own again.

"God, I'm knackered," I mumbled inside my oxygen mask, but Phinjo Dorjee couldn't hear me over the howling wind.

I looked up at the stars, trying to place myself on the South Col route charts I'd memorized. Elevation. Pitch. The topography I could once visualize so plainly was abstract to me now. I was stumbling through Picasso's *Guernica*—white-on-white snow and shades of cold darkness. From the corner of my goggles, I saw Phinjo Dorjee waving at me, motioning that it was time to hydrate. I had my first water bottle strategically tucked inside my summit suit for body warmth. I pulled it out and found it frozen hard as a hammer. *Shit.* Okay. Try the insulated bottle. When I put it in my backpack, it was so hot I couldn't touch it, but now, when Phinjo Dorjee dug it out of the pack, it was frozen solid. *Oh, those fuckers!* Those false advertisers! Those shit-eating, glad-handing, retail-promise-breaking assholes! "Oh, no, this won't freeze—no, not even on *Everest*." In a rat's ass, it won't freeze! In a rat's motherfucking ass!

Swearing inside my face mask, I dug under the summit banners in my backpack. My last hope was a Nalgene water bottle I'd carefully wrapped in a pair of down booties. I'd planned it for my descent, but I could think about that later. When I pulled it out, I was delighted to see the comforting slosh of liquid inside. Just one problem: neither Phinjo Dorjee nor I could get the cap off. Over the next twelve hours, I would ask twelve other people to give it a go, to no avail. My one source of liquid. I was so thirsty, I wanted to smash that bloody thing against a rock, but I couldn't risk breaking it and letting the liquid run out, so I continued on, carrying the extra weight of all that water, hoping I'd be able to access it at some point, but that never happened.

Keep calm. Carry on.

I'd survived dehydration before. Obviously not my first choice. It sucks, and there are consequences. But I would rather have faced those repercussions than drink from anyone else's bottle. Everyone around me was sick by now. Bronchitis, Khumbu cough, chest infections, cold, flu, pneumonia, pulmonary edema, diarrhea. Emma and I had been looking around camp with that uncomfortable last-man-standing feeling of impending doom. Dehydration would slow me down. Possibly make me hallucinate. I was fairly sure I could count on Phinjo Dorjee if I seriously lost it. Or not. Maybe. I vacillated. *I can do this. This is impossible. Do this. Fuck this. No, do it.*

I read an article in *Alpinist* magazine about mountaineer Don Bowie, who climbed Annapurna with Ueli Steck in 2013. He talked about "wrestling with an inner argument, vacillation between confident 'I CAN DO THIS' and disparaging 'THIS IS JUST A BAD IDEA.'"

That is so where I was at.

We kept moving. My mind kept wandering. Now my face mask was bugging me. The oxygen respiratory piece was so big, it took up the whole lower part of my face, from the bridge of my nose, across both cheeks, and under my chin. My goggles— battery powered, with a built-in fan to keep condensation at bay—were also huge, extending from the bridge of my nose to the top of my head. That left no real estate on my face for my headlamp, which would have been attached to my helmet, but— well, we don't have to revisit that. The headlamp kept slipping up into my hairline. I kept pulling it down. It kept slipping up. I kept seeing my helmet bouncing down the mountainside. Trying to find my feet, using one hand for my mountaineering axe and another to find something in my pocket, I felt the elastic band on my headlamp snap with a classic Bugs Bunny *sproi-oi-oing*. The headlamp shot off and bounced down the mountain into the darkness.

"Noooo! Fuuuuuuuuuuck!"

Dammit. Now I was really pissed off. I had another headlamp, but it was down at Camp 4. When Daniel went over extra kit we should carry to the summit, instead of the extra headlamp, he made sure we all had extra batteries. Plenty of extra batteries. And they'd last even longer now that I had no fucking headlamp.

Without speaking, Phinjo Dorjee and I choreographed a way to share the single light from his headlamp, and we continued upward. He took ten steps and turned to give me a glimmer of light—just enough to show me the next ten steps—and then he turned his light upward again. Ten steps in the dark. Glimmer of light. Ten steps in the dark. Glimmer of light.

I was in the foulest mood imaginable. *Why am I doing this? I have nothing to prove to anyone. I'm higher than I've ever been. I should just cut my losses. I should turn around. Daniel's not here. Why am I here? I'm so tired. I'm so thirsty. I'm so tired.*

As that toxic internal voice ranted on, I tried to pep-talk myself with uplifting messages like *You've trained so hard*, but that quickly morphed into *You've just spent seventy-five thousand dollars.* When Phinjo Dorjee turned again, there was snow falling. I looked up at the stars, but they played tricks on me, dodging in and out of the clouds. The stars, falling snow, and distant headlamps all merged into a grainy eight-millimeter film.

The mountain rose up beneath me, profoundly icy, infinitely white and indifferent. All around me, climbers slumbered beneath the snow. The melting glaciers of Everest keep revealing them in gruesome reality, but trudging through the frigid darkness, it was possible to imagine that it wouldn't be a terrible way to go—that curling into a warm fetal position, that closing of the eyes to sleep.

Stop it. Stop it. Get a grip.

I felt myself spiraling, down, down, down, clawing to self-arrest. Ten steps in the dark. Glimmer of light. Ten steps in the dark. Glimmer of light.

Ninety-nine bottles of beer on the wall
Ninety-nine bottles of beer

It started out as an earworm, demanding attention, and then became a mantra, steady as a heartbeat.

Take one down and pass it around
Ninety-eight bottles of beer on the wall

I breathed with the downbeat and forced my feet into a rhythm.

Ninety-eight bottles of beer on the wall
Ninety-eight bottles of beer
Take one down and pass it around

We used to go on car trips, my family and I. Every weekend we went somewhere. A state park. A carnival. Camping. Canoeing. Staying home was more dangerous than any of the outdoorsy activities we undertook.

Ninety-seven bottles of beer
Take one down and pass it around

We hiked. We fished. We went everywhere.

Ninety-six bottles of beer on the wall

The back seat of the family car was littered with books and snacks. Ben and I played games to pass the time. Sang songs. Bickered. Slept with our sweaty foreheads against the window.

Ninety-one bottles of beer on the wall
Ninety-one bottles of beer

I still remember his face. He is forever fourteen, frozen in that moment just before he disappeared into the darkness.

Take one down and pass it around

I forced myself upward through the night. Ten steps. A glimmer of light.

Eighty-two bottles of beer on the wall

Eighty-one bottles of beer
Take one down and pass it around

Seventy-three bottles of beer on the wall

Fifty-six bottles of beer
Take one down and pass it around

Forty-nine bottles of beer on the wall

Forty-three bottles of beer on the wall

Thirty-three bottles of beer
Take one down and pass it around

Twenty-nine bottles of beer on the wall

Twenty-one bottles of beer

We reached the relatively flat area called the Balcony at about 8,400 meters. There was enough room for several climbers to stand there and change oxygen bottles, and one of them called my name.

"Vanessa?"

"Johannes!" I offered him a clumsy gloved fist bump.

"Good to see a familiar face," he said. "How's it going?"

"Great," I lied. "Super."

I tried to down an energy gel—a sticky-sweet ooze that's supposed to give you a superabsorbent blast of energy, or at least a little jolt of caffeine. Over the past eighteen months, I'd tried every flavor and hated them all until an adorable guy appeared out of nowhere on Shishapangma and offered me a new flavor called "Espresso Love." Dispersed oxygen molecules, an extra shot of caffeine, and an electrolyte blitz. What's not to love? But I still had no water, so it coated my dry mouth like a glaze of honey inside a dead tree.

Above the Balcony, the incline pitched steeper and steeper. I switched to the French technique, proceeding sideways with my crampons, one foot, then the other. The stars were out again but not quite as piercing. The sky was awash with the thin light of pre-dawn. The icy slope in front of me was easier to see now. A spotty thread of headlamps twined upward between the glow of Phinjo Dorjee's headlamp and the small knot of lights at the summit, about 400 meters above us, but the majority of the traffic was below. We were making good time, all things considered. Ten steps. Glimmer of light. Thank God for Phinjo Dorjee. His father would be proud.

A leg cramp sank its teeth into my calf.

Shit. Shit. Switch sides.

Take one down and pass it around

Ten steps. Glimmer of light.

Seventeen bottles of beer on the wall

The wind whipped up from below, and I leaned into the blast, crunching and uncrunching my fingers inside my mitts, rubbing them against the palms of my hands. I located my inner General Patton.

Wake up! Forward!

Oh, my kingdom for a headlamp! Between the 2,400-meter drop-off on the southwest face and the 3,000-meter drop-off on the Kangshung Face is this narrow, single-file path. I traced Phinjo Dorjee's footsteps.

Two bottles of beer on the wall
Two bottles of beer

We reached a knife-edge ridge, the cornice traverse, which leads
to the Hillary Step. It's not like there's a billboard: WELCOME TO THE
HILLARY STEP! The rocks grow ever larger as you ascend, one increasingly massive boulder after another, until this truly gargantuan
colossus presents itself—one that needs a bit of effort to get up and
over—and that is the Hillary Step. (I would be one of the last to experience this iconic treasure, as the Hillary Step would be severely al-
tered after an earthquake in 2015.) I clipped my carabiner that acted
as a safety onto the rope and started climbing. It was up and down
with some twists and turns, which was tricky with my short arms
and legs. Here and there I had to drop down with a triceps dip, praying that my feet dangled and landed properly. Shorties do not get the
benefit where rock is concerned.

One bottle of beer on the wall
One bottle of beer

It was a classic bottleneck, but because it was still dark and
early, all the traffic was heading up. I feared what would happen
when we had to make our way down against a tidal wave of climbers motivated by summit fever. But first it was my turn at the top.

I reached the summit of Mount Everest at 4:12 AM on May 19,
2012.

I'd been pushing toward this moment for two years, thinking
that when I got here, the summit would be the only thing that
mattered. But as I said, when I'm wrong, I am willing to admit it.

12

Dear Lord, please don't let me fuck up.
—THE ASTRONAUT'S PRAYER, ATTRIBUTED TO
ALAN B. SHEPARD, THE FIRST AMERICAN IN SPACE.

The area defined as the Everest Summit is just a bit more than the length and breadth of a king-size mattress. A hard wind scoured the gritty summit, driving ice crystals into drifts of trash and tattered prayer flags. I'd be lying if I said I was elated. I was too fatigued and adrenaline-spent to experience what I would call pure joy. It was not everything I imagined it would be, but I was there, and for a moment, that was everything enough. I stood at the top of the world, my body trembling with exhaustion, my mind numb with fatigue.

Phinjo Dorjee and I were the first of our team to arrive. We radioed this information to EBC. We'd beaten the thick of the crowd. Twenty people milled about, fiddling with their flags and cameras in the first light of a cold, milky dawn, and no, not one of them had enough strength in their wooden fingers to open my damn water bottle.

So. Right. What's next? Summit photo. Flags. Camera. Why wasn't it working? *Batteries are frozen, dammit.* I dug around in my backpack for the backup batteries I'd carefully wrapped in down, and those were dead too. No summit photo meant no summit certificate.

"Johannes, up here!" I waved as he mounted the jagged ridge below, an excellent candidate for hero of the day. We met with a cumbersome hug and a hearty high five with our chubby mittens. "Well done, Johannes, well done."

"You too," he puffed. "Cheers."

"Johannes, is your camera working? Can you take my summit photo?"

It was and he did.

"I owe you an orange Fanta, big-time," I said. "Wow, how many banners have you brought?"

He had loads, but I waited for him to take pictures with them so we could head down together. Meanwhile, our teammate Perry arrived. Johannes and I offered weary high fives. No hugs. No jumping up and down. We were just there. Because it's there. And now other climbers were arriving. They'd earned their moment on top, and I was already thinking ahead to the treacherous traffic jam forming on the Hillary Step below.

The summit is only halfway.

This had been drummed into my head along with the warning that most deaths happen on the descent. I'd been mentally preparing myself, calculating how much oxygen I might dedicate to descent line etiquette, but nothing could have prepared me for the massive queue forming below us. My heart sank. I'd heard horror stories of frostbite and edema that set in because people stood still for an hour or more, waiting for someone else to give them permission to pass, lingering in the Death Zone longer than the human body can take it. I was not going to let this happen to Phinjo Dorjee and me. This was Kami's son. I felt a bolt of protectiveness toward him that was surprisingly maternal, a mama-bear instinct I didn't know I had.

It wasn't that Jonathan and I made a decision to not have children. That was decided long before I knew him. When I started high school, even though I hadn't really begun to date yet, my mother became obsessed with the thought that I might get pregnant and "ruin my life." First, she focused on birth control, but she quickly moved to sterilization. She and my father were young when I was born, children having children, ill equipped for the challenges of raising a family. She framed that scenario as the worst possible thing that could happen until the worst thing that actually could happen—my brother's death—took her mind off it.

Growing up, I watched my grandmother mourn the son she'd lost in World War II. He was part of the First Battalion, Ninth Marines, nicknamed the "Walking Dead," a handle that crossed my mind many times on the long slog up one mountain or another. My grandmother never recovered from the loss of her son. Now I saw my mother repeat that behavior, disappearing into that same fog, completely unaware. A few weeks after Ben died, she and my father filed for divorce. They both moved out, leaving me to live alone in the family home, and the memories there made it too painful for them to visit. Awash in survivor's guilt, I took full responsibility. I tried to atone. At first, I wanted to help them. Later, I wanted to hate them. Eventually, I understood that their implosion had nothing to do with me. I was just the collateral damage. Functional point: I was on my own.

For reasons I will never know, my mother felt strongly that I should get a tubal ligation, and the way I looked at it then is not so different from the way I look at it now. I simply couldn't guarantee a child's happiness. There were too many outliers. Clearly, being a mother exposed one to a terrifying level of vulnerability. I agreed to the surgery, and when the doctor dragged his feet, she pushed past him, obtained the necessary authorization, and organized the paperwork. The sterilization surgery was performed before I ever even considered having sex for the first time. My body still did everything it was supposed to do on its monthly cycle, but there was no risk of pregnancy then or ever. Whatever creative energy I had I devoted to school and eventually to my career. I directed any caregiving impulses toward charity and environmental causes. I relished my freedom and enjoyed the idea that I was safely insulated from the type of loss that had wounded my mother and grandmother more grievously than the loss of a limb.

But standing above the Hillary Step with Phinjo Dorjee at my elbow, I suddenly felt fiercely protective of him. He's climbed Everest many times, but he's Kami's son, and Kami is a dear friend who led me up my first 8,000-meter peak. When Kami couldn't be there with me on Everest, he sent his own son in his place. Phinjo Dorjee and I had come a long way together, a hard climb in more ways than one. Maybe this was the moment for which I'd stashed away my maternal instinct. Or maybe it was a moment of my mother being with me in a way she was never able to be when she was alive. I don't know how else to rationalize the burst of protectiveness that moved through me. All I know is, it felt uniquely *genuine*, like the stories you hear about a mother lifting a car to save her toddler. I looked down at the implacable queue of climbers, and I had to get Phinjo Dorjee down, and fast.

Transfer of risk is a foundational principle to almost any business. A deadlocked transaction moves forward if someone steps up to assume a greater level of risk in return for an incremental reward, which is ultimately for the benefit of both parties. When you buy a house, a mortgage company assumes a large risk by allowing you to own and occupy the house with a down payment and comparatively small monthly installment. I had to transfer the risk, I realized. The one who takes the risk earns the step.

I took my oxygen mask off and yelled to Phinjo Dorjee, "Follow me." I clipped in on the fixed line and motioned for Phinjo Dorjee to stay close behind me as I led the descent, facing the oncoming traffic. No one was about to let us take the step into the single lane on the impossibly narrow staircase, but I wasn't going to stand there while we ran out of oxygen. There were so many people coming up now, with no rules granting the right of way to climbers moving in one direction or the other and no way to communicate with this other person who, like me, had his mouth and nose stuffed with an oxygen apparatus, thick black goggles on, and (unlike me) a helmet making a good impression of an astronaut on a mountain.

I gripped the line with my left hand and unclipped the carabiner/safety with my right hand. Phinjo Dorjee grabbed the back of my summit suit, and I held the carabiner up in front of the face of the person climbing up directly in front of me, showing them that I was unclipped. Then, with my right hand holding the carabiner/safety, I took the step down and moved the carabiner around their waist to the fixed line behind them to clip in again. It seemed that everyone understood this nonverbal way to communicate and enlist their cooperation, with many people grabbing my elbow to help me reach the fixed line. I took the risk, so I deserved the step. There was no more guessing which one of us should go up or down. With gravity on our side, we made our way down, quick and efficient, and people had two fewer climbers to contend with.

Allow me to inject the standard disclaimer: *Do not try this at home.* Fellow climbers, I'm not saying this is the way it should be done. Just reporting. That's what I did to get out of the traffic jam during that first year of the now dreaded Everest Queue.

On our way down, we spotted a climber on his knees. "Please," his climbing partner begged, "anything you can do to help."

I knelt down and took my mask off. "Hi, I'm Vanessa. Do you speak English?"

The stricken climber nodded, unable to move, his breath staggered and choppy.

"I'm not a doctor," I said. "Do you understand me?"

Another nod.

"Is there any reason you shouldn't take oral dexamethasone?"

He shook his head no, and I dug into my pocket to find it. I gave it to his friend with instructions. Now, I do not recommend dispensing or accepting meds from random people on mountaintops. Just reporting. That's what I did. Because climbers must sometimes navigate unnavigable situations, understanding that armchair explorers will lecture us online about what we *really* should have done. It's easy to lecture a mountain climber from a barstool. Pardon me if I don't give a fuck.

Phinjo Dorjee and I left the two to continue their descent and still made it to Camp 4 by 10 AM, less than six hours after summiting. When we radioed our arrival to EBC, they were surprised to hear from me so soon.

"Camp 4, copy. Well done, Vanessa and Phinjo Dorjee! Well done. Is anyone else with you?"

"Johannes was right behind me, but I lost track of him. He's not here yet."

I didn't try to explain the blast of let's-get-the-hell-out-of-here energy that carried me. Pretending I needed to get Phinjo Dorjee down—it was all in my head. Phinjo Dorjee was a seasoned climber. He didn't need any mollycoddling, but by nominating myself as his protector, I rose to the challenge, and it felt real. It was powerful. I was glad to know I had it in me. I'd always felt shut out of that particular kinship with people like Pippa, who was a tigress when it came to her boys. Since that moment, I've

Me and Ben at an
amusement park.
Vanessa O'Brien

Me and Dad.
Vanessa O'Brien

Me, Mom, and Ben on vacation.
Vanessa O'Brien

Climbing the Penitentes of Shishapangma.
Ang Chhiring (Kami) Sherpa

Receiving a blessing from Lama Ghese.
Kurt Wedberg, Sierra Mountaineering International, Inc.

Mount Everest acclimatization hike.
Bob Berger

Descending after
Mount Everest
summit.
Phinjo Dorjee Sherpa

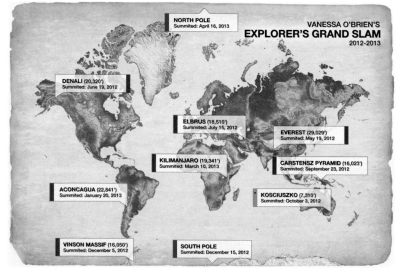

The Explorers Grand Slam.
Courtesy of Thomson Safaris

Training for the North Pole on Revere Beach.
Jonathan O'Brien

Skiing to the geographic north pole.
Doug Stoup—Ice Axe Expeditions

K2 Season 1 acclimatization to Camp 1.
Alex Buisse—www.alexbuisse.com

K2 Season 1 with James, Gul Muhammad, and Major Satti.
Zaheer Chaudhry

K2 Season 2 group photo with goat on route to K2 Base Camp.
Courtesy of NSE porters

K2 Season 2 acclimatization to Camp 2.
Estalin Suárez Valladolid

K2 Season 3, Sylvi, Dawa Gyalje Sherpa, and me at Camp 1.
Ang Chhiring (Kami) Sherpa

K2 Season 3 summit with UN Women flag.
Dawa Gyalje Sherpa

taken ownership of my own brand of parenthood: compassion; empathy; a desire to make a difference; a homemaker's custodial vigilance for the planet; and unconditional love for the people of my adopted countries, Nepal and later Pakistan.

No such deep thoughts at the time, of course. Only thirst. After fifteen hours without water, breathing bottled oxygen mixed with ambient air, my mouth and throat were like sandpaper. When I tried to guzzle a water bottle, my lips were so cracked and numb, I couldn't form the right mechanism to drink and swallow. The water just dribbled down my chin. I had to sip a little at a time, craning my neck like a baby bird, taking in a tiny bit of water, then a cup of hot tea, then a bowl of noodles and broth. I waited until noon, wondering why Johannes had not arrived. I couldn't wait much longer if I was going to make it to Camp 2 that day. Camp 4 was still well within the Death Zone; it wasn't safe to linger. Phinjo Dorjee and I made our way down to Camp 3, paused long enough to hydrate, and then continued down, arriving at Camp 2 around five in the afternoon.

The cook stepped out of the mess tent to greet us. No one else was there. I radioed Daniel, down at Base Camp.

"Congratulations," he said. "You did it."

"Yes, and where's my high five? I thought you'd be here."

"Nah, I'm buggered. Had to come down. Are you coming down tomorrow?"

"Maybe," I said. "Did everyone summit?"

"Almost." He wouldn't confirm who'd summited and who hadn't, which was irritating. "They're staying at Camp 4 tonight. Heading down tomorrow. You should head down tomorrow too."

I assured him I'd take it under advisement, but it was safe to spend two nights at Camp 2, well below the Death Zone, and I wanted to be there to greet the rest of the team. Listening to cross talk on the radio, I was happy to gather that Emma did summit, but not everyone's summits had been accounted for. In my tent, I peeled off my summit suit and boots and crawled into my sleeping bag, profoundly weary. I was more than halfway down, but I had a long way to go before I was off this mountain.

"Vanessa?"

Whoever was trying to wake me up, they'd better have a damn good reason.

"Camp 2?" It was Daniel's voice on the radio. "Camp 2, copy."

I could tell it was morning. There was gray light coming through the tent flap. The Camp 2 cook grinned down at me and held the radio forward. I sat up in my sleeping bag, feeling like I'd been dragged under an oxcart.

"Hey. Hi. I'm here. I'm awake."

"How's it going?" Daniel asked. "Are you ready to head down?"

"No way. No one showed up here yesterday. I'll wait for the team to come down from Camp 4."

He tried to talk me into going down to Base Camp, but I was having none of it until I thought about Phinjo Dorjee. I was sure he was more than ready to get back to his family, and I didn't want to keep him here longer than necessary. If the team were to arrive here early enough, then perhaps Phinjo Dorjee and I could head down today, but if they did not, I would have to stay.

"I'll start packing my gear," I said.

"Right, then," said Daniel. "See you soon."

It had taken me five hours to get here, and I knew the team wouldn't loiter at Camp 4. I expected to see them any time now and figured we could either say a quick hello and leave or stay one more night, unless the weather turned. In the mess tent, I listened to more radio chatter over breakfast. I repacked my gear so it would be easier to handle in the icefall. It was after noon. Still no sign of the team. I lay on my sleeping bag, reading, my mind drifting. The later I stayed, the less likely I was to go down today.

Finally, around 3 PM, the team began to trickle in. Big group hugs. Perfunctory high fives. We congregated in the mess tent and sat there staring at each other in silence.

"I don't know about you guys," I said, "but I think that's probably the hardest thing I've ever done in my life."

Everyone burst out laughing at the understatement of the century. We'd left Kathmandu eight weeks earlier, hearty and healthy, a diverse team of intrepid climbers. Now we were shadows of ourselves, each having lost twenty-five to thirty pounds, with scabby necks unwashed, unshaven, or both and faces red and purple with windburn and sunburn. One climber's eye was pointing a quarter turn to the outside. Another couldn't figure out why his ass was bleeding. Perry said he couldn't feel his toes.

"Did you use Hotronics?"

I squatted down and pulled off his socks. His feet looked fairly normal—a bit pink maybe, like he'd dipped his toes in scalding-hot water. I tickled the top of his middle toe, and he didn't react.

"Lucky for you, I read only mountaineering tragedy books while climbing mountains." I smiled up at him, briskly rubbing his feet between my hands. "Point is, just this morning, I happened to be reading *Snow in the Kingdom* by Ed Webster. Really well written. All about climbing Everest, but up the Kangshung Face in Tibet."

"Is there a moral to this story?" asked Johannes.

"Lots of frostbite involved."

"And?"

"We need to soak his feet in lukewarm water," I said. "Hold fast, Perilous. Webster says it hurts like hell."

Anticipating the worst, we called the Himalayan Rescue Association, and they set plans in motion to evacuate Perry by helicopter first thing in the morning. He tried to be optimistic, but time is vital with frostbite. He'd already spent the night at Camp 4 and would spend another at Camp 2. This is a bittersweet story, because he did lose all five toes on one foot, but a few years later—though there was no spark of romance between them at the time of the expedition—he and Emma reconnected, got together, and had twins, so if you do the math, that's a net gain of fifteen toes.

There wasn't much for dinner besides the infamous four quadrants of crap. The climbing company had offered military MREs, but early in our journey, when I'd pointed out to Daniel that most of them were a couple of years out of date, he'd just shrugged. A man of simple needs.

We picked through our food and sipped hot tea, sharing our climbing tales of woe. Mine didn't take long; I had the quickest summit and least eventful descent. Others had struggled with their masks and regulators or ran out of oxygen altogether. The only one who didn't summit had turned around somewhere between the Balcony and the South Summit. It would take him six months to recover from pneumonia. Another team member complained that he never got the oxygen he paid for. Emma had been chilled to the bone waiting for her Sherpa, who kept having to stop and vomit, and because the Sherpa controlled the radio, he tried to blame her. She eventually took over the radio and asked for another Sherpa to be sent in his place. Sam had disappeared for a while, and the consensus was that he had gone off with summit fever. Everyone was feeling a bit jaded, laying their distress at the feet of the Base Camp manager, climbing company, and Daniel himself.

We agreed to leave Camp 2 at 4 AM to make an early bid for the icefall, so I was up at 3 AM to get myself ready. Every part of my body felt bruised and used. My eyes ached. My tongue felt like an argyle sock. I was so eager to go. Emma woke up, pensive and a bit downcast. She'd had a rough go. Instead of heading down with the rest of us, she had decided to stay another day. I gave her a hug and wished her well, and we promised to stay in touch. Something I learned from those weekend car trips with my family: if getting there is half the fun, being there is the other half, and getting home is a no-damn-fun grinding slog. While others took a helicopter, I walked a whole day to a teahouse in Pheriche to lower costs. I took plenty of pictures. I didn't expect to be back.

It's not unusual to leave Everest feeling shell-shocked. Every one of us had put 110 percent of our heart and soul into the summit bid, leaving nothing on the table, mentally, emotionally, spiritually, and physically. In the wake of all that adrenaline came a free-falling sense of *What next?* What could possibly follow the hardest thing you have ever done?

Daniel and Johannes were off to Denali, continuing Johannes's Seven Summits quest. For years, I'd been bombarded with stories about the Seven Summits, but with my whole focus on Everest, I never let myself consider the logistics—or the cost. Most people start with Kilimanjaro, the shortest, and work their way up to Everest. I could tick both those boxes, but there's some debate about what comes between.

In the 1980s, a businessman named Dick Bass coined the phrase *Seven Summits* and set himself the challenge of climbing the highest peak on each continent: Australia's Mount Kosciuszko, Antarctica's Mount Vinson, Europe's Mount Elbrus, Africa's Kilimanjaro, North America's Denali, South America's Aconcagua, and Asia's Mount Everest. He accomplished his goal in 1985, but the following year, mountaineer Reinhold Messner challenged the Bass definition, suggesting Australia's Kosciuszko (nickname Kozzie since no one can spell it) was little more than a molehill and should be replaced with Carstensz Pyramid in Indonesia, which would widen the definition to include Australasia and introduce the only pure rock climbing by substituting Carstensz Pyramid (the Messner list) for Kosciuszko (the Bass list).

"Are you doing the Seven Summits?" people routinely asked me, and I automatically answered, "No, just Everest." Now I wasn't so quick to shut the idea down, and I knew if I took it on, I would include both Kozzie and Carstensz. I would climb all eight of the Seven Summits according to the CYA (cover your ass) list.

By the time I boarded my flight for Boston, another penny had dropped.

If you reach your goal, and you think, *All righty, then! Done and dusted*, you've lost the curiosity that dares you to grow and drives you to change. Better you should reach that seemingly unreachable goal, see that it's only about the length and breadth of a king-size mattress, and embrace the reality that this goal was just a bus stop on a far greater voyage of discovery. Only then can you find your real path: a never-ending series of aims and ambitions that add up to a life compelled by a sense of purpose. Then you'll know what you love to do, and hopefully that has something to do with what you're good at. And how you can contribute to the world.

13

Why do mountain climbers rope themselves together?
To prevent the sensible ones from going home.
—UNKNOWN

"Summertime in the northern hemisphere," I said to Jonathan. "It's not a good time to be job hunting or starting a business venture. If there's a way to do the Seven Summits over the next few months and learn a bit too, well . . . why not?"

Why not? is a dangerous question to ask an English chartered accountant (the equivalent of a CPA in the States). *Not* is their specialty.

"What mountains?" he wanted to know. "In what order? And what will it cost?"

Armed with spreadsheets, fresh data, and climbing company estimates, I promised, "It's not like Everest. Most of these are five- or ten-thousand-dollar mountains, excluding Vinson Massif in Antarctica. And I'll go back to work after. I promise."

"Are your fingers crossed behind your back?"

"Yes," I confessed, "but not because of the cost of the mountains. It's the uncertainty of going back to work."

I did not get my way immediately. It took some cajoling. I listened with rapt attention to several long lectures, but I couldn't afford a lot of time for haggling over the details. Denali can only be summited from May to July, so it was time-sensitive. I was too late to join Johannes and Daniel on their post-Everest expedition to Denali, as Daniel's team had been full for months, but Daniel referred me to his boss in Alaska, Colby Coombs, founder of Alaska Mountaineering School, who said he would take me himself. He liked to stretch his legs every other season or so and wouldn't need to acclimatize any longer than I would, as he's usually out on different locations doing interesting things. With the right weather window and a small team, we could summit in less than twenty-one days, taking the West Buttress route: approximately sixteen miles and about 4,000 meters of vertical gain.

I hadn't even finished unpacking my Everest kit when I started repacking for Denali, the third-highest and most northerly of the Seven Summits. Asking around about this mountain, the one consistent comment was "so fucking cold." Getting there was an adventure in itself: Boston to Chicago to San Francisco to Anchorage—return flights available only on Tuesdays and Thursdays, with a four-city connection and a $1,000 change fee—and when I landed in Anchorage, I had a three-hour bus ride to the town of Talkeetna, during which the driver talked at great length on the PA system about her divorce, her move to Alaska, and how she landed her job driving this bus. By the time we rolled into Talkeetna, I was ready for the kind of silence only nature can provide, and she was about an hour into the stream-of-consciousness saga of her dysfunctional family, which I must say, at the risk of being a calamity snob, was not half as dysfunctional as mine.

First thing in the morning, the team—Colby, his assistant, an apprentice named Troy, and I—met at the mountaineering company. Colby was an experienced mountaineer, easy on the eyes with a long-suffering, vaguely ironic sense of humor. It didn't surprise me to learn he'd attended English boarding school as a kid.

Flights to Denali were grounded by bad weather, and you do want to fly to Denali Base Camp (DBC) as Denali National Park alone is about the size of Massachusetts, so he sent me off to safety training to kill some time. We had fun simulating crevasse rescue (Alaska has some of the deepest crevasses in the world) and practicing crevasse travel, pulling sleds that were roped together in the event one of us fell through the ice.

We packed within strict weight limits. I was allowed only one set of clothing: base layer, midweight, outer layer, one vest, one jacket, one puffy coat, and one pair of down pants plus two pairs of socks and liners. I snuck in some moisturizer and an extra pair of underwear, but while most men shrivel at the word *tampons*, Colby was unflappable. When I brought out my headlamp, he laughed and reminded me, "We're two hundred miles south of the Arctic Circle. It won't be dark here until after Thanksgiving."

I thought I might see Johannes and Daniel somewhere along the way, so I also managed to squeeze in the orange Fanta I still owed Johannes for taking my summit pictures.

Gear check negotiated, we presented ourselves at the park ranger station and viewed the required videos about safety, frostbite, and how serious the rangers are about leaving no trace, including yes, human waste. Conrad Anker, climbing Denali with Jon Krakauer, was famously fined for taking an unauthorized dump on the glacier. "They were taking a shit," Supervisory Climbing Ranger John Leonard told the amused media. "I don't have much tolerance for people shitting on the mountain." Following the protocol of "leave no trace," we carried a supply of plastic bags on our way in and packed our solid waste to take with us on the way out.

The staff ranger also humbled us with some hard truths about the awful summit success ratios. More than one thousand people attempt to climb Denali every year. This year, the weather had been particularly volatile; the success rate so far was a dismal 40 percent. Seven climbers died in 2011, five in 2012. Colby was unfazed, having heard all this before, but he had to admit that the weather forecasting on Denali was a crapshoot. There was a huge element of luck involved in summiting, and our luck was off to a shaky start. The plan was to fly to DBC that afternoon, but the flight was postponed again, until that evening, as a result of bad weather. A stray dog bit me as I was walking up the street for dinner, and then the evening flight was postponed to morning. *Is that two strikes or one?* I wondered, but the next day, we caught a flight. Flying over the national park, I looked down on incredible views of the mountains and great, ancient glaciers that form the six-hundred-mile arc of the Alaska Range.

Geologists are still trying to sort out the complex history of the magmatic, plutonic, and volcanic rocks forged in the fiery belly of our planet and then shoved up into a cold new world—forever bleak, forever frozen, and utterly forbidding—to be ice-carved and reinvented over and over again for millions of years. Denali is startling when you first see it. Wickersham Wall, Denali's north face, jabs up out of Peters Glacier and soars nearly 14,000 feet almost straight into the air. From base to summit, Denali is a mile taller than Everest. I didn't fully process that reality until I actually set eyes on it.

After we greeted the Base Camp manager who coordinated communications between climbers and air taxis, we kitted up, put on our harnesses, and began pulling our sleds up the Kahiltna Glacier. It was hard work, but I budgeted a bit of energy to tease Colby about his outfit, a one-piece climbing skin with alternating color blocks of royal blue and gold, which made him look like he was preparing for an upcoming role in a Marvel Comics film.

Twenty-four-hour daylight plays tricks on the mind. I found

myself losing track of time as the day stretched on and the wind picked up. After five and a half miles and very little elevation gain, we stopped for the night to build Camp 1. A few of Colby's employees came out of their tents to welcome him. *He must be a good boss*, I surmised, because they seemed happy to see him and were quick to lend a hand, helping us dig out a platform for our tent. After dinner and a game of "Name That Tune," we turned in for the broad daylight night, and I lay awake, feeling weirdly wired and frozen to the bone. My teammates had tucked into one tent all together, snug as bugs, and I would have preferred not to stand on ceremony, but Colby, thinking he was being gallant, put me in a separate tent by myself. We were less than 2,400 meters up, and already the extreme cold sank its teeth in.

The next day, hauling our sleds toward Kahiltna Pass, we took short breaks, stamping our feet to get the blood flow back, anxious to get moving and warm up again. We set up Camp 2 at just over 11,000 feet, five hours above Camp 1. It took a little longer to build without the help of Colby's loyal employees, and it was bloody cold. I couldn't wait to get settled so I could boil hot water for tea. Normally, climbers would only carry equipment to Camp 2 and then descend to sleep at Camp 1. I had pre-acclimatized, coming from Everest, so Colby wasn't worried about me, but by late afternoon, Troy said he had a massive headache, the first sign of mountain sickness. We cozied up, four in one tent, alternating heads and feet—forks instead of spoons—so I figured I'd be warm enough to get some decent sleep, providing no one sweated too badly in their socks.

The next morning Colby declared a rest day, so I walked along the little village of Camp 2 to stretch my legs, took photos, and then took a power nap. We set off again early the following morning, heading toward Motorcycle Hill. I hoped ascending it might get us above the clouds. I tried to keep track of time, following the shadows on the snow as the hard, bright sun moved across the sky, never setting, but never giving off a speck of warmth. I focused on the rope in front of me, maintaining the appropriate length and tension for crevasse safety, which meant slowing my pace to keep step with my teammates, who weren't as recently acclimatized as I was. We climbed up two steep sections, Motorcycle Hill and Squirrel Hill, and traversed a glacial basin on the way to Windy Corner—name self-explanatory, and it lived up to its brutal reputation.

Less than three miles, but a substantial vertical gain at 975 meters, and we arrived at Camp 3 at 14,200 feet, almost even with the summit of Mount Hunter. No time to stare at the grand scenery. We were knackered and had our camp to build, and Troy was looking worse for wear. The poor guy had been handpicked by Colby for this trip as a reward for his hard work, but our abbreviated acclimatization schedule was quite unfair to him. They were both wise enough to know without discussion that it was time for Troy to descend. Plenty of other teams were headed down, so he joined one of them the following day. The three of us who remained broke down Camp 3 and walked a couple of hours to the base of the headwall, knowing 250 vertical meters was the only thing separating us from Camp 4. This day was not about distance. It was all upward mobility and awesome views. Out came my ascender and my camera. I was in my element: pure Himalayan climbing. One step, one push up with the ascender, one rest step, repeat.

At 17,200 feet, Camp 4, High Camp, was one of the most inhospitable nooks on the planet, exposed to the raw wind and raging storms, but this was the launchpad for our summit bid. When you look at it on Google Earth, you see two yardstick-straight ridges that form an arrow pointing up: "This way to the summit!" We huddled over the radio, listening to the chatter. No one had summited from High Camp for more than two weeks. There were reports of serious frostbite. A number of climbers had been hanging out here for weeks, some aborting their summit bids because they'd been grounded too long, others anxiously awaiting any sign of a break in the weather, all comparing notes.

Colby studied the sky and said, "I don't trust the weather reports. It's a lot of crap. I'd rather talk to people and get a feel for what the conditions are like."

"What does it feel like now?" I asked.

"Rest day."

"Day" is a relative term when the sun never sets. The "rest" was actually a few hours, so I made the best of it. I stashed my boots, pulled off my socks, and stuffed them in the bottom of my sleeping bag.

"Whoa, whoa," Colby said. "What are you doing there?"

"Trying to dry my socks."

"No, no, no. Observe." He showed me his mountaineering party trick, laying one sock over each shoulder between clothing layers. You can even sleep with them that way. They do, in fact, dry fast, and I was grateful for that as I layered on clothes for the summit bid.

"Anchor . . . clear . . . anchor . . . clear . . ."

The call took on a familiar rhythm as the weather cleared and we traversed a broad snow slope called the Autobahn (irreverently named for the speed at which a German climber once fell down it) and angled left to the saddle at Denali Pass, and then it was up, up, up to Pig Hill. (I don't even want to know what that's about.)

I summited Denali by the West Buttress route, 20,310 feet, at 7:30 PM on June 19, 2012, one month to the day after summiting Everest.

Standing on the summit ridge, I had an airplane-window view with azure skies above and tumbled clouds below. A ragged atoll of mountaintops cut through the cloudscape. Every once in a while, the wind was enough to sweep a clear view of the copper-colored boulders and black ice cliffs in the distance, but then the clouds would fill it in, a dense layer between our bluebird day and the socked-in fog we could look forward to on our way down. After summit photos, drinks, and snacks, we began our descent, and this time I was in the lead, delighted to be setting the pace as we went down, down, down.

Passing through High Camp, I finally met up with Johannes, who was over the moon when I handed him the contraband Fanta. I gave Daniel a high five, and he rewarded me with a bowl of soup. We didn't linger long. Our goal was to get all the way back down. We'd started the summit bid at 11 AM, and we got back to the original Base Camp about five in the morning, which was 9 AM in Boston, so I felt fine about calling Jonathan to tell him I was safely back at sea level.

"Bloody hell," he said, surprised to hear from me so soon. "Seven days to summit Denali."

"It was unbelievably good luck. If I'd come two weeks earlier, I'd have been parked there, freezing my ass off, waiting for this weather window."

"Your spreadsheet predicted three weeks." He couldn't resist doing the math.

"No refunds for shorter time," I said. "I'll call you when we get back."

After an ice bivvy for a couple of hours at DBC, we hopped on a flight back to Talkeetna, and I was returned to the land of technology. There in my inbox was a message saying that an opening had come up on Daniel's Elbrus expedition with IMG in July. When I called Jonathan to tell him about this development, he was quiet for a moment and then said, "Your luck seems to be improving."

I didn't disagree, but I believe luck has a lot to do with who you are when things don't go your way. It's dangerous in business to confuse luck with chance, especially if your business is climbing mountains. Chance is whatever weather blows in, everything you can't control. Luck is what you create from it, marshaling all the skill you've acquired and all the resources you've squirreled away, not knowing how they would come in handy. It starts with a winning mind-set. You ask, *Will I like it?* instead of *Can I do it?* Voicing it that way sets the stage for success. Unafraid, you take calculated risks by pivoting, stepping up to the plate. Failure is just a data point. You take that first step, and one step is behind you. So what are you waiting for?

14

Close only counts in horseshoes and hand grenades.
—FRANK ROBINSON, MAJOR LEAGUE BASEBALL PLAYER, *TIME*, JULY 1973

I popped home long enough to do laundry, repack, and celebrate the Fourth of July before I left for Russia. Having my gingerbread man summit suit cleaned was becoming a pleasant ritual. I loved getting it back all fresh and fluffy, but it was beginning to show signs of wear, proof that I was becoming a seasoned climber.

Quick Elbrus wiki: dormant volcano located in the Greater Caucasus range near Stavropol Krai, Russia. It has twin summits; the west is higher, elevation 5,642 meters, the fifth-highest of the Seven Summits and the tallest mountain in Europe, which is a surprise, considering the Alps, which are so very—well, *alpine*. No disrespect to formidable Elbrus. She's earned her rank. But poor Mont Blanc! The indignity.

According to Greek mythology, Zeus had the Titan Prometheus chained to a rock somewhere in the Greater Caucasus as punishment for stealing fire. Every day an eagle came to eat Prometheus's liver, which grew back every night. Extrapolate what you will, but I imagine this might have something to do with the dour outlook of the great Russian novels: hulking in the background of all those stories is Elbrus.

This wasn't my first time in Russia. I'd been to Saint Petersburg on business years before, and while there, I'd taken in all the main landmarks, museums, shops, restaurants, and hotels a person could stomach. Now I didn't want to spend my limited time riding around on a tour bus tchotchke shopping, so I joined the expedition the night before the team departed for Mineralnye Vody (Min-Vody for short), a small town close to the border of Georgia. Two Russian guides, Igor Tsaruk and Nadia, were providing Daniel with local support, and Igor had arranged a nice barrel hut on Elbrus, which was important. There are no tents on Elbrus. Ingenious shelters have been created using repurposed tanker and diesel barrels, which are sturdy but not very spacious—just enough room for bunks, a small kitchen, and hooks for hanging gear. Any inside connection to a less crowded barrel hut with a less crowded toilet is a major plus.

Driving to Terskol, we passed through checkpoints manned by the Federal Security Service of the Russian Federation (FSB), which succeeded the KGB and handles all of Russia's internal affairs. Young men carrying AK-47s stopped us as we neared the border of Georgia, and we waited, quietly avoiding eye contact, until higher-ranking officials came to clear our passports. A member of our expedition took a picture of the men in uniform, and almost instantly, other uniformed men swooped in to examine the camera and delete the photo. One teammate was held up because he was a chemical engineer. According to rumor, we were near the training camps for Chechen rebels, so there was zero latitude for climbers suspected of a "secondary agenda."

Our hotel in Terskol was a stolid holdover from Soviet times with a *banya* (dodgy steam room) on the main floor, complete with *venik* massages. As leisure activities go, one would imagine that lying naked on a wooden table while two shirtless Russian men whack your back with oak leaves would appeal only to a rather special group of enthusiasts, but apparently there is a market for it. The dining hall served heavy meat and potatoes. There was no Wi-Fi, but the rooms were clean and utterly silent except for the wind that whistled through the wooden shutters. By day, we acclimatized, hiking the winding roads deep in rural Russia, wandering hills and visiting observatories, climbing rocks and cramponing on the ice. In the evenings, we returned to the hotel to drink vodka and watch the Tour de France. We spent one day at Mount Cheget Ski Resort, which regrettably shares the name of the Russian "football" or nuclear briefcase. Fun fact.

To begin our climb on Elbrus, a cable car took us high enough to glimpse the Baksan Valley and the sawtooth peaks of the Caucasus Mountains, and at the end of the line, we hopped on board a single chair lift that looked more like an amusement park ride. Daniel had enlisted about a dozen climbers, so we stood in line and positioned ourselves one by one on the platform as the single chairs came around. I waited, watched, and strategized, and when my turn came, I stepped onto the platform and turned my back to the approaching chair. When I felt it smack the back of my legs, I leaned back and let my feet rise, sliding my bum into the seat. Igor yelled, "Catch!" and threw my backpack.

"Got it!"

I sailed off, slinging up into the sky. No locks or safety belts, of course. That sort of thing is for silly Americans, not serious climbers, don't you know. Every time another chair came around the wheelhouse, a shiver went up the wire and jerked the chairs suspended high above the snow. At the top of the lift, it's jump off and step aside in two seconds flat if you want to keep your head attached to your shoulders. If a climber lost his nerve, he had to ride around the whole circuit again.

We put on crampons and passed the site of the old Pruitt hut built by scientists during the golden era of Soviet mountaineering, occupied by Germans during WWII, and burned to the ground in 1998 by someone who apparently didn't know how to use the cookstove. Or a fire extinguisher. You still hear stories of climbers leaping from the third-floor windows into the snowdrifts below. The site reportedly became famous in 1993 when *Outside Magazine* referred to it as 'the worst outhouse in the world.'

Igor had arranged a private hut farther up the mountain. It was small, simple, and perfect for our needs. We slept two to a bunk bed and ate at a picnic table in the little kitchen. There was just enough space for each climber to hang their gear at the edge of their bed between acclimatization hikes. The snow was too deep for crampons to work effectively. Snowshoes would have been excellent, but we didn't have any of those. So we left our crampons behind on these hikes, but on the slippery uphill, I felt unsteady without them. On summit day I would wear crampons, I decided.

On summit day, we hiked to the Pastukhova Rocks at 4,663 meters and began our summit bid from there. It was a long, cold day, twelve hours up and down, and Daniel scolded me for "insulting the guide" by cruising past him in my crampons, but I kept my own pace, which is what I prefer to do when the steepness increases. As we approached the true west summit, the wind pelted us with loose gravel and stinging snow. It was the windiest ascent I'd ever experienced and still is to this day. We had to link arms and fight our way forward together.

I summited Mt. Elbrus by the Baksan Valley route, 18,510 feet, at 10:50 AM on July 15, 2012.

It was an effort posing to snap summit photos at the knobby rock marker, and in every shot, my face is scoured as red as a Bing cherry. We weren't even tempted to hang around. The descent is usually a breeze for me, but this time I was at a disadvantage. Almost everyone else on the team had experienced downhill skiing, and this is a whole year before I would glissade down Mont Blanc, so I intended to use a black plastic bag as a sled of sorts, which was a disaster. I was last to arrive back at the barrel hut, but it was my third summit in three months.

I emailed Jonathan: "Three down, four to go, and Killy done."

Pippa and her boys always followed my progress with smiley-face stickers on a big map, so I emailed her as well.

"Congratulations," she shot back. "You've earned a spa week."

"A lovely thought. But sadly, no. All funding must go to climbing. I'll be lucky to go home and get a foot massage in Chinatown."

In Moscow, our team threw a birthday party for Daniel at the Hard Rock Cafe. It involved lots and lots of vodka. As we were leaving, Daniel said, "If you're interested, the company has just released Vinson Massif dates."

"I'm interested," I said.

Meanwhile, Austin, my Everest climbing mate, was nudging me to set dates for Aconcagua and Kosciuszko. The outlier was Carstensz Pyramid, which required serious rock climbing skills; I had sort of compartmentalized the little detail that I didn't know much about pure rock climbing. Flying home from Russia, I thought about my spin class teacher, an appallingly cheerful woman who used to badger us on as we pedaled faster to the beat of the music.

"Run! Faster! Run toward something you really want!" Then she'd switch tactics, eyeing those she didn't believe were pedaling fast enough. "Okay, ready? Now run away from something you're afraid of, quick!"

I can't speak for other climbers, be they optimists or pessimists, but I know which one made me run faster.

15

There is no foreign land; it is the traveler only that is foreign.
—ROBERT LOUIS STEVENSON, *THE SILVERADO SQUATTERS*

It was a high-diving horse trick, but I managed to get all my mountains on the docket: Carstensz Pyramid in Indonesia and Mount Kosciuszko in Australia in September and October, because they're close together. Vinson Massif in December, because that was the best time for Antarctica. Aconcagua in Argentina in January, because that's what worked for Daniel. You've got to allow for a certain amount of serendipity, but most of my decisions were based on budget, weather trends, and training.

My Everest buddies pointed me to a company called Adventure Indonesia and a guy named Farrell helped me put together a no-frills, "get in, go for it, and get out" expedition.

"It's that or the whole three-week shebang with another expedition in October," I told Jonathan, and he weighed in for the fast and furious negotiation, as I figured he would. Ruth, my Mount Rainier climbing mate, decided to join, and Farrell introduced me to Andrea Cardona, another experienced climber.

"Andrea's on a tight schedule," he said, "but she needs Carstensz Pyramid to complete the Explorers Grand Slam—the Seven Summits plus North and South Poles."

I already knew what was involved in the Explorers Grand Slam, but this is probably the moment the idea started germinating in the back of my own mind, like the white milkweed feather that settles and begins to quietly change the landscape without anyone noticing. For now, I was focused on finding a fourth climber for Carstensz. I pitched the idea to Kurt Wedberg, who'd saved my toes on Lobuche and joined us on Everest.

"C'mon. It'll be fun!" (My usual opening line.) "You're Mr. West Coast Rock Climber. It would be worth your while to check out Carstensz and see about adding it to the list of mountains you guide, plus it'll give you your seventh summit on the Messner list.

"Besides," I added, "I'd be grateful for your expertise and having a manly man with three women traveling through Papua, New Guinea, wouldn't be such a bad thing."

Kurt came on board, and while I herded cats to bring everyone's schedule into alignment, I worked my body, mixing and matching endurance days with Pilates. Vinson Massif would require brute strength for sled-pulling, and Carstensz Pyramid would require serious rock climbing practice. My alpine mountaineering skills were solid, but rock climbing was different. I didn't know what I didn't know. Finding the right answer is always easier than finding the right question. To find the right question, you have to go out on a limb and just do the damn thing.

I spent some time scrambling up and down New Hampshire's White Mountains, and of course the real thing was nothing—*nothing*—like the indoor rock climbing walls I'd practiced on. A typical newbie mistake, which I readily made, is hauling oneself up using upper-body strength. Proper rock climbing technique requires a relaxed upper torso, keeping the body light, using mostly legs for strength and stability. A seasoned rock climber relies on her legs, barely touching the rock with her fingertips. "Look, Ma! No hands!" Or so it felt, at times.

I was accustomed to climbing frozen waterfalls, suspended by two ice axes and a monopoint crampon sticking out from under my boot. I knew not to slam that ice axe in. No, you place it with purpose. Triangle the feet. Stick your butt out. Let the endorphins flow, lobster face matching your lobster claws. That was my milieu. Now I was trying to scramble up a wall clinging to cracks that were little deeper than the grout line between the tiles in a shower stall. The balance, the breathing, the patience required—pull-ups, triceps dips, drops, knee bends, overhangs, underhangs, twirls—it was like a sweaty, grappling performance of Cirque du Soleil.

I had two amazing instructors. One was Freddie Wilkinson, who was in the tent with Ueli on Lobuche, a badass northeastern climber known for his gracious nature as much as his Velcro-like ability to stick to sheer walls of rock. The ease with which he climbed made it seem not just possible but perfectly natural. Learning from him was osmosis more than observation, inspiration more than instruction.

My second instructor for rock climbing was Jay Mills, a talented Canadian with the patience of a saint. In Canmore and Banff, he pushed my limits and waited for me to figure things out. Even as the mountains were teaching me patience, I understood there was always a limit. I was on a safety harness, so if I hit that limit without falling, that was cowardice.

Years later, when I was climbing Mont Blanc, a French guide was fascinated by my unusual technique. "I do not often see people climb like this," he said. "The way you are choosing which place to put your fingers and feet so as not to go out of your way."

So there you go. What is it they say about "Frenchmen can't be wrong"?

On my way back to Boston, I felt ready for Carstensz, but I was hurting. Tendinitis throbbed in my knees and rotator cuffs, and I was facing the perplexing task of packing and repacking, debating unfamiliar items I would need for the hot Indonesian jungle. Knee-high Wellies? That was a new one for me, and not what I needed for the snow on top of Carstensz. This was going to be a challenge: layering for jungle heat, rain, swamps and mud, the summit cold, and everything in between. This turned out to be the least of our worries.

Less than two weeks before we were set to depart for Papua, Indonesia, another team attempting to summit Carstensz Pyramid was held for ransom traveling on the Illaga route. The tribe initially demanded something outrageous like several hundred thousand dollars per person, but quickly realized they weren't going to get anything approaching that and dropped the ransom to a bargain price of $5,000 per person.

"Stupid," Farrell told me later, searching for words in English. "That company don't pay well, get the right people, or negotiate correct. We'll take the Sugapa route. A day less—maybe eighty kilometers."

"Well, at least it's not five grand per climber," I wisecracked, but Jonathan wasn't amused. He reminded me that Michael Rockefeller, the son of the New York governor and future US vice president Nelson Rockefeller, disappeared in New Guinea in 1961 while looking for art to add to New York's Museum of Primitive Art, founded by his father.

"According to rumor," he said, "Rockefeller was killed and eaten by the local Asmat people."

"It's been fifty years, Spousey. I think we've all moved on."

"We'll see." He raised a skeptical eyebrow. "Don't come crying when you're baked into a soufflé."

The ill winds kept blowing. I started sneezing on the flight to Jakarta. My immunizations for Indonesia included a shot for Japanese encephalitis, and the nurse had suggested adding a flu shot.

"I know it's good for most people," I said, "but it always seems to leave me sniffling, achy, lethargic . . ."

She nodded. "Common side effects."

"So how is that better than getting the flu?"

She sold me with statistics about severity and contagion, and a compelling case for not heading into a swampy, muddy, mosquito-infested part of the world without the best defenses. Like an idiot, I ignored my gut, got the damn shot, and spent the long flight feeling pretty bad. The next flight, to Timika, was mercifully short, and in this bustling little city, a climber could stay in a lovely hotel for less than thirty bucks.

In 1623, Dutch explorer Jan Carstenszoon reported seeing ice and snow on Puncak Jaya, a 16,024-foot peak near the equator. He was soundly scorned. The equator is *hot*. Any fool knows that. Puncak Jaya was renamed Carstensz Pyramid by the Dutch in the early 1900s, an exciting time for "discovering" things cherished by locals for thousands of years. In 1962, Austrian climber Heinrich Harrer (played by Brad Pitt in the movie *Seven Years in Tibet*) was the first mountaineer to reach the summit. On a map of the Southern Hemisphere, the island of New Guinea looks a bit like a kangaroo hopping over Australia. Carstensz is the highest point in the Sudirman Range in the vicinity of the kangaroo's shoulder.

Waiting for a tiny airplane to take us to Sugapa, Andrea, Ruth, and I sat in the airport manager's office, where there was a God-sent fan blowing.

"We should discuss tenting arrangements," said Andrea.

Ruth agreed. "It can be tricky."

"To be fair," I said, "we should rotate. It's impossible to know up front who's going to snore the loudest or smell the worst."

Kurt is quite a looker, so I didn't actually know if the girls were lobbying for or against sharing a tent with him. In their innocence, they did not anticipate Kurt's love of sardines or the horrifying toe-picking ritual he had to go through, caring for his previously frostbitten feet. I have to laugh when people ask me about randy climber-on-climber action in the camps. First off, I can't imagine sparing the oxygen for it. Second, it's forbidden in many areas because it would disrespect the mountain. And third, I'm sorry to say it, but I can't think of a situation in which human bodies could possibly be less attractive. You just try to keep as clean as you can and hope to ignore each other in unavoidably close quarters.

Getting off the plane in Sugapa was like stepping into another century. People in surprising states of undress rushed the plane, but when the first wave of sultry air hit me, I realized I was the one inappropriately attired in my safari pants, long wicking shirt, and red La Sportiva Trango boots. I was already sweating without moving a muscle. We walked about two miles to an empty room in an administrative building, where we would sleep on the floor before setting out in the morning. I sat on my sleeping bag, eyeing the dark corners for roaches, spiders, and centipedes, listening to the elaborate negotiations taking place outside between Farrell, our guide Joyo, and the Moni and Dani tribal leaders.

As far as I understood, both tribes worked as porters for expeditions, taking turns but never collaborating. They finally decided it would be better for business if they cooperated, but how many from each tribe would be selected? How often? What about the number of men and women, since both participated as porters? Daniel told me later that someone had threatened to kill his team in revenge if a porter died on the expedition, so these negotiations were no joke. The complex selection process took more than three hours, during which they took two breaks. There was a lot of shouting, communication breakdowns, and threats from both sides to call the whole thing off. Several of the men were naked except for penis gourds—exaggerated wooden phalluses that encased the actual item and left testicles dangling below. Note to would-be world leaders: based on my observation, the guy in charge was the one with the widest gourd, not the tallest.

As the negotiations labored on with Farrell doing his best to keep the peace, Kurt, Andrea, Ruth, and I wandered up the street to look around for a while before getting settled for the night. Everyone had a great laugh at my expense when I rigged my elaborate mosquito netting and performed my nightly spider check.

"That's fine, peasants. Have a go," I said, tucking into my sanctuary. "Enjoy your little bedfellows. You'll be all carbuncles in the morning."

We woke up to find that the Moni and Dani had resolved their issues. In an official ceremony, with both tribes looking on, a non-aligned leader called out the chosen ones from among the two tribes, and I was impressed to see that almost half the porters called were women, who stepped forward with bare feet and balanced food and gear bags on their heads and backs.

Joyo directed us to mount motorcycles that would take us to the trailhead. I bounced along, clinging to a hard leather seat on the back of a bike piloted by the Indonesian Evel Knievel. He roared up the road, lurching over mud puddles, tangled roots, and potholes, leaving the others far behind.

Go with the flow, go with the flow, I told myself. It had been a while, but I'd been on a Harley before.

It started pouring rain, so I let go of the seat and gestured to him to pull over, which he eventually did. Relieved to see the others coming up the hill, I took off my backpack and dug out my raincoat. Indo-Knievel gestured emphatically, taking hold of my jacket while I piled the rest of the stuff back in my pack. I thought he intended to hold it for me, so I turned, thinking, *Oh! What a nice fellow!* But when I looked over my shoulder, he was putting the jacket on himself.

"Oh . . . um. Okay." Not wanting to insult or embarrass him, I just let him keep it. Ruth rolled up, took full stock of the situation, and laughed her ass off. Holy hell. I'm such a sucker sometimes.

A short distance later, we stopped again. Two young men appeared out of nowhere and stepped up, blocking the road with their torches before drawing a line in the mud. No communication barrier there. *Do not pass.* I didn't feel particularly threatened—they were all of eighteen, and one of them had a daisy tucked behind his ear—but then they started arguing, gesticulating, voices rising. I stepped between them and offered two candy bars, the international language of chocolate. They accepted, and we stood there, eating our chocolate, smiling at each other, until the chief came with Joyo.

"They want money," Joyo said. "To allow passage."

"What do you mean?" I asked. "Do they own this land?"

"It's a matter of local negotiation," said Joyo. "Let's wait for the official."

We waited for a local official, the mini-ransom payment was exchanged, and that was that. We were allowed to proceed to the trailhead and start our climb on foot. We maintained a strong pace, passing small villages and remote farms, and camped for the night in huts that were almost as nice as those the villagers kept for their prized pigs. I fell into a paranoid sleep, swathed in mosquito netting, listening to the scuttle and squeak of rats in the dark. At least, I think they were rats.

The next morning, we awoke to find that the men who had not been selected to guide had followed us and were sleeping on the ground next to their wives, who had been. They trooped along behind the expedition, keeping an eye on the women—never offering a hand, of course, but lending plenty of vocal support. The men sharpened their machetes, and children dashed around, dodging between everyone's legs. Several of the small ones had thick yellow mucus running from their noses, so I stayed well away, but not for fear they'd make me sick. Quite the opposite. I knew I was carrying the virus from the flu shot and worried that I would be the one introducing them to an illness their immune systems were not conditioned to fight.

We marched through the jungle, crossing rivers and streams. Game on, Wellies. I slogged through the morning, relatively dry and leech-free. We came to a bridge, patrolled (or just trolled) by a muscled individual swinging a broad machete. After an hour of what sounded like another negotiation, I asked Joyo, "What's the holdup?"

"He wants employment on our expedition in order for us to use his bridge," said Joyo.

"There's nothing we can do," said Panuta, our other guide. "All the jobs are taken."

"Nonsense." I did not get my MBA to get stuck in a Billy Goats Gruff fairy tale. This was a no-brainer. I shrugged off my backpack and dropped it on the ground in front of them. "There. I've just created a private contractor position. I need someone to carry my backpack. How much will it cost?"

My fellow climbers thought this was genius, but the guide bristled.

"Madam. The Moni and Dani will not allow him to join us, as he was not part of the original negotiations."

"Fair enough," I mumbled, withered by the look he gave me as I resituated my pack. "So much for social engineering. Let's pay the man and move on."

Once the troll was paid another mini-ransom for our bridge passage, we continued up the road. I was mortified to have acted like such a brash Westerner, throwing down the pack, ignoring the whole penis-gourd protocol and making an ass of myself. How would they manage the existing labor contracts if they let anyone with a machete barge in and change the rules whenever they wanted? Then again, that's what was happening now. Somehow this cycle had to be broken if tourism was to survive.

With the fatigue of the late afternoon came a creeping realization that the road had become a path through a forest, and soon the forest became a dense jungle, choked with undergrowth, raucous with the noise of birds and bugs. The temperature and humidity were over 100 degrees and 100 percent. We were so hot and filthy, the rain should have been a pleasure, but I assure you, it was not. The muddy ruts became streaming gullies and wide patches of grainy quicksand. Twisted roots rose up from the mud, enough to trip us at first, but eventually enough to make us step up and jump over, landing in the viscous ooze. There was no way to know if you were stepping into a six-inch puddle or a thigh-deep rut, water and mud up and into the Wellies. I fell into camp that night and barely remember eating dinner.

Day three, the thick jungle canopy protected us somewhat from the rain as we slogged through the slippery mud puddles. I tried to land a giant step over a log and heard the crotch of my rain pants give way with a cartoonish *rrrrrriiiiiiip*. What could I do but carry on, mooning the people behind me? I was carrying a GoPro, but I had to delete a lot of lush green footage that was nothing but me cursing and yelling profanities at whoever was listening. Scrambling up and over a fallen tree trunk, I yanked my boot out of the mud with such force that—*fwock!*—I smacked my forehead against an overhanging tree trunk with a dull, wet thud. I stumbled to my knees, stars reeling in front of my eyes.

"Oh my God!" Ruth and Andrea came running.

"Shit. Who put that tree there?" I tried to play it off, laughing at first, then fighting tears of pain and embarrassment.

"Vanessa, are you okay?" My teammates peeled me off the ground and picked bits of embedded bark from my forehead.

"I'm fine. I'm good."

I was not good. Every part of my body felt shocked and soggy and hurting. My pants were ripped, my clothes were full of mud, and my feet were wrinkled and soaked. I took some aspirin and continued on, but my foul mood and body aches had blossomed into a prize migraine. Twilight fell, and the mosquitoes came out in force, but we sprayed ourselves with DEET and trudged on by the light of our headlamps. Every once in a while, someone in the lead would call back, "Tree!" or "Rock!" and we'd focus our lamps upward in the mist to avoid hitting our heads. When we stopped for the night, Joyo nudged my elbow and said, "Less jungle tomorrow. More rocks."

"Hooray."

That might be the only time I've ever welcomed rocks.

Supper was delicious. I will say that. We had the most flavorful meat and rice. Otherwise the whole day was pretty grim. We hung up our wet clothes and tried to dry our waterlogged feet, lined up like mushrooms on a log. The next day, we crossed our first big river, walking a mossy log like a balance beam over roiling Class IV whitewater rapids. Andrea went first, a surefooted pro. I went next, taking my time, praying and breathing. *Step. Add weight. Steady.* Ruth followed me, but Kurt took one look at the churning water and shook his head. His feet were frostbitten, his pack was overweight, and he didn't trust that slimy green log. He got down on his bum and shimmied all the way across, pants be damned.

We made camp in the dark, soaked to the bone, reeking of DEET, but we woke up the next morning to see that we were above the tree line. We traversed wide-open fields and felt the humidity drop. Finally, we caught a glimpse of the object of our desire, Carstensz Pyramid, off in the distance, a great limestone saw blade shrouded by fog that billowed up from the jungle. The mountain cuts into the sky with such force, you can almost hear echoes of its creation, a massive collision of the Australian and Pacific Plates. Rocky steps popped up on the trail, and we scrambled over them, hanging on to the rocks as our boots collected mud and morning dew.

Another full day of this, and we arrived at Base Camp, just over 4,000 meters, next to an aquamarine lake at the foot of Carstensz Pyramid. We could see the Grasberg mine, the largest gold mine and second-largest copper mine in the world. It was a huge source of income for Indonesia, so it was politically important. Although helicopters used to fly people to Base Camp over the mines, this was not allowed after early climbers allegedly took photos of what appeared to be a strip mining operation. In 2012, as I understood it, mine owners rarely granted anyone permission to pass by, overhead or on foot. There was a story about a guide who entered the mine zone and ended up spending two weeks locked in a shipping container. Hence the five-day journey through the jungle instead of a two-day trek through the mine.

That night, after another amazing dinner (roasted pig with sweet potatoes this time), we gathered for a gear check. We'd used no climbing gear so far. Now, out came the harnesses, ascenders, rappel devices, and carabiners for the task ahead. I reminded everyone to wear gloves. The temperature had dropped to 40 degrees. Anticipating difficult rock climbing, we talked through the route, and Kurt went over how to execute a Tyrolean traverse, when two or three pieces of rope are suspended for a half mile or so between two rocks, allowing one to clip onto the rope and dangle—face to the sky, great void at your back—as you pull yourself arm over arm to the other side.

We were up at 2AM for our summit bid. The cold felt clean and sharp, high above the stifling heat of the jungle. I never thought I'd say it, but I was thrilled at the thought of seeing snow. The climb got real almost immediately.

"Trust your feet," said Joyo. "Keep moving upward."

I flung myself forward and grabbed hold, heart racing, and pulled myself up the slope. The rock was almost vertical, and my hands were getting sweaty. Or maybe the rock was wet with mist. Condensation made narrow ledges glassy and slick, but I was wearing my three-season Trangos. So far, so good. Most steps and arm grips were generous, and the cool, misty environment was strangely calming. I couldn't overthink or plan ahead. The mountain offered me only one opportunity at a time, so I took each one as it came and moved on with gratitude. Dawn rose with an eerie silver horror-flick fog, but I was focused on the black rock in front of me, focused on where I placed my feet, focused on keeping my upper body loose and light.

The top of Carstensz Pyramid is a tricky SOB; you're up there on that narrow blade, but to get to the actual summit, you have to traverse a series of jagged fangs that appear to be connected. When you get right up to it, however, there are gaps between the teeth.

When Joyo jumped over and landed on the tip of a rock shaped like a needle, I thought, *Oh, hell no! There is no way I can jump on that shark's tooth.* It wasn't going to happen for me. I would fall short or overshoot.

You got this, Vanessa.

I summoned my inner Stretch Armstrong and extended myself across far enough to grasp Joyo's hand. Using his knee as an extension of the rock, I was able to make it. On to the Tyrolean traverse, which wasn't as bad as I anticipated. I clipped in and worked the ropes, hand over fist. The rope sagged in an elongated U, so gravity helped push me to the middle, but I had to work harder to pull myself uphill on the receiving end. I confused the choreography a little and reached my destination the wrong way round, so I had to turn to climb up. Soon enough there was another gap-toothed grin I was too short to jump over. I don't remember how I made it happen, but I'm certain it wasn't pretty.

I summited Carstensz Pyramid, Sugapa route, at 16,023 feet, at 8:30 AM on September 23, 2012.

Standing in the silence of the hard-earned summit, I looked down on the Grasberg mine, a gaping wound where a rare equatorial glacier used to be. I don't recall what I was thinking at the time, but when I revisit the moment in my mind, I feel a sisterhood with this mountain, Puncak Jaya, her strength and her scars. I do remember how good it felt when the snow began falling. I turned my face up and stuck out my tongue to catch a few airy flakes, almost able to forget the heat and humidity below. With gravity on our side, we rappelled like freewheeling dragonflies, down from the cold fog to the cool boulders to the warm timberline and back into that impenetrable blanket of moist jungle heat.

The bridge had washed out, so on our way back to Sugapa, we didn't see hide nor hair of the troll with his machete, nor did we encounter the young man with the daisy behind his ear. Not quite out of the woods, so to speak, we dodged a confrontation with some axe-wielding locals and negotiated for souvenir penis gourds and ornate bows and arrows on our way to the airport.

Inches from a clean getaway, we thought, but our plane didn't come. Later that afternoon, a Kiwi cargo flight came in, and the pilot explained that the guys with the axes had radioed him to say if he landed for us, they'd mess him up. Industrious souls, the axe-handlers. They weren't just trying to shake us down for cash, they were trying to force the guiding company to give them jobs on the next expedition.

Eventually, an agreement was reached, which means a transfer of money, of course, and we were able to leave the next day. We'd missed our connecting flights to Jakarta, so we found a hotel in Timika, where the cockroaches were as big as cocker spaniels. Sometimes tents offer the safer, cleaner space.

On to Australia. Trying to be cagey, batting my eyelashes like mad, I passed through customs with my giant bow and arrows wrapped tightly in newspaper and covered in duct tape.

"What's this?" the customs officer asked.

"A souvenir."

"What's it made of?"

"Wood."

Wrong answer. He pointed to a quarantine area. The customs officer wanted details. It didn't really help that the arrows were as long as spears and smelled like a pig hut.

"Wood, eh? Is this a weapon of some sort?"

"*Not in the first world*," I said, under my breath.

"Let's open 'er up and have a look," he said.

"Do we have to? This is a gift, elaborately wrapped."

"Come again?"

"Look," I said, "I'm only here for three days to climb your tallest mountain. What if I leave the package with you and pick it up on the way out?"

"What?"

"I know, I know. It flies in the face of common sense and breaches a hundred customs rules. But I trust you with this antique. You can scan it, no problem. I'm asking you to trust me."

Five minutes later, I was in a taxi with my climbing kit and my unopened bow-and-arrow package, bound for a posh hotel where Austin had negotiated a good rate. I could rest for a day or two before we left for Kozzie. Austin had come all the way to Oz to climb with me, moving mountains, as it were, with the dual purpose of visiting his two dads. There was snow on Kosciuszko, so we arranged to rent snowshoes from K7 Adventures, and threading the needle, gave ourselves only a few hours to accomplish this climb, rain or shine, snow or sleet, bluebird sky or whiteout blizzard.

Double sixes. We got the bluebird day.

I summited Mount Kosciuszko, via Thredbo, at 7,310 feet, at 11:30 AM on October 3, 2012.

Flying home, I thought about a Hong Kong fortune-teller I'd visited, purely on a lark, before I went to Everest. He said, "2012 is the year of the black water dragon. As a wood dragon in the year of a water dragon, you will reach new heights, your character strengthened. Could be a lot of ups and downs."

He looked at me, perplexed, while I laughed, and later, Pippa came up with dragon decals for the North Face duffel bags I took with me to Everest.

"We do not believe one necessarily has a good year when it is 'your year,'" the fortune-teller said. "Rather, it is your year to be tested."

I am certain this is true.

16

Hold on to your knickers. It was actually Jonathan who said, "How can you go all the way to Antarctica and not complete the South Pole?"

"Trick question," I said. We both knew I'd been thinking about it, so no use pretending.

"Extremely remote," he said. "Wicked expensive. You wouldn't want to go there twice."

"Not on purpose."

"Maximizing a single trip seems prudent."

Mountain math. He was catching on to the trickle-down economics of exploration: it's actually imprudent to do the highest peak on Antarctica without doing the South Pole, and if you do the South Pole, you're just one pole away from the Explorers Grand Slam.

"Is it possible to piggyback a South Pole trip?" I asked Daniel.

"So it's not just the Seven Summits," he said. "You're going for the Explorers Grand Slam."

"I'm not going for it. I'm doing it."

There was no lightning bolt moment of decision this time. I'd come to understand that such decisions are not made in a vacuum.

Every climber with whom I'd shared a meal, a tent, or a rarefied summit moment had a story to tell about the people who cared if they came home alive, the people whose lives were impacted by their decision to climb and climb again: the trickle-down economics of love.

When I first met Jonathan in London, I was on a mission from the corporate mother ship to sell the business, shut his office down, and put him out of work. He wasn't supposed to know this, of course, but he's smarter than the average Joe and picked up the scent almost immediately. In the film version, we will now cut to a romantic ballad montage of J and V, played by Ralph Fiennes and Charlize Theron, ogling each other over a succession of hedonistic "working dinners" paid for with his doomed expense account. That dear little AmEx card had been given a terminal diagnosis, and we were determined to fill its last days with bliss.

This was an apt beginning for our long partnership: a happy amalgam of making do and stepping out. Neither of us came from a cuddly childhood. We both had everything a child needs, with the pesky exception of that one thing a child needs most. In those early days, we learned to seek pleasure in pleasurable things, not as a substitute for love, but as a flawed world's best effort at reparations. You can't always get what you want, as the song says, but what you need—well, that's why God created AmEx.

For all the time we spent on separate continents, Jonathan and I were never far apart in any other respect, but my first three years climbing tested all that. We were forced to redefine what we were to each other, what was truly at stake in our relationship. I make light of the naughty-chair discussions, because I don't want it to sound like we were fighting all the time. I make light of the moment he suggested the South Pole, because I'm not comfortable gushing about him.

So. On with it. I'd already booked Vinson Massif with Daniel and IMG in early December and managed to connect with Antarctic Logistics & Expeditions (ALE) for their December South Pole Last Degree expedition. ALE would fly us to a drop-off location at 89 degrees latitude, and we would cross-country ski sixty-nine miles to the South Pole at 90 degrees. With favorable weather, we might make it in seven days, so it was prudent to prepare for ten.

Less than four weeks after I returned from Carstensz Pyramid and Kosciuszko, I was back in the gym every day. Training for the poles, I had to tip my world sideways, thinking latitude instead of altitude. For three years, training had been all about the blood oxygen budget, all about cardio, but pulling the sled on Denali, I learned that this expedition was going to be about endurance. I needed a solid core, kangaroo-caliber legs, and a cast-iron back, chest, and shoulder muscles. I kept up my usual runs around the Charles River, because breathing was key to everything I would be undertaking. To supplement my polar training, my research advised rigging a tire and dragging it around.

"It's really easy," said everyone.

Everyone has no clue. Dragging a tire is about as easy as *dragging a fucking tire*. First off, one must acquire, transport, and store a tire suitable for dragging. Cruising a junkyard on the outskirts of Boston, I told the attendant, "I'm looking for your worst tire. The cheapest tire."

"What size?"

Ah. Devil in the details. I had no idea. He escorted me to a pile of nineteen-inch car tires, which looked about right, and nineteen-inch truck tires, which were heavier.

"How much?" I asked.

"On the house."

Free is a climber's favorite price. I took one of each. He helped me load them into the back of my car. Next stop, my local hardware store to get holes drilled for the rope. It's not easy to play the damsel in distress card in the context of "I need help rigging this tire so I can pull it across a parking lot," but a helpful soul at the hardware store came out in the middle of Charles Street to drill the holes, which is tricky because there's a bit of metal in there, you know. At home, my neighbor stepped up to help me jam the rope through the holes, which is even trickier, because the rubber creates a suction effect. We tackled the truck tire first, an all-afternoon process that involved hammers, screwdrivers, and more drilling.

Finally—*yippee!*—we pulled the rope through. One down, one to go. But when we leaned forward to lift the tire—*wham!* Epic headbutt.

It happened so fast and hit so hard, we both rocked back, stunned, stars circling. Tears rushed to my eyes. We were both embarrassed, but he'd caught it at a bit of an angle while I took a straight-on shot to the cranium. A massive, all-encompassing migraine came over me in one nauseating wave. We mumbled apologies and pushed the rope into the car tire. I thanked him and stumbled into the house. (Sidebar: I didn't see him again for six months. I suspect he was avoiding me.)

No training that day. Or the next. I couldn't manage anything more strenuous than Googling: *Concussion symptoms. Concussion complications. Can this concussion kill me?* As any rugby player will tell you, a headbutt can be a serious thing, and making matters worse, though I didn't know it at the time, my sinuses had already begun to backfill like a retention pond. I was intent on training, though, so as soon as the headache subsided to a level I could endure, I went to town with the tires.

"You can train anywhere," said Doug Stoup, founder of Ice Axe

Expeditions and my future North Pole guide. This may be true for him; he lives in the middle of nowhere. The City of Boston, however, doesn't take kindly to black skid marks on public sidewalks.

A friend suggested Revere Beach, five miles away. In winter, with everything closed for the season, people still came to walk their dogs. Couples strolled hand in hand. Teenagers flirted and shoved. It was a popular spot for newly arrived immigrants to enjoy a beautiful view of their new city. Occasionally a homeless person appeared from under a blanket and wished me luck, or an early-morning drunk slurred something encouraging. Children came running up to me for a free tire ride across the sand, and it always seemed like the biggest kids jumped on board just when I was on my last legs. Dogs barked at me. Seagulls gave me the eye. The *Boston Globe* sent a videographer to chronicle my Explorers Grand Slam attempt, and she followed me around the beach, shooting a lot of unflattering footage of me sweating, swearing, and babbling off-the-cuff minutiae about what I was doing and why I was training like this. Soon enough, an odd tire or two were spotted on the beach. Seemed like a training trend was getting started, but I had no time to pay attention to what anyone else was doing. I just kept dragging that tire back and forth, day after day, channeling my inner General Patton: *You do not quit when you're tired. You quit when you're done!*

Three miles up the beach.

Three miles down the beach.

Repeat.

Antarctica is the coldest, windiest, driest continent on the planet. It's about the size of the United States and Mexico combined, twice the area of Australia, with an ice sheet around 16,000 feet thick at its maximum, covering most of the continent. Antarctica contains about 68 percent of the world's fresh water and

90 percent of the world's ice. If that ice sheet melts, it could raise Earth's oceans by 180 feet.

The travel paperwork was a jigsaw puzzle. Antarctica has no central government, no indigenous population, not even a brave invader willing to step up and take charge. The Antarctic Treaty signed by twelve countries in 1959 cobbled together an agreement for the purpose of research and exploration. No commercial flights go there, but a few established providers like ALE can charter a flight from Union Glacier, a remote camp in the southern Ellsworth Mountains. Nothing is cheap in Antarctica because everything is imported, and the fuel cost is prohibitive, so once you get there, you pack your sled, and start hauling.

As word of my Explorers Grand Slam attempt spread on the climbing grapevine, I heard plenty of horror stories about both poles, but most people were psyched for me, and that sort of networking always breeds sparks of information and assistance. Doug recommended a certain brand of boots and sent a wolverine-fur-trimmed hooded jacket for warmth and to shed accumulated frost.

Vinson Massif is known to be cold, though it's only 16,050 feet high. It can be a short trip if you're lucky, or you might get stuck for three weeks at or below the summit due to high winds. The South Pole might be doable in one week, or you could be struggling through the snow for ten days. These variables make packing an unwinnable game of roulette. Either you end up dragging the weight of extra supplies or you run out of essentials in the middle of frozen nowhere.

Thanksgiving weekend, I met my Vinson Massif team in Punta Arenas, Chile, the farthest south you can fly in the Americas, north of the Strait of Magellan, a gateway to Patagonia. At the airport, Daniel introduced me to Tim, a fellow Bostonian, and Deacon from California. I'd met Deacon earlier that year when he was on Denali with Johannes (the orange Fanta moment), and we'd all climbed with Daniel before, so our dinner conversation was comfortably lively. No turkey, because Thanksgiving Day in Chile is just another Thursday, but ever the Martha Stewart of climbing, I supplied chocolate turkeys and a festive stuffed animal turkey centerpiece.

Everything would be tightly rationed, as Daniel was the chef and made the grocery list. Shopping for supplies at a nearby market, I was excited to see Zuko, my favorite orange drink mix. (It's the closest thing to the taste of fresh juice, and I can pound a liter of it in a nanosecond.) We took our supplies back to the hotel, removed all the excess packaging and wrappers, and divided the contents into meals, making sure we carried nothing but the essentials. What a different world we'd be living in if packaging were stripped down to the essentials to begin with! The authorities are dead serious about "leave no trace" in Antarctica. On Vinson Massif, you capture urine in pee bottles and bring it to urine-only dumping stations along the route. GO Anywhere toilet bags are issued for your feces, which you carry back to Union Glacier, where it's collected and flown off the continent. No shit. (Pun intended.)

We split the group gear, and then Daniel made the rounds to check everyone's kit. We weren't coming back this way between expeditions, so Daniel and I were both packed for the South Pole in addition to the mountain.

"I'm nervous about the cross-country ski piece of this," I said.

"Just keep shuffling your feet," said Daniel. "It's easy."

"Oh, like dragging a tire?"

I wasn't completely inexperienced. Jonathan and I had done a weekend in Chamonix when we were first married. The French ski instructor said I showed great promise on the bunny hill, and he was French enough to lure me onto the ski lift, knees wobbling.

Green and blue slopes ensued. I built confidence as the instructor skied backward in front of me. I figured if all went wrong, I'd fall into his arms. Not the worst fate one might meet on a mountain.

Daniel put together the Vinson Massif expedition, but ALE runs the operations on the ground in Punta Arenas for all guided trips to Antarctica for climbing companies, scientists, mountaineers, polar explorers, diplomats, and general visitors. At an ALE orientation session, we learned more about Antarctica and the many expeditions taking place. Studying the maps, I could see Vinson Massif in the Ellsworth Mountains, which are named after the American pilot to make the first Antarctic transcontinental flight. The term *massif* usually means a group of connected mountains, but for whatever reason, it gets used in a haphazard fashion for individual mountains here and there, and while you regularly hear "Everest" without the "Mount," you rarely hear people call it "Vinson" without "Massif."

December is summertime in the Southern Hemisphere, so we expected balmy averages between 0 and –30 degrees Fahrenheit with twenty-four-hour daylight. Only about 1,400 climbers have summited Vinson Massif because of costly logistics and the short weather window, but the mountain itself is a pretty straightforward slog up a relatively stable glacier—sort of Denali Lite. There have been many incidents of hellacious frostbite but no deaths on Vinson Massif, which is remarkable.

We flew in a Russian Ilyushin Il-76 cargo plane to Antarctica, a lucky break; teams sometimes spend weeks waiting for a lift. The flight crew never sat down, even for takeoff and landing. They stood around in big furry Dr. Zhivago hats, drinking vodka and cracking each other up in Russian until we landed on the blue ice runway at Union Glacier, a proper tent city. I stepped out onto the White Continent, an otherworldly landscape of snow and sparse tentlike buildings, one of which housed a great library full of old photos of the original explorers, Amundsen and Scott. We boarded Twin Otters equipped with skis for the forty-five-minute flight to Vinson Base Camp (VBC), sitting on jump seats, ears stuffed with cotton to buffer the scream of the engines. VBC consisted of one little covered shelter for the operations director who assisted climbers with weather reports and rescue, as needed. There was no wind, but as we set up tents for the night, I could feel the cold deep in my nose every time I inhaled.

The next morning, I left my South Pole kit at VBC, stashing my South Pole boots and wearing my La Sportiva Olympus Mons. I ended up taking more kit than I should have—basically an extra week's worth of food, clothing, and toiletries—a mistake I would bitterly regret once I started pulling my sled. Daniel was in a bad mood and tried to pile on additional group gear when he saw that I was overloaded.

"You need to shift more weight to your backpack and take it out of the sled," he scolded.

"I'm much stronger with my legs and core than upper body."

"Yeah, tell me that eleven hours from now."

Good times. Awesome. This was going to be a nightmare.

My backpack weighed eighty pounds, and the sled weighed one hundred, which isn't that much, but the whole shebang just sucked. My battery-operated Smith goggles were designed to relieve condensation and had worked beautifully on every mountain so far, but now they kept steaming up. I mule-stomped along, overheating, stopping to peel off layers, and because we were roped together, everyone had to stop every time I adjusted. How could this be so much harder than the tire? How could I feel so out of shape at this nothing altitude? I plugged in the music that usually spurs me on and tried to Patton-talk myself, but it was no use. Five miles on, we stopped to hydrate, and as I chugged my Zuko, Tim cocked his chin toward my sled and said, "Vanessa, is your brake on?"

"What? No, it's—oh, *for fuck's sake!*"

Moral of the story: You know how strong you are. If something seems harder than it should be, instead of blaming yourself, try checking the bloody brakes.

The remaining six miles were a breeze, but the damage was done. I pulled off my boots in my tent at Camp 1 and found a blister the size of a quarter on the back of each heel. This worried me for the South Pole more than for Vinson. With back-to-back trips, I'd have to take great care.

The climb to Camp 2 was too steep for the sleds, so we stuffed our packs as tight as we could, stashed the goods at Camp 2, and came back to Camp 1 for the night. My back was in spasms, and my feet were a complete mess. The blisters yawned open, two raw red holes. I aired them out, gingerly dabbed them with triple antibiotic cream, wrapped my feet and ankles with duct tape, and hobbled to the mess tent.

"Weather's moving against you," the ops director opined from VBC. "Winds at fifty miles per hour for the next forty-eight hours."

This didn't bode well for Camp 2 in the morning, but we'd made our carry. No point going up higher with that weather forecast. The teams sitting at Camp 2 were faced with the tough call: come down or try to run up during this tiny weather window. Two bold opportunists did run up to tag the summit—and hooray for them—but everyone else came down to wait out the windstorm at Camp 1. We knew what was coming, so we chopped ice blocks and built walls to shelter our tents. As other teams piled into Camp 1, igloos, arches, and other ingenious designs popped up.

Daniel had located our camp a little bit away from the other expeditions, because he liked his privacy. I do too, but it meant longer trips to the loo, and Daniel was getting on my last nerve anyway. He decided to call our mess tent the "Bob Marley Café"—and I was certain this was just to wind me up—repeating the same playlist of Buddha Bar meets electric chill-out rock/jazz/funk. Tim was playing a cover version of Kate Bush's "Running Up That Hill" but had no idea who Kate Bush is or that he was listening to a remake. (1985, dude!) I can handle Bob Marley's greatest hits or my favorite mix, Bob Marley vs. Funkstar De Luxe's "Sun Is Shining," but a little reggae goes a long way for me, and now I was trapped—on my birthday, no less—trying to read while the same fourteen songs played over and over again, powered by the longest solar battery life since the vestal virgins.

A week went by while we were grounded by storms, which gave my feet a rest, but we all started feeling cabin crazy. One day the blizzard let up a little, and a woman from another expedition offered a yoga class. Climbers of every nationality came out of their tents and did downward dogs with boots, hats, and gloves on. The southernmost yoga class on record, as far as I know.

When the wind ebbed to a stiff but passable 15 kph, we unanimously decided to give it a go. Terrible idea. Maybe we'd had too much rest. Maybe the hill was steeper than I remembered. I was afraid to set my heavy pack down, because I wasn't sure I'd have the energy to pick it up again. I felt the backs of my heels grinding to a fresh pulp. When it came time to build our tents at Camp 2, I was useless. I mumbled an apology, crawled into my tent, and tended to my ruined feet.

The next morning, we headed for the summit. My hands were so cold, I couldn't zip my jacket. Daniel lent me a hand, but then I never heard the end of it. All I could do was pray for the unforgiving wind to drown out the mosquito drone of his snarky voice.

We dropped our packs on the summit ridge and made our final ascent to the true summit. The summit pyramid is steeper and more exposed, so scrambling up those last few yards, I made a conscious effort to look away from the ground and take in the incredible view. Diamond-white snow cut the jagged granite. Billion-year-old rocks jutted into newborn blue sky. The entire continent seemed frozen in time.

I summited Vinson Massif, 16,050 feet, the highest point on Antarctica, at noon on December 5, 2012.

We paused for summit photos and headed down. The uphill had been hard on my back, but the downhill was tough on Deacon's knees, so I didn't do my usual Tigger bounce to the bottom. We stayed together at a moderate pace all the way to Camp 1, where we packed our sleds and began the long drag to VBC, powered by twenty-four-hour daylight and energy gels.

The next day, back in Union Glacier, I was exhausted but eager to repack for the South Pole and get in a little ski practice. Daniel did a final gear check and signed off: "You're ready."

"Copy that," I said. "I just hope you know how to use a compass."

17

*Polar exploration is at once the cleanest and most
isolated way of having a bad time which has been devised.*
—APSLEY CHERRY-GARRARD, *THE WORST JOURNEY IN THE WORLD*

If you think of Earth as a lollipop, the South Pole is where the stick
goes in. The altitude is subject to change but stays in the neighborhood of 9,300 feet, which was not a big deal for those of us just coming off Vinson Massif, but we certainly weren't expecting it to be a
cakewalk. Southern Hemisphere summer temperatures average between 10 to –15 degrees Fahrenheit, and ALE warned on its website
that the trip is "extremely strenuous, may include severe wind chill
and storms," and includes "hauling heavy loads for many days in a
row." The only thing they left out was "safe return doubtful."

There's slightly different kit involved when you're pulling sleds
instead of climbing. First, you need a harness that fits around your
waist and over your shoulders, eventually hooking up to two separate pulling lines with carabiners to actually pull the sled. The un-
derbelly of the skis are protected with nylon or mohair "skins" to
prevent slipping. "Pogies," which look like neoprene oven mitts,
are attached to your ski poles, and you slide your gloves into them
to protect your hands from frostbite.

The plane dropped us all off at the eighty-ninth parallel south,
about sixty-nine miles from the South Pole. Two teams of five

would be skiing the last degree, about sixty nautical miles. Team A was led by American member Scott Woolums and Team B was led by Scot member David Hamilton. When we arrived, Team B chose to set up camp first, but my team, Team A, decided to start out right away.

Dressed and ready to go, I put my headphones on low and let my legs fall into a natural rhythm—*shhhhoos, shhhhoos*—back and forth, back and forth. Rounding the math: seventy miles in seven days is ten miles per day—or more than that if we wanted to reach our goal in less than a week. That assumed no storms, that we wouldn't get lost, no one would get sick or injured, and planes would run on time. The statistical probability of everything going right is approximately zero, so clever Team A decided to put in extra miles to plan for worst-case scenarios, and with that rationale, we ended up covering about five miles that first half-day. At this rate, we'd soon be a full day ahead of Team B.

When we made camp, I shared a two-person tent with Daniel. One of the Brits and the other Americans shared the cook tent, which was larger, but had people coming and going early in the morning. Our guide, Scott, was on his own, which must have been colder, but he seemed unbothered by that. The superlight, single-walled, tunnel-shaped Hilleberg tents had very little hardware, so they were easy to set up and looked like bright red caterpillars on the stark white snow. While the others boiled water and made dinner, Daniel and I built a quasi-loo where we could all go to use our toilet bags: a round hole with steps leading down and blocks built up for privacy and shelter from the wind. I won't lie, I hated the ice outhouse. It was too fucking cold. If it was humanly possible, I always waited for Daniel to be otherwise occupied so I could use the vestibule in the tent.

There was homemade food and chocolate truffles for dinner the first day, and we made the most of it, knowing we'd be eating pack-aged rations for the rest of the trip. Once our chores were finished, Daniel and I designated our "his and hers" areas, each about the size of a beach towel, and we settled in with drinks and snacks. He'd brought me some Zuko he had left over from his last trip to Acon-cagua, and I chugged an entire liter while we listened to music, read books, and sorted our electronics. I slept like a baby, which I do on most expeditions, at altitude or not. I take melatonin, on and off expedition, so while others complain of nightmares, I'm off to sleep. I'm so physically and mentally knackered at the end of every day, there's no way I could stay awake if I wanted to.

"Eat up," Scott, our new chef, scolded us over breakfast. "You'll expend a lot of energy today."

I was about to say something funny, but the Brit leaned over and vomited all over the sleeping bag belonging to his tentmate who was out taking a wee. Daniel did a remarkable hands-in-the-air leap out of the way, somehow holding on to his breakfast bowl. It reminded me of a moment when I was out ice fishing with my dad, and he fell through the ice but managed to hold on to his beer. (Priorities, people, priorities!)

The tentmate was remarkably stoic when he came back and discovered what disaster had befallen him.

"No worries," he said as the napkins got sent around. "I have a baby at home."

The whole "eat up" thing wasn't a popular morning pep talk in the future.

We all agreed to split the stricken Brit's share of group gear. It was kind, on the face of it, but on the ulterior side, none of us wanted him to slow us down. *Eat up, indeed*, I thought. Hauling my heavy sled eight to twelve hours a day, I tried to stay focused and calm. There was nothing to see for miles but a 360-degree view of abso-fucking-lutely nothing but snow upon snow upon snow. It was like reading a book with all blank pages. It was hard to keep my bearings, searching the horizon for a little bump to fix my eyes on, following the sastrugi, long sharp grooves sculpted by wind currents cutting into the snow. Time slipped, the sun hardly dipping between high noon and another high noon. The merciless wind made my ears ring. Nothing—I repeat, nothing—was exposed. Not a single body part. Whenever we stopped to rest, we all had our forty-below jackets handy at the tops of our sleds.

At night, I lay in my sleeping bag, reading a book called *Captain Scott* by Sir Ranulph Fiennes, who laid out the agonized history of early Antarctic expeditions. Captain Robert Falcon Scott, a British Royal Navy officer and explorer, announced to the world that he was going to be the first man to reach the South Pole, but when he got there, he found a note from Norwegian explorer Roald Amundsen that basically said, "If we don't survive the return trip, please tell the Norwegian king the truth about who arrived at the South Pole first." Can you imagine what a demoralizing throat punch that must have been? I have to wonder what effect it had on their physical and mental stamina. Still, being a true gentleman, Captain Scott took the note, in case Amundsen did not make it home. (Ultimately, he did, only to disappear on another expedition over a decade later.) Scott and his men perished in a storm, exhausted and starving, just eleven miles from the closest food depot and point for rescue. Religious men, they would not take morphine to hasten their deaths, lest their souls be damned to hell. Instead, they let hypothermia do its work. I'm haunted by the story of Captain Lawrence "Titus" Oates, who left his tent on his thirty-second birthday with the final words, "I am just going outside and may be some time."

On the third day, we covered more than twelve miles, and

Daniel was navigating for much of that, so he crawled in bed and crashed to sleep that night, out soundly enough that I was able to sneak in a bivvy bath, scrubbing myself all over with Wet Ones. I like to clean my face, feet, and privates every day and hit the rest as often as opportunity presents, which is easier with a female expedition partner. I peeled off my socks and sucked in a deep, cold breath. Three toes on my right foot had taken on the clammy purple hue of a rotting plum. I squeezed them between my thumb and index finger, and they were as numb as beach pebbles.

"*Shit!* No, no, no no . . ."

I'd been so focused on my heels, I'd seen no sign of frostbite on my toes until now. A sickening slide show flashed through my head: Perry trying to rub life into his frostbitten foot on Everest. All the gruesome YouTube videos. Worst of all, my mind settled on the stump of my mother's maimed foot and the plastic prosthetic with its purple imitation flesh.

"Daniel?" I nudged him. "Daniel, wake up."

"Huh. What is it?" He rolled over, shielding his eyes from the sunlight. I pointed at my foot. He rubbed his temple and said, "Oh. Wow. When did that happen?"

"I don't know," I said. "I don't care. I just want to know what to do about it."

He was groggy and useless. I threw on clothes and went to Scott's tent. He examined the toes and said, "We'd better keep an eye on it. Take some ibuprofen. I'll ask for advice on this evening's call to Union Glacier."

"Sounds like boot bang," the Union Glacier doctor said that night.

"Boot bang?" I echoed.

"It happens with cross-country skiing," said Scott. "Repetitive banging of the foot into the boot and the boot into the ski. Especially for feet like yours, where the second toe is taller than the big toe. It creates tissue damage that mimics frostbite—that's the purple—and it can blister too. I won't lie: it's painful."

"Wonderful. More blisters. And pain."

"Are you picking up your foot or sliding it?"

"A combination, I guess."

"Okay. Let me watch you tomorrow."

After dinner and hot chocolate, we hit the sack, but at one in the morning, I jolted awake with the most incredible stabbing pain in my foot. My toes throbbed and tingled. It felt like they were being seared with a branding iron. *Fuck!* The pain came and went without warning, flashing like lightning every time I dozed off and let my foot brush against my ankle or touch the seam of my sleeping bag. Eventually, exhausted and alarmed, I dug through my med kit for some Vicodin and finally fell asleep. I was afraid of what the day would bring, but oddly, I skied all day and never felt a thing. But the next night, and every night after that, as the tissue began to thaw after hours of cold, it was like a rattlesnake sinking its fangs into my foot, yanking me from a deep sleep. I lay there trembling, trying not to groan or move, willing myself to rest, even if I couldn't sleep.

I read the last pages of my book and lay there contemplating the advice of Sir Ranulph Fiennes, an explorer himself, who opines in *Captain Scott* about the care that must be taken when reading and interpreting the expedition letters and journals of others. After a hard day, one might slag off a teammate for being less than helpful, using harsh words in a diary entry. But imagine if one or both parties were to die the next day. Someone reading that expedition journal would assume the writer hated his teammate when in fact it was just one hard day. I love that Fiennes points this out. God knows, if I'd kept a journal, anyone reading it would have gotten an earful of how what's-his-bucket was completely useless and how so-and-so walked like she had a piano tied to her ass. It would seem like I hated everything and everyone, because there's no energy for reflection or perspective at the end of a long day. In the moment, the challenges loom larger than the rewards, but in retrospect, you know the deal: Little challenge, little reward. Tremendous challenge, tremendous reward. And we're all just trying to get through it alive.

I finished reading *Captain Scott* and tore the book in half to share with the boys. In the morning, which looked no different from midnight, I gingerly pulled on my socks and boots and went back to my sled, unable to shake the weight of the story. Frozen glory, shattered ambitions, stumbling twists of fate—it was all too prescient in combination with the searing cold in my nostrils and the dull ache of the concussion that had never fully left me. On the seventh day, the sprawling structures of Amundsen-Scott South Pole Station appeared in the distance.

We arrived at the geographic South Pole at 2 PM on December 15, 2012.

Team B was a full day behind us now, so we got to spend the night at the South Pole, waiting for them. We made camp and toured the station, where more than two hundred people were employed for the summer. It's nerd Nirvana, filled with history and scientific research on big bang theories, neutrinos, melting glaciers—an overwhelming array of ideas. Amundsen-Scott South Pole Station is on New Zealand time and we kept Chilean time, so I have no idea what hour of the day or night it was for them, but they stamped our passports, gave us a tour, and allowed us to use US dollars to purchase South Pole memorabilia in the store. Sadly, we weren't allowed in the cafeteria, which is the only thing we desperately wanted.

We took pictures inside and outside, posing at the Ceremonial South Pole, which is marked by a candy-striped pole with a mirror ball on top and a circle of international flags all around, and at the geographical South Pole, where all lines of longitude meet. I had fun quite literally "walking around the world." The next day, Team B arrived, and a ski plane took us all back to Union Glacier. I managed to sneak in a melted-ice shower before the Russians arrived with their beaver hats and vodka to fly us back to Punta Arenas. I sat in the back of the cargo plane, making lists and trying to wiggle my purple toes inside my boot.

I had only three weeks to train for Aconcagua. The worst thing you can do is show up for any mountain unprepared, and it's particularly ill-advised to fudge it on the largest mountain in the Western Hemisphere. I was so utterly absorbed in what needed to happen next, I neglected to call Jonathan and tell him I was safe.

18

Only bullfighting, mountain climbing, and
auto racing are sports. The rest are merely games.
—BARNABY CONRAD, AUTHOR, BULLFIGHTER, AND BOXER

When I finally did call Jonathan a couple of days later to tell him I was boarding my flight to Boston, he didn't have to raise his voice above a simmer.

"So you made it," he said.

"Yes, I'm—oh, shit."

British people don't rage-erupt like Americans do. Brits seethe quietly, which is somehow more unnerving.

"Couldn't be bothered to call?" he said.

"There wasn't much reception. Or time."

"Uh-huh. You managed to call from Everest Base Camp in the middle of nowhere, but surrounded by a massive full-service private camp at Union Glacier, you couldn't manage it? Why bother paying for the satellite phone?"

"I'm sorry, but we were completely . . ." No. No excuses. Not the endless, penetrating cold. Not my toes. Not the shit internet. I decided to own it and said, "Spousey, I'm sorry."

I immediately understood how deeply I'd hurt him, and I hated it, but I didn't know how to fix it. When I got home, I apologized all over myself. Of course I apologized! Repeatedly. And I meant it. Repeatedly. Jonathan received my regret with the same chilly decorum he showed when I offered up the South Pole tea mug I'd gotten him for Christmas.

I grew up in a house full of unbridled rage. When someone was angry, words flew like hatchets, doors slammed, plates exploded against the wall, fists balled up tight and occasionally bashed into eye sockets. Jonathan's anger was the polar opposite of that, pun intended. His tightly contained wrath was like a silent monster under the bed. It was worse, in some ways, than the alcohol-fueled free-for-all fight nights of my childhood, because none of that was my fault, and this was entirely.

"Does it help that I have a punishing training schedule?" I tried to tease. "Fifty shades of cardio?"

He harrumphed. We are not amused.

All I could do was go to the gym and run on a steeply raked treadmill, hoping he'd get over it and etching my brain with a mental note to never ever—*ever*—neglect to call him again. And I had to suck it up when he said he'd like me to accompany him to Maine for a long holiday weekend. I was counting on each precious day of training between the South Pole and Aconcagua and hoped to spend what little downtime I had checking my gear, catching up with friends, and attempting a bit of homebody normalcy. But the better part of valor won out. Eager to make amends, I said, "Sounds like a plan, Spousey."

I'm not sentimental about Christmas, but I didn't want to spend the holiday in the doghouse. As a kid, I hated holidays— Christmas, Independence Day, even my birthday—because I knew my parents would drink even more than usual.

My dad always took Ben and me to see Detroit's Thanksgiving Day Parade while my mom made the traditional feast. He parked his truck, hauled out two ladders and a sheet of plywood to lay across them, and said, "Climb up and scoot over." We scrambled up onto the makeshift scaffold so we could wave to Santa Claus from the best seats in the house while our dad knocked back a bottle of peppermint schnapps, which he was happy to share with us.

We celebrated mass on Christmas Eve at Saints Cyril and Methodius Slovak Catholic Church, just off Van Dyke Avenue in Detroit. The ornate old sanctuary had begun to crumble a bit, and what remained was demolished in 2003, but back then it was still imposing enough to put the fear of God in you. On the arched proscenium over the altar, inscribed in big Gothic shouty caps was KLANAJME SA VECNE SVIATOSTI OLTARNEJ! ("We kneel before the eternal holiness of the altar!"). Saints Cyril and Methodius were the apostles who converted the Slovaks to Christianity in the ninth century, and masses were still held in Slovak or Latin, which were equally Greek to me.

Ben and I attended church with our maternal grandparents almost every Sunday, and occasionally we'd go as a family with our mother and father. I'd watch from the corner of my eye as my father inevitably fell asleep during mass, and then there was a big Sunday lunch at our grandmother's house. Before we tucked into the spiral-cut ham and au gratin potatoes, we had to wash our hands with a silver fifty-cent piece to bring wealth. After we were excused from the table, Ben and I played for hours in the attic, a vast, dusty treasure trove of memories, mysteries, and fascinating objects, including my grandfather's pickaxe and headlamp, essential tools for a coal miner. Like his father, for whom he was named, he had labored inside that dark mountain. They'd each sacrificed at least one finger at work in the coal mines. Now when I'm climbing, I can't swing an ice axe without thinking of them—these hearty characters built stronger by suffering, by swinging an axe and leaving their blood on the rocks, humbly invincible, always moving forward.

When my brother and I played in the attic, my grandfather loved to scare us by whispering into the heating vents, knocking and rattling his keys. The ghostly voice echoed out of nowhere.

"Whoooooooooo . . ."

Ben and I stood perfectly still, trying to make out what it was until we couldn't take it any longer, and then we flew down the stairs, screaming our little heads off, certain the attic was haunted.

We spent a lot of time at my grandparents' house when I was little. My mom was the youngest of their six children. Her oldest sister was twenty-two years her senior. I remember my grandmother teaching me to kneel down and bring my hands to prayer. She patiently waited as I memorized the Lord's Prayer. She talked about how to be grateful, stay humble, and have faith. My grandmother told stories, stories, and more stories—short, pithy fables that always ended with a moral lesson and long, involved tales of our ancestors, who came from Austria-Hungary.

"I'll tell you a story about my dad's mother," she said. "It's a beautiful story and yet sort of sad. She came from royal birth. My cousin found a picture, so you can see for yourself, she was very pretty and well educated, but she married a commoner, so she was disowned by her people. They sent a coach loaded with her dresses. As if to say, 'You made your bed, now lie in it.'" She brushed her palms together to show how they dismissed her. "Now, about my mother's side—she was very poor. Had to take sheep to the meadow every day with her dad and bring them home every night, so she never went to school. Never could read or write until she married my dad. He taught her to read and write. His mother was well educated, so he was too."

I listened to those stories about choosing love over money and rising above one's bitter circumstances, and then I went home with my parents, who were half-drunk when they got in the car and fully hammered by the time Ben and I pulled our blankets over our heads and tried to sleep. Over the years, the area surrounding Saints Cyril and Methodius declined and became a desolate, burned-out ghost of the old neighborhood. The last time I set foot in it, I was there for my brother's funeral. Sometime after that, the church became a haunted ruin. Being sentimental, my mother took Jonathan and me there for a tour before it was completely torn down. I carved off a sizable chunk of marble from the facade, and it has traveled with me to every home I've lived in, all over the world.

Christmas 2012 was as festive as I could fake. Maine was relatively close, so going there didn't take too much time away from training, but this is all you need to know about Maine in the winter: I returned healthy from *Antarctica*, only to be laid low with a miserable cold caught in Maine. A barking bronchitis lingered, clouding my chest and sinuses as I packed to leave for Argentina.

Furthermore, my feet were still a mess. The doctors at Union Glacier couldn't agree on a diagnosis—frostnip or boot bang—but the podiatrist in Boston assured me there wasn't a big material difference. My blistered toes were purple, numb, and swollen with fluid. I took cayenne pepper and capsicum capsules, which were supposed to bring down the swelling, but all that did was upset my already wretched stomach. I could count on two hands the number of days I was actually able to get in a decent workout. I was comforted by the idea that I'd be climbing with my trusted buddies, Austin and Daniel, until Austin emailed to unload the tale of how he'd failed to summit Aconcagua the first time. Searching the blogs of my peers, I saw a lot of that going around.

What is it about this mountain that trips people up? I wondered.

There was the height, for starters—almost 23,000 feet—not only the highest mountain in South America but the tallest peak in all of the Americas and in the Southern and Western Hemispheres. Many people attempted it early in their quest for the Seven Summits just to get what they perceived as altitude. The Normal route via Horcones Valley typically takes about twenty-one days and begins from the south as you climb the western flank of the mountain. The mountain itself sounded fairly straightforward, except for the summit bid, where we would have to cross a 700-foot incline traverse to get to a rocky couloir, a steep gash, and then ascend another 1,500 feet to the summit pyramid. Bottom line: not everyone makes it to the summit, but very few climbers die.

I thought the three of us booking with IMG—Austin, Daniel, and I—could be there and back in less than three weeks. A small team has a unique agility. I left Boston, resolved that—come hell or high altitude—I would not be the one to slow us down. Without adequate opportunity to train, I'd have to rely on knowledge, muscle memory, a burst of adrenaline, and hopefully, a good acclimatization schedule.

Aconcagua is in Mendoza, Argentina's wine country, which reminded me a lot of California's Napa Valley, with nicely arranged vineyards in the rolling hills around the quaint towns. After I arrived, we picked up our climbing permits and planned our departure over thick steaks and lots of local malbec at a charming eatery on a tree-lined plaza. The next day, we were driven to Puente del Inca near Aconcagua Provincial Park to start our climb. It was only seventy miles, but it took two and a half hours, which was not terrible, because the driver had an amazing playlist, and I impressed him with my "Name That Tune" knowledge base. I could usually call it based on the opening guitar riff.

"Jethro Tull: 'Aqualung.' "

"Oh! Oh! Oh! Deep Purple: 'Highway Star.' "

"Puh-lease. That's Pink Floyd. 'Time.' "

I got a million right and only three wrong. Take that, Bob Marley Café.

We arrived at Grajales, a local logistics provider, near the Aconcagua Provincial Park entrance. Our duffel bags were weighed for mules to transport. In the meantime, we chatted up the staff regarding weather and conditions. Balmy summer nights above 16,400 feet were usually only a few degrees below zero, while the typical temperature at the summit was −22 degrees Fahrenheit, so I figured I was fine with my Olympus Mons and alpine gear. Austin and I decided to do a quick thousand-foot acclimatization hike while Daniel sorted out some paperwork.

You know I love my Himalayas for unbeatable girth and grandeur, but the Andes—snowcapped, skirted with vibrant green foothills and flowered meadows, sporting a silvery band of clouds like a feather boa—this was the prettiest mountain range I'd ever seen.

"First day is mostly flat," said Daniel. "About eight hours to Confluencia Camp at eleven thousand feet."

"Confluencia," I said. "Sounds like a lung disease."

We set a nice pace and got there in five hours, well ahead of our mules, so our Grajales friends let us post up on bunks in one of their big tents and fed us a dinner of meat and potatoes that rivaled the best Russian fare we ate on Elbrus. The next day, we hiked up to Plaza de Mulas at over 14,000 feet, and made camp, planning to stay for an extra day to hydrate and acclimatize. Daniel warned us that a doctor would be there to check everyone's pulse oxygen levels and blood pressure.

"They're authorized to hold you back if they don't like what they see," he said.

I have factor V Leiden (a genetic predisposition to blood clots), and I have low blood pressure, but I always consult cardiovascular specialists. Dr. Hackett, my high-altitude specialist, helps me assemble a high-altitude medical kit for every expedition. I take it seriously, but I was a little concerned that a doctor who didn't know my particular physiological makeup might misinterpret or take something out of context, and Daniel was concerned about a rumored conspiracy to hamper Western guides. We went warily to the medical tent, and—fuck my luck—my blood pressure was 100/60 and my O_2 sats were 89 percent, which I thought was normal. Austin's numbers were a bit better, and Daniel's were close to mine, but the doctor signaled me to step out.

"I'm sorry, you won't be allowed to climb," she said. I started to bluster, but she pinched that off like a pill bug. "Drink some fluids and check with us tomorrow."

I worried that my sats were likely to get worse, not better, especially if I was up all night at this altitude drinking and peeing instead of sleeping. But this was not a suggestion. She pursed her lips tighter than a clamshell and tipped her chin toward the door.

"This is bullshit," Daniel fumed. "No other mountain has anything like this. Not even Everest."

"Maybe I could go for a run," I said. "That would get my heart rate up."

"Maybe." He was unconvinced.

I jogged to the internet center, thinking I'd spend some time researching how to get my blood pressure up without further dehydrating myself, but I got distracted by all the art on the walls.

"The highest art gallery in the world," said the owner, who was also the artist. I roamed around, looking at the color-saturated Fauvist paintings of mules, women, children, mountains. I was rather taken with a unique chalk drawing of Aconcagua. It was framed with an old Polaroid of the artist as he was creating this chalk landscape and inscribed with the date of his summit.

"It's not for sale," said the artist, who noticed I had paused too long at this particular piece. "Why do you like it so much?"

"I guess because it's a picture within a picture," I said, "which seems to be created partially from memory of your own summit. And it's the only picture in the gallery that has a date on it."

"Very good observation."

Won over, he was willing to negotiate a price, and I told him I'd be back after I summited. He wanted me to dance with him and share a bottle of wine to celebrate, but I politely declined.

Back in the common area tent, I found Austin and Daniel lolling on bean bags with a group of American, Italian, and Russian climbers from Silicon Valley. I flopped down next to a sporty blond named Alisa and struck up a conversation that would continue throughout the years as we became climbing buddies.

The next morning, I ran around camp, trying to get my heart rate up before I joined the queue outside the medical tent. I stood for about fifteen minutes, shaking my hands and jogging in place. There was a different doctor today; I felt a surge of hope that he would at least listen to me plead my case if my sats weren't up enough. He wrapped my arm and put the oxygen gauge on my finger. He noted it on my chart. *99/59 and 85% oxygen saturation.*

"I normally run low on these tests."

Before I could launch into the whole explanation, he said, "I see here that you have climbed many mountains. You should be a good judge of what is normal for you. How do you feel? You feel good?"

"Yes. Yes, I feel great."

"Very good, then. Have a good trip." He signed the form and handed it to me, and we beat it out of there, stopping only briefly to say goodbye to Alisa and the Silicon Valley Mafia. We applied ourselves and reached Camp Canadá at 16,570 feet by the end of the day. The summit looked close enough to touch, ancient volcanic rock, mottled gray shot through with blue-green marine deposits and reddish cinder intrusions. There was no snow or ice, so we had to fetch water from a stream and disinfect it with my Steripen, a little gadget that uses ultraviolet light to make iffy water potable. All water purification tablets take on a strange taste after a while, and on principle, I don't go for anything that hasn't been boiled—and sometimes not even then—but I was parched, and I'd slowly grown to trust this handy gadget I picked up from Cliff on Shishapangma. Knock on wood, we wouldn't get diarrhea.

The next two days, we passed Camp Nido de Condores and moved up to High Camp Colera on the north ridge.

"Camp *Cholera*," I said, looking at a map with what I hoped was a mispelled name. "Again, what marketing genius . . . ?"

"I don't like this weather tomorrow," said Daniel. "We'll have to hang out for another day."

I was fine with a day to rest, acclimatize, and sort my gear. I spent hours sorting my gear. I swear! Hours. I went to bed feeling super prepared. I don't know what poltergeists got into my kit during the night. The next morning, we got up at four, anticipating a quick breakfast and five o'clock departure, but somehow I couldn't find anything. I'd packed the wrong face mask, wrong snacks, wrong layers. As I thrashed and swore, Daniel stood outside my tent, bitching and lecturing, "Christ, Vanessa! This many mountains under your belt, and you can't get your shit together?" and so on and so forth, as if I weren't saying all these things to myself already.

Having summited Aconcagua many times before, Daniel expected to be first. We finally trudged out of camp, half an hour late and barely speaking to each other. He's a guy who doesn't like to get stuck in the middle, as I learned years earlier trying to keep up with him on the rocks and scree. This is the problem with having only two people on a team, by the way; in a larger group, you can rely on someone else to muck it up and be late. With only two people, it's a flip of a coin whether it is you or the other guy with the dunce cap on your head. With our team of three, the odds were only slightly improved. It's fair to say we weren't quite awake. Austin was so discombobulated, he put his heated hand warmers in his boots to pre-warm them and forgot to take them out. I don't know how he didn't feel that—super focused on the summit bid, I guess—but it resulted in some hellacious blisters.

To make up time, Daniel opted to take us through a shortcut up a particularly steep bit of the mountain. This was a great call. A few hours later, we were in the lead and looking good despite the rising wind and hard-biting morning cold. I rummaged my pack for sport gels or anything with the word *energy* on it. It was about to get trickier, steeper, icier. It had taken me a few hours to find my feet that morning, but Austin was the one lagging as we hit the traverse across the Gran Acarreo. We finally stopped for a break outside a big cave at the base of Canaleta, the summit couloir, and from there, we pushed for the summit. The terrain raked steeper and more strenuous. Daniel scrambled up the rocks, hopping from boulder to boulder like a ruddy mountain goat. *Bastard.* I picked it up a notch, in crampons on solid footing. I turned a corner and saw the path disappear over the edge of a cliff.

"Daniel?" I called.

Silence. I stepped closer to the edge, craning my neck to see how far down it went. It went a long way down. My heart lurched in my chest.

"Daniel? *Daniel!*"

"Up here. I had to take a shit."

"TMI, Daniel, thanks for sharing."

"Aconcagua!" he crowed. "Last to depart, first to arrive!"

"How many times am I allowed to say *I told you so*?"

"Just get your ass up here."

He pointed to a path that veered sharply upward to the final summit pyramid. I climbed hand over fist. Almost there. The jagged layers of rock told their story, how they met and were disowned by the earth, pushed upward, broken, and remade.

I reached the seventh of my Seven Summits, Aconcagua, via Plaza de Mulas, 22,841 feet, at 11:30 AM on January 20, 2013.

Austin arrived a few minutes later, and we took summit photos of each other under the brilliant blue sky—posing with a cross made from lead pipes, standing on a pointy, wide-brimmed rock formation that resembles a witch's hat.

Clouds gathered and soon enough there were snow flurries all around us. *The summit is only halfway*, I reminded myself. Daniel motioned for us to head down, and I focused on the steep rocks. As I started across the traverse, I realized I was getting dehydrated. Weariness started in my core and oozed to my extremities like a dark sap, thicker and heavier with each step. Every day that I hadn't trained demanded its due now. Payback is a bitch, as they say.

A blinding snowstorm rolled in out of nowhere, borne on a steely wave of cold wind. With all Daniel's obsessive weather checking, I seethed quietly, how did he not see that coming? How did I not see it myself? I secretly fancied myself some sort of weather savant. From the time I was a child, I've been fascinated by storms, tuned in to the sky on an intuitive wavelength. Ben and I used to count the number of seconds (one Mississippi, two Mississippi) between the lightning and thunder, divide by five, and guesstimate how far away the storm was. We generally ignored the old adage "When thunder roars, go indoors," waiting instead for the more urgent, "If you can see it, flee it," and then taking shelter. I love a good storm, in theory, but this was an endless, pelting beatdown. I don't even remember how I made it all the way down to Plaza de Mulas.

I could see it now—why this mountain is so hard, how it throws people off. Easy, except for the summit day. It's like the old joke: "Other than that, how was the play, Mrs. Lincoln?" Our Grajales friends took us in, warmed us up with snacks and tea, and let us roll out sleeping bags on the floor of their mess tent so we didn't have to pitch our tents. The artist stopped by to bring me the artwork I bought, and when Daniel was taking a picture of us, this strange man swept me up in his arms. The photo is hilarious, but I was startled to feel my body so easily scooped up, as if I were a rag doll.

The next day, we hiked out in a cold, pouring rain, three drowned rats. Austin couldn't keep up because of the holes in his feet from the hand warmers, but I was afraid of getting hypothermia if I slowed down. I could feel the body heat leaving me faster than I could produce it, so I kept motoring along, cajoling, "C'mon, you guys, it's Miller time. I mean malbec time."

Back in Mendoza, finally clean and dry, we indulged in a boozy celebration lunch, but before I stumbled off to sleep, I called Jonathan. Oh, no, I did not forget to call again. Not after the bollocking I received last time.

"I made it! And I'm bringing home some amazing malbec for you to try. It's quite good."

"Not as good as a French Bordeaux or Burgundy."

"C'mon, Spousey. It's a new world. You can't always be stuck in the Old World."

In the local market I found colorful Inca bags and bracelets for Megan and Lara, our goddaughters in London, and for Pippa's boys, I bought I CLIMBED ACONCAGUA T-shirts.

Back in Boston, I breathed a shaky sigh of relief. I had my Seven Summits, and I was one pole away from the Grand Slam.

19

There are many paths to the top of the mountain,
but the view is always the same.
—UNKNOWN

I had two months to train for the North Pole, and I resolved to make the most of them. I was still coughing, but my feet were healing. Time to get out and drag that tire. I would never short-change my training again, but I was also determined to work in a little bit of normalcy—time with Jonathan and with friends. I wasn't fully aware of how disconnected I'd become until I was walking down the street in Manhattan with Stephanie, who was visiting from Hong Kong. As we strolled along, window-shopping, I said without thinking, "I need to take a quick wee. Let me pop behind . . . oh."

I caught myself, and we both laughed.

"No, darling," Stephanie said gently. "You're back in the *concrete* jungle now."

We laughed, but I had that rag doll feeling again, startled to find myself swept up in something out of the blue.

Over lunch, Stephanie said, "I've been looking at the Seven Summit statistics. The fastest woman to complete the Seven Summits took almost a year. You could beat that record if you climb Kilimanjaro again."

"I'm not following," I said. "I've done the Seven Summits. I climbed Kili."

"But that was before you were *climbing* climbing."

"Before you came into my life, you mean."

"Well, exactly," said Stephanie. "I've done a little homework. You have time to climb Kilimanjaro before it closes for the season, but you have to go in early March, before the rainy season kicks in."

"That would mean ten days away from my North Pole training." I shook my head, trying to dislodge the idea that was already digging in like a weevil. "I was lucky to get by this time. One time lucky, two times foolish."

"You could do this."

"And you could climb Everest!" When she didn't flinch at that, I said, "Okay. I'll go if you come with me."

"I'm pretty sure I have to stay home and wash my hair that day."

I tried to badger her into it, and when that didn't work, I put out a call to a few other friends. Jonathan suggested our friend Serena, a marathoner and Ironman competitor he'd met at the Ashram, a California retreat center where he soldiered through five-hour hikes, weights, yoga, pool volleyball, and nonstop activity on a 1,200-calorie-per-day regimen he describes as "half a blueberry and a blade of grass." They didn't allow stimulants, so there was no tea, which is cruel and unusual punishment for an Englishman. Serena, thin as a rail, gave him her egg every day, so like a puppy, he was forever indebted. Ashram-trained with an old soul and solid sense of humor, she was the perfect candidate for Kilimanjaro.

Serena and I chose a fast-track expedition with Thomson Safaris via the Umbwe route—a new route for me. I spent February training for the North Pole—core, cardio, Pilates, and tire-dragging—

but all that would be useful for Kilimanjaro. In between, I was still making that valiant attempt at normalcy, but that always seemed to go sideways.

One day, a neighbor—not the one I'd headbutted—asked me, "How are you not tweeting about these amazing adventures?" As an entrepreneur and TV personality, he was appalled to learn that I wasn't on Twitter. He requested my phone and helped me create a profile on the spot, advising me to tweet something every day. That seemed excessive, so I lurked at first, observing how other climbers were using this new platform, before I retweeted a few things and started posting training snapshots.

Historically, getting sponsorship has been trickier for climbers than it is for other athletes, because no one wants to take the chance that their logo will be prominently featured in photos of a frozen corpse. And what's "tricky" for a man translates to "forget about it" for a woman. But in January 2015, President Barack Obama tweeted, "So proud of @TommyCaldwell1 and @KJorgeson for conquering El Capitan. You remind us that anything is possible." Thousands of retweets later, everyone was talking about the first free climb of El Capitan's Dawn Wall. Sponsors crave that sort of viral visibility, so people try to conjure it wherever they can. It was motivation enough for me to set out across the social media minefield.

Between flights in Amsterdam, I dove into my Kilimanjaro research, pulling out a few tweetable facts.

Kilimanjaro and Elbrus are the only volcanoes of the Seven Summits, composed of layers of hardened volcanic ash, lava, pumice, and tephra. #funfact

147 characters. Shit.

#Kilimanjaro has six different climate zones: cultivated, rainforest, heath, moorland, alpine desert, and arctic. #funfact

121 characters with spaces. Boom.

When I posted that I was on my way, I received a flurry of good wishes, but I could see how easily Twitter might become a dangerous distraction and how quickly comment threads turned to bickering and backstabbing. #notimeforthat

Serena and I were climbing with another woman, a guy, and three Tanzanian guides with English nicknames: Stuart, Peter, and Gregory. Wanting to meet them in the middle, we gave ourselves Swahili names: Tongaa (me), Manca (Serena), Mtoto, and Leloo. We followed the Umbwe route through lush, rolling farmland in the cultivation zone, into the twisted, mossy rain forest, and up to the verdant green heather and wildly beautiful moorland zones. We took our time, making sure everyone was properly acclimatized and hydrated. Freedom, the medical porter, let me take a turn carrying his pack on my head, which lasted only long enough to get a single "pics or it didn't happen" shot for Twitter. We laughed a lot, played tricks on each other, and shared stories about our lives back home.

Stuart told me about his wife, his children, and their many, many cows. I told him about Boston's restaurants, universities, and severe winter storms.

"But what about your cows?" he asked.

"Oh, I don't have any cows."

"I am so sorry." His eyebrows furrowed in an expression of deep sympathy.

"No, we're good," I assured him. "My place in Boston is not big enough for cows." (I realized later that this would make him worry more.)

At our final camp, I tried to sleep for a few hours before our midnight summit bid, but my thoughts raced with what Alain de Botton, one of my favorite philosophers, calls "the mind's revenge for all the thoughts you were careful not to have in the day." Snow was falling as we met in the mess tent for tea and then set out for the summit. It was steeper than I remembered, and I saw Serena slipping and sliding ahead of me. Her legs were too tight, her steps too small.

"Manca, be careful," I called. "One step up, shift your weight to rest on your back leg for a second, and then go. One leg should be in front of the other for balance, never side by side."

"It's too slippery," she complained during a break. "Do you think I should put my Yaktrax on my shoes?"

"No, you won't need them. Just keep going up," Peter replied.

Wearing Yaktrax on your shoes is like putting snow chains on your car tires. I didn't see any need for them going up, but they can be psychological crutches. By 3 AM, Serena's performance was deteriorating along with her self-confidence.

"Hey, Peter," I said, pulling him aside during a break, "I think you should let Manca use the Yaktrax. Not for the mountain—for the mind." I tapped my temple.

With Yaktrax in place, Manca bounded up the trail, but as she was getting her mojo back, I was bowled over with gas pains. Bloating and diarrhea are common at high altitude, but this felt like being squeezed by an anaconda. I had to wave the others on and excuse myself to an unlucky patch of African violets. Luckily, Manca, like a clever little squirrel, had packed one of every pill on the planet. I took her Imodium along with some Cipro of my own.

I confided in Freedom that, given my situation, it was more stressful to be going along at this snail's pace than it would be to speed up. He agreed to keep up with me, and we took off, arriving at Stella Point forty-five minutes ahead of the others. This gave me a private moment to settle my intestines with tea and biscuits and rescue my dignity while the meds kicked in. It was lovely just sitting there watching the sun rise. Watercolor clouds glowed amber and magenta and snowdrifts went from indigo to silver as dawn washed the horizon.

We all trekked together to Uhuru Peak, where signs and a stone cairn mark the summit. I suppose I should paint a picture of it here, but I think I already have. No one wants to admit it, but truthfully, most summits look the same in many ways. If you're lucky, you see familiar miles of sky, blue eternity above, self-important clouds below. The air has the same ringing clarity. The sun has the same relentless glare. The far horizon has the same broad arc, and if there's any trace of mankind, it's the same vanishingly small wisp of smoke or distant freckle of civilization. You might see the top of a mountain range, maybe one or two mountains scattered beneath. Perhaps a glacier below, depending on the angle of the mountain. If it is a volcano, the smell of sulfur hangs in the air.

What makes each mountain unique is everything under the summit: your team dynamics, the gut-checking effort it takes to get there, and the new eyes it's given you by the time you reach the top.

I summited Mount Kilimanjaro via the Umbwe route at 7:07 AM on March 10, 2013, and stepped into the record books as the fastest woman to summit the highest peak on every continent.

20

*Unfortunately, my expeditions are no
longer about being first, but rather being last.*
—ERIC LARSEN, POLAR EXPLORER,
COMMENTING ON THE MELTING ARCTIC SEA ICE

Kilimanjaro was my first summit tweet, a picture of me in front of
the green sign at Uhuru Peak with 114 characters:

> Tongaa (me) on summit of Kilimanjaro 7 am 10 March. That's 7
> Summits + Carstensz in 10 months. Now about that NP ☺

My GoPro footage from the descent was a radically bumpy
mess as I awkwardly boot-skied down the snowy scree and negotiated the slippery rocks of a steep riverbed in the pouring rain. I
fell on my butt as I was arriving at camp, but no one was handy
with a camera, thank God. I did my best to capture the certificate
ceremony and trip home to Boston, but all in all, my social media
platform was off to a tepid start.

Fortunately, my entrepreneurial neighbor introduced me to
Penny Vizcarra, a PR maven who pageant-coached me over coffee.

"You'll learn," she said. "For now, congratulations! You did it.
You're the fastest woman on record for the Seven Summits, and by
the end of April, you'll be the fastest woman to complete the Explorers Grand Slam." She scrolled around on her iPad for the data.

"I went through every Explorers Grand Slam biography. The male record holder is a Welsh rugby player. He did it in seven months. I couldn't even find a female record holder."

"Annabelle Bond completed the Seven Summits in a year," I said. "I invited her to the South Pole, but she wasn't available."

"*What?*"

"It seemed like the right thing to do after we cracked open a bottle of Pol Roger in Hong Kong."

"Okay, new rule," said Penny. "Don't help the competition."

"It's not a competition. She's a friend of a friend."

"Yes it is, Vanessa. Whether you like it or not." Penny was relentless. "Did you know that a Russian woman and a Chinese woman were also going for the Seven Summits speed record while you were on Kilimanjaro?"

"No. I didn't know."

"See, this is why God created Twitter," said Penny. "If you do the Explorers Grand Slam in eleven months, that's another world record. All you have to do is get to the North Pole."

"And get home."

"Of course! If you get killed, your sponsors would never forgive me."

"Sponsors?" I was skeptical. We were only thirty days out, and I'd never had any luck getting sponsors before. On the other hand, I had several successful expeditions under my belt.

"Brainstorm with me. Let's create a short list."

"I used to work for GE Capital," I said, "and I've seen GE's logo on a North Pole sled. In fact, when I worked there, I won their Pinnacle Award, which is a big deal, a prestigious award for high performance."

"*Pinnacle* Award?" Penny pecked away on her laptop. "How perfect is that?"

"That year, the theme was all about the Land of the Midnight Sun, including a trip to the Arctic Circle. The folio says, 'You've reached the top of the world,' and commemorates the date we crossed into the Arctic Circle."

"That's almost *prophetic*."

It really did feel like fate for a moment, and Penny was optimistic. When I got home from my afternoon workout, I found an email from her.

Subject: NEED SEXY PICTURES!

WTF. Gulp.

She was probably not talking about me in my gingerbread man suit. I found a few photos of myself in classic little black dresses and cocktail attire, but I was always midguffaw with a drink in my hand. More smashed than smashing. Penny checked these out and gently suggested it was time to invest in a proper photo shoot.

"I need video too," she said. "For the sizzle reel."

"What's a sizzle reel?"

"It's a little marketing video montage. Just three or four minutes of you being fabulous and all extreme sports and everything, plus some footage of the action and scenery and all that from your GoPro."

"My GoPro footage is roughly two percent summit splendor, sixty percent looking down at my feet, and thirty-eight percent Daniel's ass as I follow him up the mountain. I figure his future girlfriend will thank me."

"We need to work on that."

"Done," I promised. "After I finish the North Pole."

I felt like a slacker. No sponsors, no sexy photos, no video. Bloody hell. Did other people set out with this endgame in mind? I certainly hadn't. For me, it was a classic case of something wary project managers call "scope creep" or kitchen sink syndrome. You start out with a singular focus, but then along comes some shiny new possibility, and now it's about that—but then, wait! What about this? And this! And *THIS*! And so it goes until you reach critical mass, and the whole thing implodes, effectively burying that singular objective you started with. We live in an era of such unlimited possibility, it's easy to confuse activity with accomplishment. Staying on message, staying on mission—that doesn't happen by serendipity. It happens on purpose, and while I wasn't looking, my purpose had evolved.

I thought about it while I dragged my tire back and forth, while I ran up and down thousands of stairs, while I lifted weights and did my daily crunches. Halfway through my training time, Jonathan and I attended a fund-raiser for the American Red Cross, and I was so moved by what I heard and saw that night, I reached out and said I would be honored to take the Red Cross flag with me to the North Pole. I love what the Red Cross does and how efficiently they do it, largely because their volunteers are such a force of nature. When the Red Cross told me that ninety cents of every dollar goes to someone in need, that sealed the deal. I wanted to help.

One of my Everest teammates asked me to take a banner for Street Soccer USA, a nonprofit whose mission is "to fight poverty and empower underserved communities through soccer." I was thrilled to be part of that. The mission aspect was starting to align with the message.

Packing for the North Pole, I had to work around restrictions I hadn't dealt with before. There can be no down at all in jackets, sleeping bags, or vests. The North Pole is wet cold, not dry cold like Antarctica. In that moist environment, anything that gets wet will inevitably remain in one of two liquid states, frozen stiff or thawed to unbearable clamminess, until you get back on dry land. Meanwhile, we'd be turtles, carrying our homes with us on our sleds. You need enough food, fuel, and clothing to last for seven to ten days. It's hard to predict how long the expedition will be, because in addition to the usual variables—weather, wind, extreme temperatures, and illness—you have to accept the potentially mind-screwing "negative drift" that happens when you and the ice go in opposite directions. You can ski north till your legs fall off, but if you fall asleep that night and the ice under your tent is drifting south for eight hours, you might wake up to find you've traveled ten miles in the wrong direction.

There was absolutely no fudging weight restrictions because we would be pulling our own sleds over open water leads and massive pressure ridges made up of angular ice blocks, some as high as large appliances and automobiles, piled up on the ice floes. I received the Street Soccer USA banner, which was lightweight and waterproof, but the Red Cross banner was approximately six feet square, weighing about three pounds. Jonathan thought it was hilarious, but I groaned, "It's a tent!"

I took a picture of it and tweeted:

Thanks for the bivvy @RedCross!

I don't think they got the joke or realized that they'd sent me something that belonged on the side of a building. We were down to the wire with no time to get something else, but nothing had changed about my reasons for wanting to carry it, and this was a tiny patch on everything they did for people in need, so I folded it down as compact as I could and worked it into my kit, vowing to tweet the dickens out of it so it earned its keep. Now all I needed was a soccer ball (which I planned to kick across the North Pole, for Twitter and posterity, of course, but mostly for fun).

During our last dinner out before my departure, a friend asked me, "Where *is* the North Pole, exactly?"

"If you think about Earth as a Christmas ornament," I said, "the North Pole is where you attach a hook."

"Yes, but, like . . . Scandinavia?"

"No. If this tablecloth is the Arctic Ocean, here's the North Pole." I set a glass of ice water in the middle of the table and gathered a few bits and bobs—salt, pepper, coffee cups, and a candle—setting out a wide, familiar pattern. "Here's Russia, Norway, Iceland, Greenland, Canada, and Alaska. And here's Michigan." I loaned my wineglass to toast the old neighborhood.

"But what *continent* is it on?" she enunciated, looking at me like I must be drunk or extremely obtuse. "Like, the South Pole is on Antarctica. The North Pole is on . . . what?"

"It's not on a continent," I said. "The North Pole is a location in the middle of the Arctic Ocean. Right now, it's covered by free-floating ice, but that's melting. It might last until 2035, if we're lucky. Anyway, we start here." I indicated a fleck of pepper off the coast of Norway. "The island of Spitsbergen. From there, we fly to a spot at eighty-nine degrees latitude—this line that circles the globe way up here—and then we ski the last sixty nautical miles."

"On a free-floating chunk of ice."

I played it off with a joke. "In the event of an emergency, your sled may be used as a flotation device!"

Everyone laughed except Jonathan. My numbers guy. He enjoys known quantities: a fixed point toward which one drives, guided by GPS, over solid ground. He did not enjoy the notion of this shifty liquid terrain. It might be an inverted mountain, substantial enough to hold up the Chrysler Building. Or it could be a flaky pie crust barely able to hold a starving polar bear. Remember all the Sturm und Drang over the Antarctic ozone layer back in the 1990s? Turns out we should have been worrying about Earth's ten-gallon Stetson of an ice cap melting down to a frosty little yarmulke.

From 1981 to 2010, Arctic sea ice declined an average 12.8 percent per decade, according to measurements by NASA. In 2012, when I was planning this expedition, sea ice extent was at its lowest point on record up to 2018. At this writing, during the summer of 2019, the continuing decline of sea ice combined with geopolitical tensions have made expeditions like this virtually impossible. It's humbling, heartbreaking, to contemplate the possibility that I am part of the last generation of explorers to stand at the geographic North Pole. It's imperative that we continue gathering data about the health of the polar ice cap, and for that, explorers must continue to go there, but we're having to change the way we approach the North Pole. As with any complicated relationship, words matter, gentleness and respect are required, and undesirable outcomes must be prepared for.

The sleds we were dragging are engineered to do double duty as a sort of streamlined pontoon float. When you come to an expanse where the ice has melted, you have two choices: 1) put on a dry suit, jump in, and swim, towing the sled; or 2) mount up on the sled, straddling your gear, and use your ski pole as an oar. I didn't like either option.

"I'll be fine," I assured Jonathan as I was leaving for Oslo, "and anyway, you'll be closer and in the same time zone on your business trip to Germany."

I didn't tell him that the possibility of open water scared me more than the certainty of punishing cold and the heavy sled. I prayed daily that I would never have to lower my body into that icy water and kick my legs, trying not to think of the abyss below. It was unsettling to think about crawling into a tent floating on a fathomless green-gray ocean, knowing that I might wake up miles from the map coordinates where I lay down.

For about three weeks every April, the Russians establish Barneo, a camp sponsored by the Russian Geographical Society, within one or two degrees of the North Pole. A team of engineers parachute onto the ice from Russian Mi-8 helicopters to build a temporary landing strip so the Ilyushin 76 cargo aircraft can deliver supplies, tents, fuel, and equipment. The Russian Geographical Society, which includes primarily scientists, oversees a number of research initiatives, studying the impact of climate change on the polar ice caps.

The starting point of all expeditions to Barneo has been Longyearbyen, the capital of Svalbard, Norway. After Austin and I arrived on Spitsbergen to meet up with our guide, Doug Stoup, we practiced dragging the sleds around the town of Longyearbyen. Polar bears have been known to stalk those traveling to the North Pole, so we carried flares to scare them off and a rifle to defend ourselves if the flares failed. We did a dry run, setting up and striking our tents. Penny texted me: "Shoot tons of video and pix!" I checked my electronics and resolved to get some beauty sleep before our early-morning departure.

In the Barneo mess tent, everyone wore massive puffy coats and held mugs of tea between their mittens, breathing steam into their chapped lips and red noses. There was a Norwegian team led by a famous Scandinavian explorer and a British team led by an equally accomplished Englishman. Our little trio lacked any such cachet, but 360 degrees of ice is a great equalizer. We had agility, simpler logistics, and the same weather tech they had. It wasn't a race, but there's no use denying the competitive undercurrent that always flows through camp.

From the curved window of the Mi-8 helicopter taking us to

the eighty-ninth parallel, I looked down on an impossibly varied palette of blue and white. Textures and hues created and re-created each other: mammoth white-tipped icebergs suspended in steely gray water, bony ridges biting into a milky sky, fresh snow shelves hanging over hoary old glaciers. The ice fields stretched in every direction, an endless variety ranging from stodgy pack ice to pale opal sheets, a veneer so thin it was hard to distinguish it from a wide swath of open water.

"Looks like older, multiyear ice, mostly," said Doug. "Probably three feet thick."

I never expected the terrain to be like Antarctica, but I wasn't prepared for the enormous pressure ridges—blocks of ice that thrust upward when two massive sheets of ice crash into one another. While everyone else marveled at how pretty they were, I was thinking, *We're seriously supposed to ski over those?*

The Russians dropped us off at 89 degrees north in the broad daylight of a twenty-four-hour sun. The wet wind was like a knife blade across my face. We unloaded gear for all three teams, and the Russians took off. We put on our harnesses, attached our boots to our skis, and set off pulling our sleds, each team going its own way.

It took less than an hour for me to realize my ski bindings weren't quite right. When we had practiced, we'd been skiing on even snow trails. Now we were bumping along over ruts and pressure ridges. The terrain was uneven at best, and at worst, impassable. Every time my ski jammed into a ragged spot, it splintered off, so the only way I could keep up was to take off my skis and drag my sled through the ice blocks on foot. Every time the sled got hung up, I had to jimmy it out, up, and over the rough patch, and then put on the skis and attach the sled to my harness and start pulling again until I hit another pressure ridge, repeating the whole process. Only now my ski bindings were coming off too frequently. I was literally too big for my boots, as they say.

The sled weighed almost ninety pounds, and I was dragging it through this obstacle course with the rope over my shoulder, so a few hours in, I was sweating inside that down-free synthetic coat that was supposed to ward off dampness. Wind chill took the ambient temperature down to −22 degrees Fahrenheit, but I could feel sweat trickling down the small of my back and soaking the inner layers on my torso and between my legs. When we stopped for breaks, I was so miserably cold and damp, I couldn't eat anything of substance, but I needed to hydrate, so I forced myself to take off my mask, chug a quick little slurp, get the mask back on. Breathe. Unmask. Sip. Mask. Breathe. Repeat this process for every little sip or nibble. It was too cold to muck around with beverages and half-frozen snacks anyway. And too cold to take off my mittens to deal with the cameras, so I had exactly zero footage of the spectacular scenery.

By the end of day two, I had developed a hacking cough and a serious failure of good humor. The binding issue kept me from getting a steady rhythm, but the negative drift wasn't bad, so all things considered, we were doing all right. Austin was feeling good; his skis fit, so he was booking right along.

"We're making excellent time," Austin said over dinner that night. "Do you think we might make it back for a black-tie dinner I have next weekend?"

He started to go on about this event at which Bill and Hillary Clinton were expected to make an appearance, and I got that this was a big deal, but I was so miserable, the sound of his blathering made my face numb. My inner dialogue started ranting:

So this is why it took you two rounds to summit Aconcagua and you didn't make it up Everest. Maybe if you weren't preoccupied with— I caught myself and unzipped my sleeping bag for air. *Stop it. Don't say something you'll regret. Don't transfer your shit onto innocent bystanders.*

My stupid kid brother saw me kissing my first boyfriend and said, "I'm telling Mom and Dad."

"Try it," I scoffed. "I'll tell them about your weed. And the porno mags."

"You're a fucking bitch!"

"Fuck off," I said as I walked away. "I wish you'd drop dead."

A week later, *he was dead.* That moment stayed with me like a sliver of glass under my skin. I feel it every time I'm about to say something that can't be unsaid.

"Look, Austin, I feel like shit. I'm getting a chest infection and sweating like a mule, and I can't go any faster with skis that are too big. That said, I would be willing to put in a couple of extra hours every day so you can get home for your dinner event if you're willing to help me get some video footage. It's important, and so far I've got nothing."

Austin was so happy with this proposal, he offered me his dry compressor jacket he'd been saving—same size as mine—and Doug stepped up to volunteer as cameraman.

"I'll make sure you get all the cool parts," he said, and just like that we were a team. We strategized for a few minutes and then zipped ourselves in to sleep for a few hours.

I drifted on that unpleasant plane between conscious and unconscious, jolting awake from daylight nightmares that took me down into the water. I kept seeing Ben there, pale blue and bloated, his slightly too long brown hair circling with the current.

21

*In three words I can sum up
everything I've learned about life: it goes on.*
—ROBERT FROST, POET, AT HIS EIGHTIETH BIRTHDAY CELEBRATION

The summer after Ben started high school—the summer everything was normal until it was not—I was working as a cashier at the marina, selling booze and gas to American and Canadian boats that came and went on the Detroit River. The drinking age in Canada was eighteen, while the drinking age in Michigan was twenty-one, so there was arbitrage, a lot of traffic between Windsor, Ontario, and Detroit. I went back and forth plenty of times myself, via the Detroit-Windsor Tunnel or the Ambassador Bridge, owned by a local billionaire.

"Phone call, kid." My boss held out the greasy receiver.

"Hello?" I was annoyed to hear my mother's voice on the other end. She sounded like she was drinking.

"It's your brother. He had an accident. I think you should come home."

"I'm working. I don't get off until five thirty."

"Just come home."

"I can't just leave. I have responsibilities." I hung up. *Bitch.*

"Everything okay?" my boss asked.

"I think so. I don't know. My mom said something about my brother having an accident."

"Do you want to go? I can take over." I appreciated the offer, but I knew it was one of those things where the person is hoping you'll say no.

"I'm sure it's okay," I said. "Let's see the rest of these boats come through first."

I stayed for an hour, stocking shelves and ringing up customers, but I kept thinking about my mom's voice on the phone. She sounded weird. Wobbly. Drunk, probably. Or scared.

"If your offer still stands, I think I should probably go home," I told my boss, "if you're sure you don't mind."

I headed home, picking up my pace, uncomfortable urgency in the pit of my stomach. I turned the corner at the top of my street. It was full of police cars. Lights flashing. Neighbors standing in the street, craning their necks toward the lights in our living room window. As I moved through the gauntlet of glances, stares, and whispers between the driveway and the front door, my mom's friend Dottie saw me and ran to escort me inside. She was talking fast and frantic. Bits of information came at me like a swarm of bees.

"He was in the water. He was hit by a boat. His body is missing."

"His *body*?" I pulled away from her. "He's an excellent swimmer. He's not—that's *bullshit*. He would not get randomly hit by a boat."

Dottie gripped my arm and dragged me through the front door. It was worse than the driveway, crowded with my mother's friends—women I hated; I never saw my mom's friends do a good thing for anyone—and everyone was drinking, clutching highball glasses in their shaky hands as the drama unfolded. Mom was hammered, a complete disaster, and her friends hovered around her, everyone crying their eyes out. Dad had locked himself in the upstairs bedroom with a fifth of whiskey, and he stayed there for three days.

Fuck this.

On day three, I sat up in my sleeping bag, pushing the heels of my hands against my eyes. I knew I was never going to sleep with the twenty-four-hour sun overhead and the never-ending trickle and creak of melting ice below. I don't obsess about Ben's death. I don't think about it unless I'm surrounded by water.

Inside the tent, it was airless and smelled like feet. Outside the tent, it was so cold it made my eyes burn. I boiled water for tea. We ate noodles for breakfast and set out across the ice field. It was fine for a while. With a bit of duct tape, my skis stayed reasonably in their bindings, but I was still going hard. An ambient trickle that was always in the background became more pronounced as we skimmed over a thin skiff of water that turned to slush, and then we faced our first expanse of open water.

"This ice is thinning." Doug pounded one ski pole between his feet. "Be careful."

We went sideways for a while, hoping to find a way around it, but scanning the horizon, we could see no other way but through it. Our limited options hung in the air. Riding that sled like a slow-motion polo pony would take perfect balance. It would take patience and calm. But the alternative, wading into the blackness—it made me think about things I was already fighting to not think about. I waited for someone else to speak up, but they both looked at me, and I shrugged.

"I don't like the idea of stripping down to get into the dry suit," I said. "As sweaty as I am, I'd be our first frostbite victim."

"If you end up in the water with no dry suit, frostbite is certain," said Doug. "You'd have to swim like hell for the other side, but any more than three or four minutes—that's no good."

I nodded. "Between the devil and the deep blue sea."

"No shit."

"I'll take the devil."

Austin agreed. We took off our skis and secured everything on the sleds. I saddled up on top of my gear and found the right purchase for my feet.

"Take your time. Keep your feet up," Doug said. "Be careful."

"Ya think?"

He laughed and braced his hands on the back of my sled. "Ready?"

"Ready as I'll ever be."

He gave the sled a firm shove. It skimmed forward across the slush, and then the ice dropped away beneath me. I bobbed on the deep water, fighting for balance, a scrolling panic prayer inside my head.

Oh God . . . Fuck . . . Help me, Jesus . . . Shit . . .

I was so cold and tired, my legs were already trembling. I forced myself to relax and breathe evenly, trying not to cough. I heard Austin skim onto the water behind me, followed by Doug. When I felt steady enough to move, I extended the tip of the ski pole over the water and gingerly dipped in. The sled lurched at an angle and swayed from side to side. I compensated, thighs clamped tight to my gear, searching for that balanced core they teach you to find in Pilates. It took me a minute to find my equilibrium and establish a gentle rhythm, paddling on one side and then the other. I didn't dare turn to look back, but I could hear Austin and Doug establishing their own rhythm behind me, each of us focused on breathing, on balance.

There was no wind. No sound. The frozen world was silent except for the alternating *plosh plosh* of our ski poles in the water and a soft *thunk* and scrape each time the blunt nose of my sled encountered a shard of broken ice. Small bits and pieces from the crumbling edge of the nearby floe rose and fell on the surface.

Larger chunks cast shadows in the clear water below, creating a haunted kingdom that extended down and down and down and disappeared.

On June 25, 1981, a powerboat, piloted by someone whose only intention—or whose lack of intention—was all about a summer afternoon party, tried to "thread the needle" between a raft and a sailboat. My brother was swimming from the raft to the sailboat. He'd made it halfway. Kids on the raft saw the powerboat coming. They waved and yelled at the boat driver to stop, but everyone on the speedboat was drinking, and between the roar of the motor and the loud music playing, they didn't notice the shouting. Knowing he couldn't swim left or right based on the boat's trajectory, Ben dove down, trying to escape. He didn't make it. When the spinning blades of the boat's motor tore into his chest, they churned his body upward and stopped the engine. According to the police report, the driver said he heard a "clunking sound" at the rear of the boat and thought he hit a piece of wood. But then he saw the cloud of blood and what appeared to be a "human subject."

Witnesses said they saw Ben come to the surface and heard him scream for help, so he was conscious briefly after impact. *Briefly, God, please.* A guy from the powerboat grabbed Ben's arm, but when he saw the extent of the open chest wound, he recoiled in shock. A boy swam from the raft and managed to grab Ben, but he couldn't hold the slippery deadweight. Unconscious or already dead, Ben disappeared into the crimson water.

Someone called my father, who came immediately. He had a friend on the police force and kept his own boat at the pier. No divers were immediately available from the sheriff's marine division, but the Detroit Police aviation unit flew over the general area, scanning the surface and shoreline. On day two, divers searched with an assist from the Coast Guard, but they found nothing. On day three, search operations were postponed due to a large number of watercraft in the area, but early in the afternoon, two joggers stopped a police car and told officers there was "something blue on the rocks" about two hundred yards from shore. The Coast Guard brought a wire body basket and removed the remains of a white male wearing dark blue swim trunks. Long brown hair. Deep cuts on the right leg and up the right side of the body and chest area. The right arm was cut through the bone. A bracelet on the right wrist was identified by a police officer and friend of the family.

Ben was pronounced dead June 28, 1981, at 3:10 PM. His death certificate listed the cause of death as 1) open chest wounds and 2) drowning. The boat driver was arrested, but to my knowledge, was not prosecuted. It was an accident. People shook their heads over God's mysterious ways and reminded me what a terrible thing that person would have to live with for the rest of his life. And I hoped they were right. I hoped it would be unbearable. I wanted him to close his eyes every night and hear that dull wooden clunk and see that oil slick of dark blood forming on the water. I hoped he would never shake the feeling of Ben's eely arm in his grasp— that all-but-severed arm—all the life spilling out of his chest. I knew hating this person would not bring my brother back. I hated the motherfucker anyway. I still do. I just don't have the bile for it that I had when I was a teenager. My initial rage settled into a deadweight of despair as I realized my brother's death was in fact the death of my family.

I tried to console my mother. She was in ruins, blasted beyond comprehension most of the time, and she had her horrible friends for whatever was left. I went upstairs and knocked on the bedroom door.

"Dad? It's me."

"Go away."

"Open the door."

"No."

"Dad. Come on."

"*GO AWAAAAAY*," he brayed like a wounded animal.

"Fine!" I yelled back at him. "I'll just sit here until you decide to open the door."

I sat outside the door, making noise every once in a while so he would know I was still there. After about twenty minutes, I heard stumbling footsteps. The tumbler turned in the lock. I got up and cautiously opened the door. The room smelled like cigarettes, bourbon, body odor, piss, and vomit. My father sat on the bed, his face haggard, his eyes bloodshot and cheeks streaked with tears.

"Dad?" I crept over to the bed and sat beside him. "I'm sorry. I love you."

"I don't care," he slurred.

There was a pause as I searched for words to say.

"You don't understand. I lost *my* son. My *only* son."

"I know, but . . . but I'm here. You still have me." I tried to put my arms around him, but he shoved me away.

"*I don't care!*" He screamed, spitting the words at me. "It's not the same. I want my *son!*"

I flinched away from his stale breath in my face. His mouth trembled and fresh tears coursed down his cheeks. His neck was bright red with pure rage, his forehead shiny with sweat. He tipped the whiskey bottle into his water glass, letting the last of it dribble over the rim.

"Go away," he mumbled. "Leave me alone."

I felt my face flush with shame, anger, and a sense of helplessness I hated. I sat there without speaking for what seemed like an eternity. There was nothing to say. I walked out and closed the door behind me. My face felt like it was on fire, but my eyes were as dry as coal. I didn't cry. There was no room for my grief in this house; all the oxygen was taken up by the blurry agony of my parents.

I don't remember much about Ben's funeral. They parked the closed casket beneath the grand arch in Saints Cyril and Methodius. KLANAJME SA VECNE SVIATOSTI OLTARNEJ! I sat numb and dry-eyed through the lengthy funeral mass said in Latin. But afterward, as I was leaving, I saw the father of my friend Gayle—my best friend all through elementary school until her family moved away about five years earlier. I'd spent a lot of time at their house when I was little and my mom was studying to be a nurse, so I suppose they had some idea of what my homelife was like. Gayle's father had had a stroke and was in a wheelchair, but he'd read the news about Ben and cared enough about me to make this effort. He cared enough to come. Cared enough to cry. Shit, he couldn't even talk, and he was crying. When I saw that, I felt my own eyes swell, and a tear fell. It was like he had cracked the car window for a suffocating puppy. That small breeze of compassion left me sobbing. It still does.

A day or two later, my father left. Then my mother left. And then there was only me, alone with my grief and anger and the understanding that no one was coming to guide me across this emotional wasteland. Tragedy sets a magnifying glass on any relationship. If the foundation is firm, those bonds become stronger. If the foundation is flawed, existing cracks widen, crevasses open between people, seracs of anger and resentment rise up, and you find yourself in an icefall of fucked-up-ness. The death of a child is potent enough to destroy a functional family; my dysfunctional family never stood a chance.

My parents' divorce was finalized less than five weeks after my brother's death. I was in high school, so the court asked me who I would like to live with, and I said I would prefer to live with my father. I was clever enough to keep quiet about the fact that I was already living alone in the house where I grew up. My mother had rented a house ten miles away. My father had moved in with a new girlfriend. He stopped by once a week to pick up the bills. When I graduated from high school, he stopped by to tell me he was selling the house.

My mother rebuilt her life with friends and a career and never wanted to remarry. My father remarried almost immediately. Not the first girlfriend, the second. Since my mother's death, I have in my attic boxes and bins, entire family albums filled with letters saved by my mother and grandmother, pages and pages of rants and remonstrations, an interminable chronicle of petty family feuds. I'm grateful that I'll never have to deal with any of that. Whenever I hear that proverb "Blood is thicker than water," I shake my head. It implies that family relationships are always more important than friendships. That is simply not my reality. In my case, often the people I know the least have come through for me the most. I trust and cherish the people I've chosen to have in my life: Jonathan and my whole crew of friends, represented and silent in this story, as well as all the other climbing mates who came after. The people fate chose for me—well, thank you above. Family isn't something I take for granted. Family is my choice.

So I balance. I breathe. I go on.

Perched on top of my gear, I felt the soft grind of slush under my ski pole. We dragged our sleds onto the hard ice, strapped on our skis, and continued across miles of treacherous terrain and expanses of open water for another day and a half.

On day five, I fell back to struggle with my boot binding, and when I caught up to Austin and Doug, they were walking in circles, heads down, looking like they were searching for a lost contact lens.

"Hey!" I waved when I was in call-out distance. "What are you guys doing?"

"Five, four, three, two, one—ninety degrees!" Austin yelled. Just as he clocked it on his GPS, the drift took it away. (Polar explorer Felicity Aston says you don't arrive at the North Pole so much as you stalk it, and I couldn't agree more.) Nonetheless, we lofted our ski poles in triumph and celebrated with a group hug. I bowed my head and whispered, *"Thank you. We did it."* It felt like the only prayer I had left.

I reached 90 degrees north, 0 degrees west, at 5:21 PM on April 16, 2013, setting a world speed record, the fastest woman to complete the Explorers Grand Slam.

And I have footage. Yes, Penny, there is a Santa Claus! Austin and Doug delivered. We pulled out the flags and banners and set up our soccer pitch, and he shot some fun video of me kicking the soccer ball into the goal. My face is covered with a ski mask, so I could just as easily be robbing a bank, but I swear, that's me. Austin and I are standing there with that ginormous Red Cross flag proudly unfurled. There's also plenty of video of me wrestling my sled over craggy pitfalls and trying to get my skis unstuck from snowbanks. It's all very ungraceful and raw-cheeked and herky-jerky, but I felt good about it.

Doug placed a call to make it official and request a pickup from Barneo. We boiled water for tea and rested for a couple of hours, waiting for the helicopter. I was exhausted, ready to collapse, but everything was rushed and hyperefficient at Barneo camp. Some important Russian dignitary was on the way, so they wanted us out. The two other teams were still on the ice. I'd hardly given them a thought, between the ski bindings and the sweat and the stretches of open water, but the Norwegians were a day behind us and the Brits were a full day behind them. We would have been glad to hang out and give them a proper welcome, but the Russian Geographical Society awarded us our certificates—names spelled correctly, which is always a plus—and sent us back to Longyearbyen.

I arrived in Longyearbyen with plans to celebrate: call Jonathan, long hot shower, crack a bottle of champagne with my mates in the hotel bar. I was probably laughing about something that doesn't matter now as I stepped up to the front desk at the Radisson Blu in Longyearbyen. A stack of newspapers lay neatly folded on the counter. Words I didn't understand. Images of Boylston Street, not far from Copley Square. Shop windows I'd walked by a thousand times were shattered, metal frames twisted, bricks broken. Bloody debris littered the sidewalks.

"It's *Boston*—where I live—this is—oh my God. The marathon."

Panic rising in my throat, I rifled through the paper, searching the horrific photographs for familiar faces, parsing the text for the few words I could understand—*bombing, terrorism, panic*—as if any of those things can be understood up close or at a distance. The story was in Norwegian, but the headline screamed BOSTON MASSACRE.

Spousey.

Was he still in Germany? I'm sure he'd laid out his itinerary, and I'm sure I'd nodded as if I were listening, but I was focused on my own trip preparations. My next thought was for my friends who were running the marathon. I would have been there myself if I hadn't gone to the North Pole, and Jonathan would most likely have been standing somewhere on the crowded street. (The following year, we were.)

"What time is it?" I asked the receptionist.

"Half past ten."

"Ten . . ." I shook my head, not sure if the window was streaming daylight or midnight sun.

"In the morning," she said.

My UK SIM card worked here, so I was able to call Jonathan from my room.

"Vanessa, where are you?"

"Longyearbyen. Where are you?"

"Still in Frankfurt."

"Thank God." I took my first real breath since picking up that newspaper. "What's happening? What have you heard?"

"Several dead. A lot of people terribly injured."

"Have they released any names?"

"No, but if you get on Facebook, the Red Cross is helping people find each other."

"My Wi-Fi's not great."

He told me what he'd been able to glean from German television.

On April 15, 2013, as I was struggling over the rugged ice floes and open water on my way to the North Pole, 23,000 people set out to run the Boston Marathon. The first pressure cooker bomb went off at 2:49 PM outside Marathon Sports on Boylston Street. A second explosion came twelve seconds later. More than 5,700 runners had yet to cross the finish line. Hundreds of thousands of spectators lined the race route. Two days later, the FBI released security camera footage of two brothers, Chechen Kyrgyzstani American fanatics, who'd built the bombs with household items and instructions off the internet. The older brother was killed during the manhunt. The younger brother was found hiding in a dry-docked boat and is now on death row.

"I imagine neither of us will be able to get back for a few days," I said.

"Probably not. The airport is closed. Even if they reopen it tomorrow, flights will be a mess." He sighed a worldly, weary sigh, but then he made a good attempt at congratulations. "Meanwhile, you've done it. The Explorers Grand Slam. Well done, darling. Really. Well done."

"Thank you."

"How are you feeling?"

"I'm okay," I said through a spate of dry coughing. "My shoulder's out of whack. I'm just tired."

"It'll be good to get home."

"Yes."

I went up to my room, feeling hollow. I'd geared myself for exhilaration, not this. I had no technology working, no way to search for information or send donations. As soon as I found the right adapter to plug in my charger, I searched for a photo of the Red Cross flag at the North Pole, certain I'd taken a few with my iPhone instead of the camera. Suddenly nothing about reaching the North Pole was as important as what the Red Cross was doing in Boston—what they always do wherever they're needed—including the huge role they play in the Boston Marathon every year. I tweeted a photo of myself at the pole with the Red Cross, a sign of hope with a brief message dedicating my endeavor to the victims of the Boston bombing.

#bostonmarathon
#handsoverhearts
#bostonstrong

I had to stop scrolling through the images. So much suffering. Standing in the precisely engineered Scandinavian hotel shower, scrubbing the sweaty grit of the expedition from my face and body, I felt jarred and humble. I lay down on the bed, wet hair wrapped in a thick white towel, and pulled the duvet over myself. I was profoundly exhausted, physically and spiritually, but when I closed my eyes, all I saw was damage. That's the difference between suffering and damage. Suffering is something you feel. Damage is something you see, something that cannot be denied.

The polar ice cap is a quintessential artifact of climate change. Surveying that expanse of mottled ice and open water is like looking at a haunted house, a venerable old mansion with smashed-in windows and broken beams. It's not a natural process of graceful aging. It's vandalism. It's damage, just as violent and wrong and life-averse as the shattered storefronts in Boston. *Damage* had this fresh avatar now, but there was nothing new about it. *Damage*, like a bullying demigod, had shaken my world from the time I was a child. In the images of the bloody sidewalk, I saw my mother's veiny stump. In the declining ice cap, I saw the carelessly disposed life of my brother. All the violence in the world mirrored the violence in my own family. All the lost parts of the planet mirrored lost parts of myself.

Whatever poet mused about life as a journey rather than a destination forgot to mention the proverbial forks in the road. I could see it now, from this perspective. The only way out was up. No matter how bad it hurt, I had to keep climbing.

PART III

FRIENDS IN HIGH PLACES

22

I returned from the North Pole in April 2013, making my way through a flurry of morning shows and media, and began speaking about my experiences to academic and corporate audiences. Penny was pleased when a Boston radio station named me Badass Chick of the Week, and I was interviewed (fully clothed) on *The Playboy Radio Show*. I answered the same questions in a hundred different interviews, and came up with a hundred kindergarten-through-college-level ways to explain the drastic impact of disappearing Arctic sea ice.

I never stopped training. In 2014, I summited Mount Whitney in April (14,508 feet), Mont Blanc in June (15,781 feet), and Manaslu (26,759 feet) in September. And then I got an email out of the blue.

Would you consider climbing K2?

Short answer: I would. I had. What serious climber hasn't?

Every time someone mentions K2, the climbers in the room sit up straight. K2 is only for the valiant, the proven, the true mountaineers among us. Women did not begin climbing this mountain until 1986, and the first five women who summited it perished on either K2 or other mountains, which spawned whispers of a "K2 curse on women." K2 kills one out of four climbers who attempt to summit. I didn't mind admitting, *this mountain scared the shit out of me*, and my answer to anything that scares the shit out of me is research. I did what I'd done for Everest. I observed, read, calculated, Googled, and spreadsheeted every nook and cranny. I studied the politics of the region and the composition of the stones. I went down the rabbit hole of history, fascinated by the early expeditions, and it dawned on me that the race to climb the highest mountains was a World Cup competition to prove a country's superiority. Inspired by those stories, I wasn't scared of K2 anymore. The most daunting aspect before me now was the dreaded naughty chair.

Before I brought it up to Jonathan, I made sure I had all my logistical ducks in well-regimented rows. I made sure we were at a good restaurant with a lovely tasting menu and matching wines.

"Climbers on K2 are having a great year." I tried to say it casually, but Jonathan's spousometer was on high alert.

"Of course. Here we go."

"Wait, wait. Before you say—"

"K2 is not Everest," he said. "It's hard. People die on it. *A lot of people* die on it."

"I know that. I've done the research. I understand what it takes to do this with a reasonable amount of caution."

"Oh, a reasonable amount of caution. Good on you. That should do the trick."

This is what passes for an argument with an Englishman. Jonathan is embedded with a *Sense and Sensibility* protocol chip I don't have. When eating fish, he must have a fish knife—not because it's the epitome of gentility, but because the end is pointy enough to pick fine bones and the scalloped blade is flat enough to remove the flesh from the skin. He rolls his eyes if you wrongly call someone Lady Firstname if she has inherited the title from her husband and therefore should be addressed as Lady Lastname. He opens doors and pulls back chairs. He would never let a woman pick up a check. At first, the feminist in me rebelled against that, but then I remembered a woman's seventy-eight cents to a man's dollar and thought, *I'm no fool*.

"It's not my job to say no," said Jonathan, "but I encourage you to think extensively about whether you really want to do this."

"I've thought about it. Extensively."

"Well, then." He folded his napkin. "So you get the mountains. What do I get?"

"Spousey . . ." I had no answer. Frankly, the candor caught me by surprise. "What do you want?"

"A boat."

"A boat?" I laughed. "Sure. Great idea."

"I felt pretty solid calling that bluff," I told my friends later. "He had a boat in Hong Kong and hated it."

I had to go along to get along, but I began training for K2. Back to running up and down the stairs. Back to the gym. Back to Jay Mills. Back to cold showers in the insanely early morning. I hoisted myself up ropes, scrambled over rocks, and hiked icy ridges in Colorado and Canada. Alone in the heavy snow on Lady MacDonald, a relatively simple 8,550-foot peak in Alberta, Canada, I traversed a ridge as narrow as a knife's edge, where I intended to place my name and the date on a piece of paper in a thermal canister on the summit. I couldn't just walk the ridge or even balance on it because of the ice and snow. When the ridge became icy and less than three feet wide, I had to drop over the edge and use my hands, placing my feet over the side. There was a sheer 3,000-foot drop on the right and about 2,500 feet of 80-degree incline on the left. I had no hiking poles, no crampons or microspikes for my shoes, no headlamp. No margin for error, one way or the other.

I forced myself to go slow, feeling my way, until I reached a snowdrift that concealed a stone cairn marking the true summit. I truffle-hunted through the snow, thinking, *What if there is no pen? Won't that be hilarious.* I found the canister and opened it. Pencil and paper. I scrawled my name and the date as neatly as I could with cold hands, and sat for a little while on the jumbled pile of Precambrian rocks, watching cloud shadows steal across the river valley far below.

Who are you when no one is looking?

The question usually goes to personal and professional ethics, but this was one of many moments when I embraced the challenge as a climber. It took me a while to know the answer. I'm the climber who troubleshoots; who scuttles, sometimes ungracefully; who doesn't care if anyone is looking or not, because I am there for myself, because it's there, and because I can.

On top of the intense training schedule, plotting the logistics of traveling through Pakistan presented a host of concerns and challenges. Decisions about what to wear were complicated by my desire to be sensitive and respectful, but at what point does "when in Rome" become cultural appropriation? I studied pictures of Mrs. Benazir Bhutto, former prime minister of Pakistan, noting the rich colors and elegant drape of her wardrobe. I was happy to rock whatever style was deemed inoffensive by high- and low-altitude porters—hijab, niqab, burka, abaya, or shalwar kameez—but how was I supposed to climb in anything but the unisex gingerbread-man getup worn by my male counterparts? The eight-week expedition would cover the month of Ramadan. I worried that porters, cooks, and other staff might feel ill, fasting from sunrise to sunset, or that they'd be annoyed to see non-Muslims guzzling energy gels and water, as I would most definitely be.

In June 2013, sixteen militants stormed a high-altitude base camp on Nanga Parbat, not too far from K2, killing a local guide and ten climbers. The incident got little press in America, but it sent a shock wave through the climbing community. Taking all my travels in stride, there's foreign in terms of geographical boundaries, and there's *foreign* in the existential *who the fuck does things like that?* sense of the word. In the peace-loving, multinational world of climbers and guides, this was unthinkable. Now I was learning everything I could about the culture and the country where the Taliban, ISIS, Al Qaeda, and any number of terrorist upstarts share a common hatred of Western ideals in general, with a particular loathing for the United States. I consulted with various US military personnel and international security firms, setting aside the fact that I had no funds for security, since every penny I had was going into equipment, supplies, and logistics.

Their expert advice: "Don't go."

"How do I get to *yes*, here?"

"Look, I don't care if you're Hillary Clinton, Theresa May, and Angelina Jolie rolled into one—pay ten grand a day—whatever. There's no guarantee someone could protect you in Pakistan. My advice is, *don't go.*"

"Okay, so *when* I go—"

I heard a distinct sigh. "Don't call attention to yourself."

"Okay. Anything else?"

"Don't be in the wrong place at the wrong time."

Fucking hell. I'd prefer to have a few specifics.

The media seemed intensely focused on how dangerous Pakistan was, but a kid from Detroit is fairly hard to impress. When it comes to talk of dangerous neighborhoods, I could name a few in the US and the UK that give Pakistan a run for its money. I was willing to risk it, relying on well-informed caution along with the Law of Attraction that seemed to draw good things my way in my past travels off the beaten path. James Michener said it quite well in *Holiday* magazine: "If you reject the food, ignore the customs, fear the religion, and avoid the people, you might better stay home."

I signed with a climbing company that had led a successful K2 expedition the year before, but the guide, Vincent, was on Everest at the moment, so I turned to my girlfriend Aurelia Bonito, who connected me with the best resource I could have tapped into: people, friends of friends, actual human beings who defied all the common stereotypes and bad press. Aurelia introduced me to her Pakistani friends, and a support network began to take shape, people in London and Pakistan who were proud to help me take on this challenge. The more Pakistanis I met, the more impressed I became. Soon I had my first endorsement from Muhammad Arif Anis and the World Congress of Overseas Pakistanis, and then I made the acquaintance of an instrumental friend who, at the risk of being mysterious, I'll just call my Wingman. (If I told you, I'd have to kill you.)

I landed in Islamabad in June 2015, wearing a colorful kaftan purchased at the airport in Dubai. At the hotel, I met the rest of the team. We were seven: two Estonian guys, three American guys, a Frenchman, and me. Not one of us had been to K2, save Vincent, the expedition leader, and Vincent had just come off Everest. He had been there during the recent earthquake that killed nine thousand people in Nepal, including twenty-two people at Everest Base Camp. We were all rightfully shaken by the event, but he'd been in the thick of it, and I could see the weight of it still on his shoulders.

Expeditions to the Karakoram were always escorted by an LO (liaison officer), a cross between a Secret Service agent and that girlfriend who always has your back. It's a procedural presence with the added comfort of having someone on your side who's a little bit badass. In the past, they were Pakistan Army officers, but our LO, Major Satti, was an air force officer. Mirza Ali, the owner of Karakorum Expeditions, would be providing Vincent with local logistics and joining us with his sister on K2, which was a new development. I was excited to meet them both, especially his sister, Samina Baig, who was the first Pakistani woman to climb all the Seven Summits. Mirza had climbed all the Seven Summits except Everest, and happened to be trying for Everest when the earthquake struck earlier this season. Vincent used Nazir Sabir Expeditions (NSE) for his successful K2 summit the previous year and I wondered why he would change things up, but I trusted Vincent, and Mirza made a good first impression, both knowledgeable and friendly.

After a quick breakfast with the climbing team, I had an appointment with the US Embassy and was hoping to meet the British High Commission while I was in the area. As the taxi pulled up, I grabbed a mint from a bowl on the front desk.

"Assalaam alaikum," I said to the taxi driver. "Diplomatic Enclave."

Islamabad is a beautiful city. As we drove past lush green belts, flowering trees, and stately homes, I felt like I was more in Holland Park, London, than Islamabad. I unwrapped the mint and popped it in my mouth, and I must have absentmindedly bit down on it because suddenly I tasted a sickly sweetness and a sharp tang of salt. *No, no, no, no, no!* I grabbed a Kleenex and spit out candy bits, blood, and my damn tooth. I flashed on a scene from a spy novel in which empty cavities were used to torture people. At altitude, the agony would be debilitating, never mind the potential for infection. *Fuck my life! What to do? What to do?* Losing a tooth was not on my risk-assessment list. It was a molar, not a front tooth, so I could do the meet-and-greet, but then what? It was Ramadan. Nothing was open. We were flying to Skardu first thing in the morning.

At the American embassy, Saba, my liaison, greeted me with a warm smile. "Vanessa! It's so great to finally meet you."

"Saba. Yes. Likewise. But—this is so embarrassing. Something terrible just happened." I tried to keep the desperation to a minimum as I explained.

"Oh no," she said. "The whole tooth?"

"The whole tooth and nothing but the tooth, swear to God," I said.

She laughed. "We'll get it sorted. Don't worry."

"You're a lifesaver."

The meeting was blessedly brief. The ambassador and I shared a few minutes of small talk and posed for photos. (I imagined his aide sidebarring the photographer: "File those, in case she doesn't make it.") Back in the lobby, Saba linked her arm through mine and steered me to the stairway. "We need to hurry. The dentist is waiting."

In the few minutes since I'd left her, she'd made a couple of calls, moved a dozen mountains, and an Embassy health care–recommended dentist was insisting I come to see him immediately.

"The car and driver will wait to take you back to the hotel," said Saba, indicating a bulky, bulletproof vehicle waiting to whisk me across Islamabad to Dr. Abrar, my angel of mercy. His office was state of the art, and he was fully versed in the high-altitude effects and danger of even the slightest bit of trapped air.

"You're lucky," he said. "You haven't cracked the tooth itself."

While he carefully cleaned it and settled it in place with bonding cement, he told me about a visit to New York ten years earlier.

"I was so lost. All those tall buildings and the subway system—

uptown, downtown, express, local—so confusing. A young woman stopped to help me read the subway map and showed me which train to get on. Someone else helped me exchange money. People were so kind to go out of their way for a stranger. It was a wonderful experience. I only wish more of my friends would come and visit me here, but they're afraid of the picture the Western media paints of Pakistan. That's an old view. Things have changed, but perceptions stay the same."

Perhaps it's for the best that my jaw was immobilized, because there was nothing I could say to mitigate his concern.

"All set," he said. "You will be safe at any altitude."

"Thank you so much. You saved my expedition. I can't tell you how much I appreciate it." I offered cash and a credit card, but he refused.

"No, no. Please, do not think of it," he said. "I never had the opportunity to repay that kindness of the people in New York," he said. "I only hope your experiences in Pakistan will make you want to share with the world that life here is not the way they might imagine."

"I will," I promised. I felt as if I'd stepped into a jet stream of kindness that would come full circle when I carried three flags—the UK's Union Jack, America's Old Glory, and Pakistan's Crescent and Star—to the summit of K2 as a gesture of friendship, peace, and solidarity. That Law of Attraction is a powerful force.

"Come. I want you to meet someone who may be helpful to you." Dr. Abrar led me to the waiting room and introduced me to a tall, silver-haired gentleman who grasped my hand with the intimidating cuddliness of a polar bear.

"So you are climbing K2," he said. "You must be very brave."

I smiled with the half of my face that wasn't paralyzed by Novocain and murmured, "Itsh shuch an honor to meet you."

I didn't know how important this man would become in my

own life—let's call him the Horseman (for his love of polo) nor that he would become "my first Pakistani uncle," but I knew from his rank and stature that he was a VIP in the complicated logistical territory I was trying to navigate.

"K2 is a savage mountain," he said, "and you are a petite girl. Please, take my WhatsApp number and send me updates so we can make sure there are no problems. When you return, we will have a celebratory dinner for you."

More than a little stunned, I thanked him and set the number in my phone, and two minutes later, I was back in the armored car. I'd been in Pakistan for less than ten hours and my whole paradigm had shifted. Those foreign military experts had advised me to not be in the wrong place at the wrong time, but they had it backward. The secret is to be in the right place at the right time.

I still had time to go to Khaadi, a popular clothing store, to shop for a shalwar kameez, a three-piece outfit with a long shirt, roomy pants, and a decorative long scarf that can be draped around your shoulders, over your head, or across your elbows in a variety of combinations. Some are over the top—beaded, embroidered, and very bling—but I promise there is no body type that doesn't look great in one. Feeling cool and classy, I was greeted at the Serena Hotel by the UN Women Country Representative, arranged by Yasmin, my contact, who presented me with the organization's flag. I wanted my climb to the summit to represent every woman's climb for equal pay and representation, the right to not be treated as second-class citizens. Even in the United States, we have a long way to go before women are equally protected under the law. While I fight my way through whatever blizzards nature throws at me, UN Women battles oppression, regulatory and legal systems, and religious persecution all over the world. Carrying this flag meant a lot to me.

Back at the hotel, my roller coaster day took another loop. The

hallway was a quagmire of suitcases, clothes, and people franti-
cally packing and repacking.

"Our flight's been canceled," said Vincent. "Mirza is suggesting
we leave at midnight on the Karakoram Highway."

"No way. That's shit. That'll take two days."

James, one of the American climbers and an IT specialist, showed
us a map online and said, "This shortcut here would only take about
twelve hours."

"No," said Mirza. "Foreigners aren't allowed to travel that route."

"Why not get the flights day after tomorrow?"

"Not enough seats."

"Mirza! *WTF?*" I said, stepping over piles of gear, quietly furious at Vincent. I called my Wingman, who had specifically instructed me: "Do not go by road to Skardu."

"How many of you are there?" Wingman asked.

"Eight, including Sherpa. The HAPs are already in Skardu."

"That's going to be hard," he said. "The planes don't fly every
day, and there is a convoluted back system of loading military, ci-
vilians, foreigners, and diplomats, not necessarily in that order.
Let me make a phone call and see what I can do."

An hour later, he called back. "I can get four airline tickets for
the day after tomorrow."

I signaled Mirza and Vincent. "Four plane tickets."

"We can't split the group," said Mirza. "Our liaison officer,
Major Satti, is supposed to accompany all of us. If you arrive before the rest of the team, there is no one with you in Skardu."

We went back and forth, Mirza lobbying hard to convince me
to go by bus, me taking him to task for not having sorted the plane
tickets in the first place, and Wingman listening to the whole
thing, getting progressively more pissed off. Finally, there seemed
to be no way around going by road.

"The minute you get to the vehicle," said Wingman, "send me a photo of the license plate. Do you copy?"

"Yes, I copy. My Garmin inReach tracker will send my coordinates every ten minutes."

"Only if there is a satellite."

"Right."

We left Islamabad at midnight so that we would hit the more sensitive areas in daylight, duffel bags lashed to the roof of the minibus. Sitting up front, where I hoped it might be less bumpy, I texted the license plate photo to Wingman, as instructed, and switched on the tracker. The night air was hot and humid, and I was too tired to be nervous. An hour or so up the Karakoram Highway, I was nodding off when the bus lurched to a halt, and a Pakistan Army soldier with an AK-47 hopped aboard. He rode with us for a while and then hopped off, and another soldier jumped on. Major Satti and Mirza exchanged nervous glances. The added muscle with the machine guns—this was something extra.

"I have never seen so much security, I have no idea what is going on," Mirza said irritably, but I smiled, grateful for the tides and eddies of a benevolent universe.

Crammed into the suffocating heat of the minibus, we couldn't drink water, because stopping to pee put everyone in danger of being spotted in the open, so we jounced along in sweaty misery, staring out the windows, traveling at a breakneck speed of twenty-five miles per hour. This dodgy dirt road, one of the highest byways in the world, is part of the original Silk Road, a network of trading routes. It dates back two centuries before the birth of Christ, and I'm certain many of the same potholes were around then. I could feel the bones rattling in my ears. The road is barely wide enough for one vehicle, so oncoming traffic was a life-or-death game of chicken.

It took us eleven hours to travel less than 225 miles, so there was plenty of time to enjoy the scenery. Scrubby foothills hunkered over raging waters. The winding Indus River seemed to have no end. We stopped for the night in Chilas because foreigners were not allowed to travel in this sector at night. Instead of eating from the hotel buffet, full of generous but unfamiliar food, I ordered a sandwich with fries and a Coke.

The bathroom had an electric light, but everything else was lit by candles, so I used my headlamp for my ritual insect scan and nodded off. The next morning, I woke up feeling a bit bilious. The sandwich. Mayonnaise. *Fuck. My. Life.*

We drove all day. Three mountain ranges—the Himalayas, the Hindu Kush, and the Karakoram—all converge here, with Nanga Parbat towering in the distance. I tried to take it in, but every time I raised my eyes, my lower intestines twisted into a knot. When we stopped for lunch, I made the one safe choice—a Coke—but the long afternoon was another 160 grueling miles of sheer misery. I managed to keep it together until I reached my hotel room in Skardu, where I was utterly wrung out by a combination of vomiting and diarrhea.

Someone knocked on the door. "Supper, Vanessa."

"I'll pass," I croaked without opening my eyes.

I was deep in clammy, wish-I-were-dead sleep the next morning when Major Satti knocked on my door. "Vanessa? Are you all right?"

Apparently, my Wingman had become concerned when I didn't answer my phone, and he sent my LO to check on me. Major Satti bustled me out the door, hastily draping something over my head to cover my hair.

"Where are we going?" I asked.

"CMH. Combined military hospital."

"Do they take women . . . foreigners?"

He didn't answer. Pulling up to the hospital, I saw two signs: ADMISSIONS and MORGUE. Heads or tails. I was carted to admissions in a wheelchair. Somewhere along the way, I threw up on some flowers. The next thing I remember is a curtained cubicle. I woke up with an IV in my arm. I winced at the sound of phlegmy coughing somewhere on the other side of the room. It reminded me of one Christmas when Ben and I wrapped shoe boxes filled with various gifts designated "male" and "female" and helped Mom deliver them to the hospital. I remember how happy the patients were to receive the gifts, how it didn't really matter what was in the box, just that someone cared. Wingman confided in me later that my CMH treatment was thanks to a second Pakistani uncle, Arif Aslam Khan, whom I would come to know and adore as the owner of the Shangrila Resort Hotel in Skardu.

The next day, the local military commander came to visit me. I mustered a wan smile and tried to sit up. "Assalaam alaikum."

"How is it that I have a mountaineer in my hospital?" he teased. "Is it not from mountaineers we learn the importance of staying hydrated?"

"Also the importance of avoiding long bus rides."

He laughed, and we chatted for a while. By the time he left, I felt I'd gained another guardian angel. Then the hospital's head doctor and his son arrived with a large "Get Well Soon" fruit basket.

"How's our special visitor? Feeling better?"

"Feeling embarrassed," I said. "I think I'm good to go. I've had three bags of IV fluid, and I have ciprofloxacin in my med kit."

"How about one more day of rest?"

"No, you've been too kind. I'm taking up valuable space here. I am extremely grateful to you and your team." It's hard to adequately express how grateful I was. The people of Pakistan cared for me with genuine respect, concern, and hospitality beyond anything I'd experienced anywhere else in the world, including the house I grew up in.

Back at the hotel, I noticed swelling in my arm. One of my teammates was a doctor, so he examined it. "The IV may have been leaking a bit," he said. "Let's mark it so we know if the redness is spreading." He used a black Sharpie to tattoo my bloated arm with what looked like two large amoebas. Whatever. As long as I could jam it into my summit suit, I was fine.

From Skardu, we traveled by jeep, on road and off, higher into the hills, past freshly tumbled boulders and landslides slick with mud—a not-so-subtle reminder that timing is everything—until we reached a footbridge. We man-hauled our equipment to the other side, where new jeeps were waiting to take us to Askole, and from there, we started trekking.

We set out at dawn, hoping to beat the July heat, and still feeling a bit wobbly, I quickly fell behind the others. Hiking along the Braldu River, I kept my eyes riveted on the silver and amber peaks, breathing through the cramps as each new wave of distress turned my duodenum inside out. When I couldn't force myself to march on, I ducked into the underbrush and squatted in the shade of an apricot grove, melting an Imodium Instant on my tongue, watching a horse graze on the riverbank. I no longer wondered how a horse could walk and shit at the same time. I was now an expert at it. Such is the glamorous life of the explorer.

I continued up the road. The sun climbed higher and hotter, hotter and higher. When I stopped to hydrate, a group of climbers and HAPs heading in the same direction stopped to chat me up.

"Who are you trekking with?" they asked.

"Mirza. And you?"

"Nazir Sabir Expeditions."

I recognized the name. This was the logistics company Vincent had used on his successful K2 summit the year before. It was owned by Nazir Sabir, the first Pakistani mountaineer to climb Everest.

One of the NSE HAPs asked, "Are you feeling okay?"

"No, not so good," I said. "My stomach."

"And they left you by yourself?" He did not like this. I assured him I was okay and they were just ahead, but he insisted on walking with me until we caught up with Mirza and Vincent, who had posted up in the shade for a snack.

"*Shukriya*," I said to the HAP, and gave him some rupees as a thank-you for his kindness.

"How are you doing?" asked Mirza.

I shrugged. "It is what it is."

"Just a little farther to the bridge and then we'll reach our camp at Jhola."

"Whatever." I slumped against the tree with my head in my hands. "Dammit, Mirza, why couldn't you get the flights? Now I'm sick. This could kill the whole expedition for me."

The sound of my own whining circled my aching head like a cloud of mosquitoes. I hated feeling weak, and the next day, I felt weaker. We were on the trail at 5 AM to avoid the heat, climbing along a sandy beach, of all things, en route to Paiyu. I was praying, eating Imodium Instants like they were communion wafers. Nothing helped. We trekked up the Baltoro Glacier to Urdukas, then Goro II, and then Concordia, seven and a half miles from K2 Base Camp. I saw K2 for the first time. So close, so high, so grand and glorious. It was humbling. As ill as I was, the intense beauty of the mountain was enough to take my breath away.

We reached K2 Base Camp on July 7, and I spent the next two days in my tent, barely moving. I'd gone through a seven-day supply of medicine and trashed several pairs of underwear, which I would now have to carry out, leaving me two pairs to wash and wear. I organized the tent that would be my home for the next seven weeks, taking comfort in the orderliness. All I wanted was a shower and a clean start to the expedition.

The next day was auspicious, so I gathered my equipment and gifts for our Puja ceremony. Looking around, I saw some familiar faces. Russell Brice had an expedition, so I was happy to see the guides I'd climbed with on Manaslu and a few other folks I'd met over the past six years of climbing and knocking about. This community could not have been more different from the circle of friends with whom I spend much of my time when I'm home, but I felt equally at home here, just as much among friends. We celebrated Masood's birthday with candles that acted like fireworks and almost set the mess tent on fire. James sorted our internet, and with the arrival of my favorite Sherpa, Kami, my Shishapangma friend and confidant, things seemed to be on an upturn.

I'd brought ten one-liter Nalgene bottles to take glacier samples that would show whether glaciers were receding and whether these snow samples contained pollution. I planned to take samples from 0 to 140 centimeters down using an avalanche probe. These glacial samples could be run through a mass spectrometer to see which, if any, lead components showed up. Events like the Soviet nuclear tests in the 1960s or Japan's Fukushima nuclear disaster in 2011 emit lead content that travels through the atmosphere and gets trapped in the glacial ice, providing a date stamp on each sample, and together, they create a pixelated snapshot of our changing climate. I was excited to participate in the science. In previous experiments, I'd used my body to see if large doses of acetazolamide (Diamox), a diuretic used to treat AMS, might lead to kidney stones, and unfortunately in my case it did. I also tested whether using hypoxic tents that utilize a gas exchange system at low altitude could be used to pre-acclimatize and change blood composition. Unfortunately, I was a "nonresponder."

We made our first acclimatization hike to the bottom of the Abruzzi Ridge, but Kami, who'd summited K2 before, suggested taking samples at some interesting glaciers up by Camp 3.

"The higher the better," I agreed.

We spent one night at ABC, and the next morning made it halfway to Camp 1 before it started snowing and we had to turn around. Okay, I figured. Early in the season. Not a huge setback. After a rest day, we got up at 3:30 AM and climbed directly to Camp 1, where the real estate for tents was limited, but the view was magnificent. I shared a tent with James, who wasn't much of a snorer, so we both slept well and felt great the next day.

We headed for Camp 2, bracing ourselves for one of the legendary hurdles on K2: House's Chimney, a vertical slot carved 100 feet high into the rock face, crusted with ice and snow. Along the steep approach, you clip into fixed lines and then start up that vertical rock face, one hand pushing the jumar up on the rope, the other hand steadying your bearing on the rock. I hate crampons on rock. It's the wrong tool for the job, but that's the tool you have, lacking Inspector Gadget footwear that sucks your spikes in at the touch of a button. (When is someone going to invent that? When!) You end up clawing the front point of your crampons against the wall, like a crow, trying to catch whatever tiny purchase you can find, even if it's only a minuscule ledge. Very unhelpfully, some long-ago climber suspended a hand ladder from the top of the chimney, so that thing dangles there in a mess of tangled ropes. At first you think, "Hey, a ladder. Great idea." Think again. Nature did not put that there. It's a terrible idea. Grabbing the hand ladder pulls your center of gravity away from the rock, making your situation more unstable, but *because it's there*, everyone makes this mistake. Once.

As I wedged my way up the Chimney, my backpack caught on

an overhang and yanked me back. Startled and groping for a hand-hold, I took a moment to regain my stability. I changed anchors, fought through the tangled ropes, and finally squeezed through the Chimney itself. My big backpack was like a cork in a bottle. To ascend the chimney, one must be creative, stepping backward, using triceps dips, applying a variety of gymnastics. "Please take a moment to locate your nearest exit. It may be behind you!" Wriggling and wrangling, you pop out the top like a prairie dog. My first time up House's Chimney wasn't pretty, but I pulled it off and was rewarded with a panoramic view of Base Camp and the Karakoram below.

At Camp 2, James and I prepared our tent and shared some Action Wipes, awesome tea tree oil and eucalyptus body wipes that renew a climber's outlook on life and make it possible to spend the night in close quarters with a relative stranger. The next day, we climbed to the base of the Black Pyramid, another technically challenging rock bottleneck almost 1,500 feet high. James and I both felt good enough to go on, debating the merits of climbing higher.

"Maybe we could go up the way they did in 1938 and '39," I said. "Americans made it to almost 8,400 meters."

"And . . . ?"

"It got dark," I said. "The Sherpa got nervous about night spirits. Dropped both pairs of crampons. So they had to descend to Base Camp. They promised a climber they'd come back up, but after twenty-six days above 22,000 feet, it was like . . ." I shook my head, and James totally understood. "So three Sherpa are sent up after the guy."

"And . . . ?"

"First four deaths on K2."

"Ah. On that cheery note . . ."

The next day, we headed down to Base Camp, rewarded by the afternoon sun as it illuminated a haze of ice crystals, creating rainbows in the air.

"Seems like the weather's shifting," I said to Kami and James.

Kami nodded. "El Niño this year."

Two days later, we were inundated with heavy snow, and talk turned to avalanche risk, so we waited, reading, sleeping, and playing games. The Frenchman played with his drone, capturing dramatic footage of the shifting mountainside. Ever-vigilant Major Satti fretted about needing government permission to do this and checked all our footage to ensure we only took pictures and film of the tents from above and nothing else. It was unseasonably warm, with subpar snow conditions—hard blue ice with a sugary snow-cone consistency on top—so the route deteriorated. Avalanches, snow slides, and rockfall were an almost daily occurrence. Another team's ABC was buried. No lives were lost, luckily, but plenty of gear disappeared. Then disaster struck too close to home.

On a mission to retrieve equipment from a higher camp, Kami was injured by falling rocks. Listening to the panicked chatter on the radio, my heart sank. It was bad. Our doctor ran to get the doctor from Russell's camp. We cleared out a storage tent, creating a make-shift hospital, and waited for them to bring him down. By the time they reached us, Kami was mumbling and sobbing, surrounded by Sherpa and HAPs, his misshapen arm wrapped in bloody clothing. I had never seen a Sherpa cry, and this wasn't just any Sherpa, this was Kami, my mate since Shishapangma, Phinjo Dorjee's father.

People crowded the doorway until the doctor shouted at them to get the hell out. He tore Kami's shirt, and Kami screamed in pain.

"Dislocated shoulder," the doctor said. "Broken arm. Broken wrist."

Kami wailed, disconsolate at the thought of permanent disability. I gripped his good hand and whispered, "Don't worry, Kami. Everything will be okay."

I passed the doctor clean wet cloths and alcohol, and he started an IV with morphine for the pain and ketamine to erase the painful memory. Kami faded into a sedated half life while the doctor attempted to put the shoulder back in place, yanking it this way and that, to no avail. The sight made me shudder. I fetched some Norco from my med kit—a combination of acetaminophen and hydrocodone for pain. Kami was going to need it when the morphine wore off. I slept by his side and saw him off when the rescue helicopter came the next morning. Now it was my turn to cry. With Kami on his way to CMH Skardu, I texted Wingman, "Please, make sure they take good care of him."

Avalanches, accidents, El Niño—it was too much. Teams were packing up to leave. Gutted, James and I made our way to Gilkey Memorial, where I'd promised to light candles.

In 1953, American climber Art Gilkey was stricken with blood clots in his left calf and if one of those clots broke loose and reached his lungs, it would prove fatal. The team attempted to lower Art, in his sleeping bag, roped together, struggling over rocks and ice during a raging storm. At one point, a teammate slipped, creating a domino effect as each man was plucked off the mountain. At the end of the line Pete Schoening had wedged his ice axe against a boulder frozen in the mountainside, and stopped the fall of all six men, including Art Gilkey.

Unfortunately, it wouldn't save Art's life, but this ice axe belay did save the others, becoming the most famous belay in history. Art was allegedly swept away by an avalanche during a stop at a camp on descent, but there were no witnesses. His friends and the HAPs gathered stones to build a memorial cairn, which now serves as hallowed ground where lost climbers are remembered. When there are no remains to inter, the disappeared are presumed dead, their passage marked with a name punched by a piton into a tin supper dish.

In somber silence, I lit candles and prayed for the dead, as if the mountains were a vast cathedral, and then we sat looking at K2, and K2 sat looking back at us.

"With Kami gone and K2 over," I said to James, "maybe we should give Broad Peak a go. It's only an hour away."

Broad Peak is the twelfth-highest mountain in the world, at 26,414 feet. Deep snow makes it hard to break trail, and there's no high camp. The round trip from Camp 3 to the summit and back again can take twenty-three hours. A few climbers from another expedition decided to go for it, but when I asked around our dinner table, Vincent was the only one who didn't say no. Everyone else was out, citing the shit weather and shittier forecast.

"Just as well," I said. "It'll be faster with only the two of us. We might be able to catch up with the other team."

Vincent called porters to take the rest of the team back to Askole, but early the next morning, at the dawn of a surprisingly clear day, people changed their minds and wanted to come with us. Trying to keep his clients happy, Vincent acted like this was perfectly fine, but I said, "Wait a minute. Their bags are packed for Askole, not Broad Peak. The porters are here. This will slow us down and cost money. And what if the weather turns and they change their minds again when the snow is thigh deep? With no other guides, who takes them down? *You*. So I'll be forced to go down too."

Voicing these concerns did not make me popular, but ultimately, indecision made the decision. It was time to go. The day turned overcast as Vincent and I headed out. The other team was already at Broad Peak Camp 2, so we climbed to Camp 1, planning to get up early, skip Camp 2, and proceed to Camp 3, but the next day, we saw climbers descending.

"Snow is too deep above Camp 3," one climber said. "It's impossible."

Gee, I'm thinking, *where have I heard that before?* People tend to exaggerate to make themselves feel better about turning around, so by way of a reality check, I said, "How deep? Can you show me against your boot?"

He pointed just below his kneecap and continued down.

Vincent radioed Camp 3. A few optimists remained, hoping for better weather.

"Okay," he said, "let's hang out here. See if they abort."

God, I hate groupthink. *Hey, here's a bold idea! Let's sit on our thumbs, and see what other people do.* Where's the leadership? Eventually, the answer is obvious because all other options have evaporated. Of course, pointing that out is—again—not popular. Well, fuck it! Popularity comes at a high price. As do summits. And corner offices. I'll give another climber the shirt off my back—I have literally done that!—but don't ask me to smile and be nice and keep my pretty mouth shut. I don't have it in me.

The next morning, it was snowing again. Perfect excuse for everyone to bail. (No, really. This time I mean it. You have to assess avalanche danger in real time with a cold eye on wishful thinking.) I saw another climber descending and asked, "How deep is it? Show me against your boot." He pointed just above his knee.

So that was the end of the Broad Peak climb.

"Sounds like it was always a long shot," my friend Maya pointed out later when I unloaded the whole saga.

"Yeah," I said, "but long shots are my specialty."

I focused on collecting the best glacial samples available in the time I had left, which meant I had to go back to ABC. James waited for me at Base Camp. I packed my avalanche probe, sanitary gloves, and a few essentials, knowing that when I returned, Base Camp (except for James) would be gone and I'd have to hustle to catch up with the descending team. I was grateful that two HAPs were game to join me, and we found a good crevasse just under 5,500 meters. We worked together, one of us marking the bottles with GPS coordinates, one of us holding the avalanche probe, and the third person chopping away the ice. It took several hours, so we were finding our way down the glacier as night was falling, a rocky balancing act that destroys boots and turns ankles with a vengeance.

The return trip to Islamabad was a comedy of errors involving another lengthy bus ride, despite being cleared for the shorter route. Major Satti insisted on doing things by the book. Wingman texted me as we passed his alma mater, Army Burn Hall College in Abbottabad, which used to operate along English public school lines. It was a signal that we were close to home.

Before I left Islamabad, I scheduled one important dinner at the Monal, a restaurant high on a hill at the edge of the city. The Monal was advertised as "a great place to enjoy the awesome weather," and who better to enjoy it with than fellow climber Nazir Sabir. Nazir's legendary career is a high-wire walk between politics and climbing, and he agrees with me that crampons on rock is no fun at all. Only a real man and mountaineer will admit that it feels like roller-skating on ice. We sat outside the restaurant, drinking green tea and telling stories into the night, oblivious to a warm, steady rain. He listened to my tales of woe, nodding, interjecting valuable advice, and coaxing me to see the humor in it. I found his climbing stories fascinating, paralleling mine in equal and opposite ways that made me laugh. That dinner cemented the start of a great friendship, and anyone looking in that night could have easily spotted the two of us for who we were—mountaineers completely soaked by the rain, oblivious and unbothered by it at the same time.

When I went to return the never-unfolded flag to Yasmin and her colleagues at UN Women, they said, "Keep it. We know you'll be back." So I flew home hopeful, thinking about those remarkable ice crystal rainbows, harbingers of the shifting weather, but also a lesson in silver linings and serendipitous connections. This expedition wasn't a success by any metric, but it didn't leave a bitter taste. I made the acquaintance of this storied mountain, which put all the tales of terror in perspective, and I connected with wonderful people who took me under their wings, educated me, and became powerful allies.

It wasn't the celebratory dinner I had hoped for, but the Horseman took Vincent and me out to dinner at the Islamabad Club with his family. I laughed when a pair of shoes and a jacket were quickly ushered in for Vincent. The maître d' couldn't do anything about the mountaineer jeans, so Vincent was instructed to sit and not move while the buffet was brought to him.

When I returned home and had the ice samples analyzed, we did find elements of pollution. Microscopic particles had ridden nomadic westerly winds thousands of miles to settle in the Karakoram. I knew that I could help the Pakistani government combat this in the future simply by providing boots on the ground to measure it. Eventually this glacier will melt, feeding headwaters, streams, and irrigation systems, reminding us that, for better or worse, no place—no person—on our fragile planet is ever truly isolated.

23

There is no such thing as bad weather, only inappropriate clothing.
—SIR RANULPH FIENNES, WORLD'S GREATEST LIVING
EXPLORER, GUINNESS WORLD RECORDS

No sooner did I choose this quote than I found popular mountain blogger and author Mark Horrell commenting on his blog, "another annoying platitude debunked by Cairngorm Ranger Nic Bullivant," who said, "It was coined for places that don't have really bad weather." I can't argue with that. There's always an element of "life goes on" while you're pursuing a static target. The mountain isn't going anywhere. It'll be there when you get back. Other people and things you love aren't as timelessly solid. My father's Parkinson's was advancing, so I made an effort to see him once in a while. My friends in London, Hong Kong, and the United States had been unfailingly supportive, so I made an effort to be a better listener and promised to say yes to more social invitations rather than train all the time.

Jonathan accepted a great job in New York, and I was happy to support the move. God knows, he's made his share of compromises for me. We found a condo bordering SoHo and Chinatown, which rather summed up where we came from. Turn right for Hong Kong, left for London. I'd lived in New York years earlier as a student, but to say I knew the city post–Koch, Giuliani, and Bloomberg—that wouldn't be entirely true. I searched out new ways and places to train, and K2 was always at the back of my mind. The tectonic plates in my subconscious kept shifting, lifting the peak's prominence, causing tremors and landslides. It was time to have the conversation.

"What do you think about a K2: Season 2," I said early in 2016, skipping the fish fork. "If I take everything I've learned, add and subtract, it would be totally different."

I felt safe promising that, because I had decided—for a lot of reasons—to lead this expedition myself. Maybe it was that tipping point Malcolm Gladwell talks about when he says if you devote ten thousand hours to a specific task, you become a master of it. Climbing mountains is about knowing yourself as much as it is about knowing how to climb, and I'd spent a lot of time inside my head since I started training for Everest. I'd rather push boundaries than dwell on limitations, but it's daunting to acknowledge the true height and depth of our own potential. Suddenly, we're confronted with the hard work of fulfilling it.

Precious few expeditions are led or co-led by women. It's rare for a team to have a female majority or a woman's name on the climbing permit. I never took for granted the opportunities, mentors, and assistance that came my way. I was grateful to all who'd lent their experience to help me get to the top of the mountains. Now I felt a responsibility to step up and set a good example, because I finally felt that solid core of *I can*. Real-time leadership and decision making are key to success on a mountain, where things move at a glacial pace right up until they move like lightning. I was willing to call shots and take risks, however popular or unpopular, and I had strong ideas about the type of team I wanted to create.

NSE would provide local logistics. This and other big decisions were easy, but team chemistry requires fine-tuning. History is littered with stories of failed collaborations, broken promises, and best-laid plans with no plan B. The teams most likely to struggle are at opposite ends of the spectrum: large groups that end up cat herding or small groups that lack the resources to get the job done. My team was in the middle: small enough to be agile, but self-sufficient with supplies, equipment, oxygen, and ropes. We were eight: Benigno, an Ecuadorian guide, joined us. Kami Sherpa had recovered and was on board, along with three additional climbing Sherpa. We had two HAPs, including Fazal Ali, who'd summited K2 before. Farman Ullah Baig, my first choice as cook, would keep the (figurative) home fires burning.

I wanted to share this experience with sponsors, hoping to offset costs, of course, but more important, I wanted to share this incredibly rare opportunity with people and products I believed in. Hard work, focus, resilience, mitigating and sharing risks—the powerful values of mountaineering—dovetail so beautifully with a company's strong statement of purpose, and K2 is the perfect vehicle for all that. My letter-writing campaign met with old-school reticence for all of the old-school reasons. When the last remnant of my savings ran out, Jonathan stepped up.

I parsed the expenses down to the last tea bag, gathered historical summit data, and cross-pollinated that with actual weather data from every day of June and July for the previous three years. In December, I went to Ecuador to study the receding glaciers and pre-acclimatize. Benigno and I summited Carihuairazo at 16,463 feet on a misty, muddy day, but the next day, as we descended a smaller volcano in the rain, my feet flew from under me. Instinctively, I braced myself for the fall, so when I landed on my butt, my arm wrenched back, tearing three ligaments in my shoulder. Every footstep forward triggered a bone-rattling javelin of pain.

As I sat in the Otavalo clinic waiting for X-ray results, I received a perfectly timed text from my friend, famed adventure journalist Jim Clash: "Keep your eye on the prize."

I pushed through the pain to climb Illiniza Norte and Cayambe, because this trip was about capturing and documenting the changes of glaciers at the equator. I went for an MRI in Quito, and Benigno tried to interpret the results, which looked something like: *adfalsdjf jafjklasdj fjafjda lks 9 dfjladjal.*

I texted Maya, who can always be counted on for support. "I just want to know what that 9 is doing in there. That can't be good."

"Nines are suspect," she agreed, "balancing on their little hind leg like that."

At times like this, you need to know a guy, as we say in New York, and luckily I knew Roger Härtl, MD. I scheduled rotator cuff tendon repair surgery for autumn—after K2—with Dr. Scott Rodeo. Meanwhile, I added ketorolac, an anti-inflammatory (NSAID), to my med kit, which is formidable, because I have a lot going on. My low thyroid plays havoc with temperature, energy, and metabolism. The screws and staples in my feet seem to conduct cold straight to the bone. Genetically, I'm at higher risk for clotting, heart attack, and stroke, but no one wants to give me a blood thinner, lest I fall and bleed out. Minor thrombosis lingered, along with a nice plump chalazion, which is basically a hemorrhoid on your eyelid. Honestly, it couldn't happen to a nicer person. Nobody—no body—is without issues, and extreme demands on the body require extreme vigilance. You try to stay ahead of all the abuse your body takes, so it doesn't get in the way.

Past expeditions, including Charlie Houston's 1953 K2, used potential summit moments to make a powerful statement promoting international friendship and solidarity, even painting the flags of the United States, United Kingdom, United Nations, and Pakistan when they forgot them. In 1990, Jim Whittaker's Everest summit promoted peace between Russia, China, and the United States. Now, friendship, solidarity, and resilience were needed here in Pakistan, so I took a page from Houston's and Whittaker's playbooks, carrying the three national flags plus the flag of UN Women.

In June 2016, I landed in Islamabad, paid a visit to Yasmin at UN Women, and touched base with friends and contacts. It felt great to be returning as a Goodwill Ambassador for Pakistan. I was excited to use my growing social media platform to chronicle my journey through this beautiful country. My work opened doors for all kinds of connections, including an earlier flight on an air force cargo plane from Rawalpindi to Skardu. My team and I spent a few days reorganizing our gear and getting paperwork in order. I was warned about an enormous landslide very close to our point of departure, but Rehmat Ali, NSE's operations manager, said, "Not to worry. The driver is bringing dynamite."

"Dynamite. Of course." I laughed.

"Don't worry. It's not under the passenger seat."

To avoid mispronouncing my name, our Pakistan Air Force LO, Flight Lieutenant Anwar, called me "Leader." He was quiet and reserved as we left Islamabad for Skardu, but the farther we went from the city, the more animated he became.

Chatting about the mountaineering course he had taken, Flt. Lt. Anwar said, "In order to get my final badge, I need you to sign a piece of paper saying we reached 6,000 meters."

"You know, I know, and the Pakistan Army knows that K2 Base Camp is only 5,000 meters—maybe 5,500 meters if you go to ABC. You'll have to join us when we go to Camp 1."

"Leader, it's just a piece of paper. Other expedition leaders sign it. I thought we get along. We like each other."

"Exactly. See, it's like this. If I didn't like you, I would sign it. Above 3,000 meters, every 300 meters count. What if you get AMS—acute mountain sickness—and you don't know the signs? You should know how it feels and what to do."

I'm sure he would have preferred that I just sign the damn paper, but he accepted my decision.

"I will make a promise to you, Leader. Nothing will happen to you as long as I am alive."

"Perfect. Then let's keep you alive, shall we?"

This was a busy season, with 112 permits issued for Western climbers, the Nepalese Sherpa supporting them, and HAPs covering K2, Broad Peak, and the surrounding mountains. Vincent was back, leading a group of five climbers, and there was also a large European expedition led by Kari Kobler. After a year of no summits in 2015, we were all eager to get up the mountain.

In Askole, we weighed and repacked everything for the porters. We trekked halfway to Urdukas and stopped for a day to acclimatize. (What a difference to do it feeling as well and strong as I felt now!) Hiking six hours each day, starting at 5 AM to beat the midday heat, we went on to the Baltoro Glacier, Goro II, Concordia, and K2 Base Camp. The first half of this sixty-mile trek was dry and dusty, but a cool breeze arose as we walked up the glacier. Mindful of the rocks under my feet—pebbles, then stones, then boulders—I focused fiercely, core tight. I wasn't going to let myself fall—and if I did, I was determined to let my head hit hard earth before I'd throw out my fragile shoulder.

At K2 Base Camp, while my team got settled, I hopped up on a rock to thank all the porters, and Farman's brother, Imam Yar Baig, helped me distribute their pay. We drew straws for who got to shower first and sat down to supper.

"Tomorrow is a lucky day," said Pasang Sherpa, who was also a lama. "Perfect timing. It's auspicious for a Puja."

We were the only team to have a Sherpa who was also a lama, so I had to let Pasang go off and lead the other teams' Pujas as well, reading the script from his iPhone, the perfect millennial

Sherpa. The next day, we began the same acclimatization pattern as the previous year, rotating and load-carrying to ABC to spend one night and climbing halfway to Camp 1 before returning to Base Camp, where I used my rest day to wrestle with the internet. I'd opted for the cheaper of two devices, which had green arrows ostensibly pointing to whatever satellite was cruising overhead, but it was like trying to align Venus with Mars. I was trying to download these bloody expensive weather forecasts, but my pay-as-you-go bandwidth was so slow, I felt like I was driving a Rolls-Royce down the Baltoro Glacier.

I was under the desk in our communications tent, splicing solar panels and rigging boxes with electrical tape, when one of the other team leaders stopped by to say hello. I'd been hearing all about this Diahanne Gilbert from the Sherpa, who are always eager to gossip.

"She's loud and obnoxious," they said. "You're going to hate her. She has pink hair and a mustache."

What an interesting microcosm of the most scandalous things that can be said about a woman: heavens to Betsy! How dare she not jump through hoops trying to make everyone like her? I came of age in the eighties, when pink hair was practically mandatory, and if you don't mind a hairy lip, why bother? She's Scottish and I was born in America, so technically we both have the wrong accent, but we're both British citizens, and we were the only two women leading expeditions on K2 that season.

She peered under the table and said, "Vanessa? Is that you? Hi, I'm Di Gilbert."

"Oh. Hi. Nice to meet you." I smiled up at her from the floor of the tent. Just then the little green arrows on my device suddenly stopped blinking, indicating the stars and moon were about to align in the ninth house. "Oh shit! Can I stop by later? I've been trying to get online all day. This internet is absolute crap and it looks like I just made my first connection."

"Sure thing." Then she walked away.

Wait. Did she just take that the wrong way? *Women*, right? Can't live with 'em, can't run a universe without 'em. Never mind all that. I was finally getting my first email via the fickle internet!

It said: "You have used $1,000 worth of internet."

WTF! That is not possible. I didn't want the fancy forecast images, just the facts. Wind speeds, direction, precipitation, temperature by height, and barometric pressure. Just one campsite down, the Europeans were receiving the very same weather reports I was grasping at, but they were not about to share. Dammit! More money I don't have to spend.

Up at 3 AM, I heard Farman shaking the tents, trying to get everyone to breakfast and out of camp to escape the heat and ensure we had tents at Camp 1, a notorious bottleneck with limited tent space. From ABC you free climb some steep terrain on what seems like a 50-degree incline. Constant warnings—"*ROCK!*"— echoed down the mountain as chips, chunks, and boulders once frozen to the earth became, thanks to climate change, unfrozen.

The next morning was another early start, this time to avoid the queue that can form below House's Chimney. Every time I approach House's Chimney, I try to learn from the last time I climbed it. It's just a rock chimney, so no big deal—if it were located anywhere else. On K2, it's not that straightforward. After a full day of climbing, we reached Camp 2, which is notoriously windy. All the tents are perched on a steep hill, with remnants of torn tents, mangled frames, and all manner of ghost gear from past expeditions embedded in the ice. With the wind howling and temperatures dropping, there's nothing better than crawling into your tent, shedding all that gear, taking off your socks, washing up, hydrating with a hot cup of tea, and preparing for a big evening meal. It doesn't matter if it's 2 PM or 6 PM, that is the ritual. These simple things offset the fierce concentration and intense physical work of getting there.

Somewhere in the world below, I had Jonathan logging on to my weather account, downloading reports, digesting them, and giving me Cliffs Notes for my Garmin inReach, which received texts but no visuals. I always feel better armed with the best information, but no one this side of Nostradamus is capable of accurately predicting the weather this high on K2. We spent two days huddled four to a tent, listening to the whistling wind and pelting snow until Farman radioed up to tell us we had to come down for an important dinner. July 6 was Eid al-Fitr, the end of Ramadan. It was an opportunity to reflect on the thirty days that many on our team had spent fasting and for all of us to recommit to our values of gratitude and compassion. The team kitchens collaborated to create a great feast. In one giant mess tent, we broke bread, tucked into the balti rice, meat, and sweets, and enjoyed an evening of laughter, singing, and dancing.

The next day, Di Gilbert and I sat in my tent, chatting over tea and biscuits, laughing at the six degrees of separation between us. She has a wicked sense of humor, and I really needed a good laugh now. The weather was taking a turn for the worse, potentially grounding us for a week. We worried about the fixed ropes we had put in up to Camp 3, whether they would survive the storms, and whether the weather would give us a break to climb again.

When it did, we raced up—Camp 1, Camp 2, through the Black Pyramid, another steep section of rock and ice on the way to Camp 3. More rock, which I hated, and a tricky traverse. The rock was so smooth, I struggled at times to find a placement for my crampon spike. I inched along, thinking, *I'm going to fucking fall.* Benigno apparently read my mind and assured me, "You're not going to fall," which was kind, but I'm five foot four. I needed longer legs. Or longer arms. Or shorter—

I fell, my crampons screeching down the rock.

I knew it! I knew it! Fuck!

I caught myself and found placement for my feet, forcing myself to exhale, taking control of my breath. I wasn't scared so much as I was anxious and annoyed, trying to concentrate on completing this traverse. I didn't look back to see the expression on Benigno's face, but I'm certain it was hilarious.

I hadn't been this high on K2 before—not that it matters. K2 never has the same weather, so one never experiences the same climb twice. You can't trust the winds of K2. It can be 10 degrees Fahrenheit with the sun shining, where one might risk overheating, and suddenly it's –40. Fucking insane. The winds picked up, and for the first time ever, I regretted not having my summit suit on. While my team rushed ahead to Camp 3, a Sherpa and his client who shared the same LO with me radioed above to Camp 3, and my summit suit was sent down to me. That's the last time I would trust K2 above Camp 2 without my summit suit. I barely made it to Camp 3 before sundown, completely knackered. Hand on heart, the climbing between Camp 2 and Camp 3 on K2 is the hardest I've done anywhere to this day. Usually I'm the one preparing soup for the latecomer. This time I was grateful to receive it. I was instantly asleep, and it felt like I'd just dozed off when I heard teams packing up, preparing to descend. A storm was coming. Surprise, surprise. To summit K2, I'd have to do all this again. Maybe twice.

Back at Base Camp, I played with the weather data, overlaying historical information with weather forecasts, trying to determine our next summit window, which was likely no sooner than July 25. With four camps and then the summit, I wondered if we would have time to fix the route up to Camp 4.

To kill time and keep everyone's spirits up, we had movie nights and I began to work on a K2 pub quiz. We had birthday parties, did the usual laundry (amazing how this builds up), and visited the other camps. Meanwhile, the kitchen staff and other assistants spent their time playing some card game that involved gambling, and this put Flt. Lt. Anwar in a foul mood. He was a righteous man, sensitive to the income disparity between climbers and kitchen boys. When Flt. Lt. Anwar heard that an assistant cook was selling his watch, that was it. These boys were there to earn money for their families, not piss it away gambling.

"Who organized this game?" he demanded, as the kitchen helpers quickly dispersed. "Never mind, I'm going to find out." And he did.

With the first available summit window, we headed up to Camp 1, which quickly became the bottleneck we feared as all the teams eyed the same small portal of opportunity. Four of us jammed into a three-man tent as I listened to climbers arriving only to discover there was no room at the inn.

"They didn't bring up tents," I said. "What were they thinking?"

Maybe they'd planned to bivouac—constructing a shelter from whatever natural materials are available—but there was no way to bivvy in this wind, and you certainly couldn't sleep outside. Voices escalated from unpleasant surprise to anger and panic.

What the fuck—whose tent is this? Can I get in there?

Do you have room? Does anybody have room?

This is exactly the kind of situation that contributes to the death toll on K2. You can climb light and fast, but you can't climb *crazy*. You need basic provisions. Skimping on essentials is dangerous and leads to an ethical dilemma in which teams try to "do the right thing," attempting to save someone who gets in trouble. But what if they start in trouble? Does responsibility shift with the wind? It's a fine moral line. I was happy to help them fill their water bottles, but given that I had Benigno's foot in my face, they needed to go back down.

Some of those heading down were Benigno's friends. So out of the blue, he was now saying, "I want to go down."

"Benigno, WTF?"

I'd climbed with him twice in Ecuador. He's a capable ASEGUIM (Asociación Ecuatoriana de Guías de Montaña)-qualified guide and an excellent climber, but he'd never been on an 8,000-meter peak, and the confusion outside was getting under his skin.

"Hey, hey, hey, listen," I said. "You have a tent. We have extra provisions. You're safe and this is our summit bid. Why waste energy going down and up again? You should stay."

The storm raged through that night and another day, and at the risk of oversharing, while taking care of private business in this somewhat compromised situation, it came to my unhappy attention that I had developed a pronounced hemorrhoid.

"No fucking way," I rage-typed to Pippa. "How do I get it off me?"

"Keep calm and carry on," comes the response.

"Fuck off. You're giving me a WWII morale-boosting slogan in my hour of need?"

"Preparation H."

"If I had Preparation H, would I be texting you? You're the mum. What are the holistic remedies?"

"Googling."

"Tick tock."

"Lemon wedge. External use only."

"But won't that ruin the taste of the lemon?"

"Hilarious. Do you want this thing to shrink or what?"

"Yes, mummy dearest. Thank you. If I don't make it, I'll be the body with the FUCKING HEMORRHOID. Kidding. Bye for now."

The next day, teams at Camp 1 braved the wind and moved up

to Camp 2, perching like pigeons inside our tents, and the following morning, despite the shit weather, I saw Di and members of her team all dressed and fighting their way through the brutal cold wind, making a move to Camp 3. I wanted to follow, but none of my teammates were willing. After a few minutes, I saw Di unclip alone and turn back.

A little past noon, the radio was full of static and chatter. "Di, it's Jake Meyer. There is no Camp 3. There's been an avalanche. I repeat: there's been an avalanche. There is *no* such thing as Camp 3 anymore. Over."

There were no casualties, but all of our tents, equipment, sleeping bags, oxygen tanks—everything we'd carefully cached above—was gone. My gut reaction was to stay at Camp 2, assess the situation with the team, and try to resupply from below rather than miss that weather window. That's what the old-school expeditions would have done. As I rationalized next steps, I could hear the larger expeditions totting up their losses, including $200,000 worth of oxygen alone. Climbing, I know all too well, is a game of economics. The larger teams were out, having invested too much money, it was as simple as that.

As teams went back to Base Camp, some of the Sherpa and HAPs went out scavenging for anything that might have been swept down the mountain. I saw one of them showing off a snazzy new sleeping bag and didn't have the heart to tell him it was mine. He was like a kid on Christmas morning, so I figured finders keepers.

The dreamer in me enjoyed the idea of the mountain god, but my logical, left-brain self doesn't buy it. An avalanche is to a mountain what water is to a dog. When a dog gets wet it shakes to get rid of the water. When a mountain accumulates snow, nature has a way of shaking it off. That is why climbers wait forty-eight hours or more after a snowfall for conditions to clear themselves.

We know this is going to happen. We expect it. Why make a decision based on fear of it now?

Di was thinking the same thing. The next morning, we got busy analyzing our own data. She's a qualified guide under AMI (Association of Mountaineering Instructors) and our analytical approaches complemented each other. Armed with fresh data, we consulted Flt. Lt. Anwar, who suggested we approach the most senior LO, a Pakistan Army officer, who was busy helping the other expeditions exit early.

"We'd like to consider staying," I said. "First, as smaller expeditions, Di and I haven't lost as much equipment and supplies as the larger teams. Furthermore, the historic summit data shows that sixty-eight percent of all summits happened on dates that are still ahead of us."

"And take a look at these," Di said, offering some photos on her phone. "I took a close look at the pictures of the snowpack that the team took from the avalanche at Camp 3. You can see, here and here, signs that this avalanche was not necessarily new. Of course, there are the obvious signs too, like the fact that we didn't see or hear anything from one camp below. We could still summit."

The officer was clearly impressed. He took all this in, and then an enormous smile stretched across his face.

"Do you mean to tell me the only two expeditions willing to continue on K2 are the only two led by women?" he said.

"Yes, sir, that's correct."

He nodded, a twinkle in his eye, and I felt the three of us reliving a powerful moment in Pakistan's history, when the founder of Pakistan, Muhammad Ali Jinnah, famously said, "There are two powers in the world; one is the sword and the other is the pen. There is a great competition and rivalry between the two. There is a third power stronger than both, that of the women."

Nostradamus had nothing on Jinnah.

Di and I gave it our best shot, but ultimately, we had to pack it in. The irony was that we could have stayed and had permission to stay. The problem wasn't in the physical equipment, supplies, oxygen, or tents. The problem was in human resources.

I knew the older Sherpa were superstitious. When the mountain speaks, they listen. Sometimes avalanches represent anger from the mountain gods. There's no motivational speech or amount of money that counters that deeply rooted belief. The millennial Sherpa don't necessarily believe this, but they lack the work ethic of their elders. (Not judging, just reporting!)

Here we were, leading expeditions, thinking we had control over human resources, when, in fact, your Sherpa may want to go home the minute they see the other Sherpa start going home. The Sherpa going home get paid the same as the Sherpa who stay, less a summit bonus, which only gets paid out if there is a summit.

Di and I met with Chhang Dawa Sherpa at Seven Summit Treks to see if some of their Sherpa would be willing to stay. He explained "minor subcontracting issues" and optics (how his clients would feel if we summited and he left), but more important, he pointed out what I thought was a valid and reasoned argument: that our Sherpa were unwilling to stay, simply because neither Di nor I were seen as a long-term employer. It was a brilliant observation. Of course, someone will go the extra mile, no pun, for someone they want to please over the long run. I would have to ponder this, if there was ever a next time.

For now, it was over. I found myself trudging up the hill to Gilkey Memorial once again, this time with Di and a couple of LOs.

"Hand on heart," I said, "I know for a fact that eighty-four people have died, but I don't see how there are eighty-four names there."

There was only one way to be sure. We started cataloguing the names on the plates, cross-referencing against a list of every climber known to have died on K2, producing a spreadsheet that showed all the names not represented. Some of the plaques were weathered and difficult to read. Others had fallen into the rocks or were hidden behind other plaques, sometimes sharing the same piton. Some names were posted twice or even three times, while others were in foreign languages, and again as part of a team. We'd been at it for two hours when heavy snow forced us to scramble down the rocks and head back to Base Camp, but we returned another day to finish the list and set up battery-operated candles.

We'd found twenty missing names that spanned thirteen nations and thirty-seven years. These were not faceless vapors. I felt connected to each and every one of them, the effort they made, the stories they left behind. Their strength lifted me in my own journey. I felt I owed them something. I wanted to make sure every dead climber had his or her place on the cairn. Before I left, I texted my Wingman. "Veni, Vidi, Victus Sum."

Sher Khan at NSE helped me find tin plates similar to the ones that had been punched with pitons and hung on the memorial.

"I bought them in Rawalpindi and had them engraved so I can place them when I go back," I told Jonathan. "Or another expedition can take them."

"Sure," he said, being kind, I suppose, but the skeptical subtext was unmistakable.

Data point versus pattern. One bad result can be accepted as an aberration. A second bad result might be an unfortunate coincidence. A third strike, though—that makes it a pattern. After two years in a row, it would have made sense to give up. If you fail once to achieve a summit, everyone has your back and encourages you to give it another go. When you fail twice, that cheerleading crowd disappears. So the risk you take if you try that third time is larger than the sum of its parts. It's make or break.

Either way, it's over.

24

How do you make one million dollars mountaineering?
Start with two million.
—JONATHAN'S FAVORITE JOKE

There were no summits on K2 in 2015 or 2016, so the question was left hanging in the air: Was it the mountain, or was it me? As long as I didn't make that third try, it was Schrödinger's cat: you can't say the possibility is still alive, but no one else can say the dream is dead.

Leaving it that way, living with the *if only* of it, was like living with a broken tooth, but there was no use even talking about it to Jonathan. Another expensive, dangerous expedition was a hard no, even for him. Six years of climbing and exploring had effectively decimated the retirement nest egg I'd worked so hard to build.

The toll climbing took on my body was beyond a price point. Headaches had plagued me ever since I hit my head on the tree trunk climbing Carstensz Pyramid and headbutted my neighbor. One day Jonathan came home and was annoyed at me for not taking out the garbage.

"How can you ignore that godawful smell?"

"What smell?" I said. And then I realized I couldn't smell anything else either.

The headaches were the result of seven blocked sinus cavities (out of eight) that had to be surgically drained, and while Dr. Ralph Metson was at it, he fixed my deviated septum. Suddenly I could breathe! After the rotator cuff surgery and hours of physio, I was still trying to improve my reach. Despite years of working my body for the specific purpose of climbing mountains, I had to spend several months dealing with the wreckage in my knees, back, and feet.

By December, I still couldn't raise my right arm more than 30 percent forward or sideways, which made it hard to wave people off in traffic and even harder to run in a straight line. Seriously, try running with one arm bound to your chest. It doesn't work. I wanted to run with Team Red Cross in the Boston Marathon in April 2017. I'd done a lot of cardio for high altitude, but I'd never run a marathon. Never ran more than six miles, in fact. I was unfamiliar with marathon methodology and jargon—slow-twitch versus fast-twitch muscles and all that. The science of it doesn't interest me the way the science of climbing does. I was still interested in promoting the Red Cross, however, so after yet another surgery in February to break up scar tissue, I worked up to running seven miles, then eight miles, then ten miles.

In March, I wanted to try running fifteen miles, but the forecast was for snow. Jonathan, being a sweetheart, checked a circumference around New York City, found a break in the weather near Washington, DC, and took me down there for the weekend. I ran the fifteen miles, realized I was lost in the middle of nowhere, and had to call an Uber. The next day I couldn't move, and there was a lump the size of a walnut below my left knee.

Inflamed patellar tendon.

"Unusual," said Dr. John Connors. "We mostly see this on teenage boys."

Every day, I asked Jonathan, "Does this thing look like it's getting bigger?"

Every day, he said, "Nope. Same as yesterday."

Inflamed temper.

Three weeks before the Boston Marathon, I was running in Central Park, falling slower and slower until I had to stop. I had a charley horse in my bum. Literally a pain in the ass. The next day, I could hardly put my right foot down on the ground.

"Do you clench your butt cheeks when you run?" asked the massage therapist.

"I'm not sure," I said.

"Don't."

I made a mental note. *Do not clench butt.*

An MRI of my sacrum and pelvis revealed a stress fracture, so Dr. Rodeo recommended I skip the Boston Marathon, but I couldn't bear to bail on the Red Cross. At the Saturday premarathon lunch, I told the event coordinator I would join them at the starting line, just to get some pictures for the team. There's a Red Cross station every mile with balloons numbered 1 to 26, telling runners how many miles it is to the finish line. When the team posed for pictures, someone handed me the 1 balloon. I took this as a sign. Run a mile, I figured. Give it a go and pull off at the first Red Cross station.

On Marathon Monday, I went to the staging area. Maya was visiting, so she and Jonathan downloaded the race app to track my badge number, which had an electronic chip.

"I don't have my cell," I said, "but you'll be able to see where I am when I dip out. Find me and we'll grab lunch."

I couldn't find my Red Cross mates in the throng, and then the charity section was called to the starting line, so I fell in and started running, hoping to see someone I knew, telling myself, *No pressure. Don't squeeze your butt.* I loped along, passing slower folks.

One ten-minute mile dropped away. It was getting hot, so I paused to take off my long-sleeved undershirt, but then another mile fell away, and another, and another. I stopped at every single Gatorade stand for a drink and chatted up every Red Cross volunteer I saw.

Meanwhile, Jonathan and Maya waited for a bit and then went into a local bar. As I heard it later, Jonathan checked the app on his phone and said, "What the hell? It looks like she's still running."

"What do you want to bet she'll go the whole distance?" said Maya.

"No. No way." He refreshed the app, frowning. "She's not supposed to be running with the sacrum fracture. She's not a runner."

"But she's more determined than anyone I know."

Meanwhile, I was just loping along. *Don't clench your butt.* *Don't clench your butt.* I realized I'd run six miles already and figured I'd go a little farther. The midday sun was blazing down now. I ran through every sprinkler and gratefully accepted every cup of water offered to me. Twelve miles down. Ten minutes later, halfway. I slowed to a fast walk while I sucked down an energy gel, vaguely surprised that I didn't need to pee. *I must be sweating out all that water I was drinking. Better watch my hydration.*

Back at the bar, Jonathan and Maya were hydrating on my behalf, watching my little avatar blip along the route, one mile after another.

"Ha!" Maya punched Jonathan's arm. "What did I tell you?"

I let my body run on its own higher wisdom. If it told me to stop, I would stop. But it didn't, so I kept running and let my mind wander.

Eighty-eight bottles of beer on the wall

My thoughts kept returning to K2. Everything it would take to try again. Everything stacked against me. Everyone who tried and tried again, the ones who died, and the ones they left behind. As overwhelming as all that should have been, I couldn't deny it. I wanted to try again.

Don't clench your butt.

Fifty-three bottles of beer on the wall

I thought about the spreadsheet, the long list of names, all the climbers whose names were still missing from Gilkey Memorial. If I never placed them there, who would? The mission meant something to me, though it's hard to explain, mostly because it's so hard for me to talk about the loss of my brother, particularly those three terrible days when he was presumed dead but his body was lost, floating in some dark, unknowable place. I know what it is like to experience death and have no body, just like all the relatives of those who lost loved ones on K2.

I didn't know how to tell Jonathan, but I knew I had to go back to K2 and try again. Everything you don't get from success was on my side now: experience, troubleshooting skills, humility. I had the fearlessness to pivot, the instinct to stay on course, and the seasoned common sense to know the difference.

Forty-one bottles of beer on the wall
Butt cheeks butt cheeks butt cheeks

When I reached Fenway Park and Kenmore Square, I figured I was almost there, so I kept going on Commonwealth Avenue, and when I turned right on Hereford Street, I was practically skipping. I rounded left onto Boylston Street, and four blocks later, I was at the finish line outside Central Library. I slowed to a walking stride, and someone threw a medallion around my neck. As I headed for the Red Cross party up the street, I saw Jonathan and Maya. She got to me first, and though I tried to warn her off my soggy shirt and sweaty neck, she shrieked and threw her arms around me.

"*Veeeeeeee!* I am so massively proud of you! We sat there following, like, 'Oh my God, she can't possibly go another mile,' and you just kept going."

Jonathan caught up to us and swept me into a hug. He didn't admonish me for ignoring the doctor or complain that he'd been told to wait for one hour and ended up waiting for five. It took him about an hour to get his jaw off the floor.

"I've never seen so much determination. I never thought you would run this marathon," he said over a celebration dinner. "You have to climb K2."

"*Yes.*" It was a profound relief not having to articulate more than that.

He nodded. "Look into it. We'll figure out the finances."

And then it took me about an hour to get my own jaw off the floor.

25

Before I left for K2 in June 2017, I stopped for coffee and tea with Jim Clash and Norbu Tenzing Norgay, vice president of the American Himalayan Foundation. We had a good chat, they wished me luck, and as I was preparing to leave, Jim said, "I have something for you."

He twisted his Mario Andretti ring from his finger. Friends, this is like a Super Bowl ring. A ring you cannot buy. A ring for which you would fistfight Vladimir Putin. Jim had to earn this by hitting a speed of two hundred miles per hour in a racecar driven by Mario Andretti.

"No. Fucking. Way." I was gobsmacked.

"Bring it back," he said, insisting on eye contact for clarity and understanding.

Caught off guard and overwhelmed, I didn't know what to say. I hugged Norbu and Jim and bolted out of there. I added Jim's ring to the collection of talismans I kept around my neck, my heart pounding somewhere between "third time's the charm" and "three strikes, you're out."

My flight from Dubai arrived in Islamabad, and for the first and only time in my present incarnation, my duffel bags were first up on the luggage carousel, but I was taking the good omens with a grain of salt this time. I went to my hotel in the F-7 Sector (*F* stands for "foreigner") and prepared for the press briefing I had scheduled for that evening. A Pakistani press conference isn't like an American press event. There are very few questions during "Q&A," as everyone wants to meet with you privately. On a previous expedition, a Pakistani journalist translated "fastest" as "shortest," so his headline declared me the "Shortest Climber to Seven Summits."

"He has a point," Pippa opined on WhatsApp. "You're only 5'4" without Ferragamos."

This time, taking great care with my words, I read from a prepared statement.

"Assalaam alaikum. Thank you for coming here before Iftar. It's great to see new and familiar faces. My name is Vanessa O'Brien, and I'd like to welcome you to K2: Season 3. My third attempt at K2. So it's like any box set: we want a happy ending."

Braced by a ripple of laughter, I talked about my previous attempts on K2, my desire to carry the four flags, our shared values, and how proud I was to be a Goodwill Ambassador for Pakistan, which had grown and evolved so much in the past two years. I spoke a little about the enormous amount of preparation that had gone into this expedition and said, "This year, we'll be successful *inshallah*."

This word—*inshallah*, "if God wills it"—rolls off the tongue a little too easily for some people, rather like "thoughts and prayers" that too often substitute for actually taking action. I see this word filled with enthusiasm and hope, not a sigh of resignation. I don't doubt the role of fate, but I'll keep hammering away to make sure it knows I'm here.

Prior experience on K2 had taught me to rely on no one but

ourselves for supplies and manpower. By partnering with Pemba, I had a long-term employer the Sherpa looked up to, and hopefully, the long-term employer they would go the extra mile for. I chose NSE to provide local logistics and sort the permits out for a solid team to embark on an eight-week expedition that would follow the Abruzzi Ridge route to the summit of K2. This team included three Chinese, another American, two Icelanders, one Norwegian, and one Singaporean. Collectively, we were attempting to set a number of records: first Norwegian to summit Broad Peak, first Chinese to climb all fourteen 8,000-meter peaks, first Icelander to summit K2, and of course, first American woman to summit K2, and first British woman to successfully summit K2. (Two British women had reached the summit of K2 in previous years but died on the descent, so it was my intention to honor their memory with this summit as well.)

For a third time, I picked up the UN Women flag, which was humbling. The unwavering support of these women brought tears to my eyes. From there, I went to meet my new LO, Lieutenant Shabbar, Pakistan Navy, which worried me. I appealed to the powers that be—"He's navy—*sea level*. He's going to get AMS." But Lt. Shabbar had been through the same Pakistan Army mountaineering course as the previous LO and quickly won me over with his intelligence and discipline.

The next day, we squeezed into a Pakistan Air Force cargo plane bound for Skardu, and the pilot let us take turns visiting the cockpit for spectacular views of Nanga Parbat and the Karakoram. We flew over the Shangrila Resort Hotel, and it made me smile to see the heart-shaped lake from the air and know that my honorary uncle Arif was there wishing me well.

Pemba and the Chinese climbers were attempting to summit Nanga Parbat before meeting us in Skardu, so I checked Facebook as soon as we arrived at the Concordia Motel, hoping to see an update. But not this update: no summit. Even worse, Pemba Sherpa was suffering from frostbite, and when he went to the hospital to get it checked out, there was no doctor there. My chin went to my chest when I saw it.

"Pemba, *think*, dammit."

Frostbite could be a straight red card, and instead of telling me, he let me read about it on Facebook? With my extended Pakistan family, I could have helped, if he hadn't been too proud to ask. By the time they arrived, Pemba staunchly insisted he was fine but requested that we stay an extra day. We used the time to repack and check weight restrictions. I was grateful to have Farman with me again, and he was grateful for another day to shop for last-minute supplies. That night, I looked around the dinner table at the strongest team I'd ever climbed with—at least, on paper. This was my third year on K2 and Pemba's second. Most team members had a minimum of four 8,000-meter summits under their belt. Fazal Ali, a HAP—and a friend—had summited K2 twice and had been with me on K2 the year before. If he summited this year, he would hold the record for Pakistani K2 summits.

The next day we went as far as Askole, stopping along the way to clear rockfall with a stick of dynamite. By the time we arrived, Farman had a tent set up, and I could smell the rich aroma of onion and garlic that served as a base for his hearty soup. While the others unpacked, Pemba and I discussed our route, calculating how many days it might take, knowing whatever we planned was subject to change for weather or due to low altitude porters, but would likely take us from Askole to Jhola to Paiyu to Urdukas to Goro II to K2 Base Camp. Traveling along this route and eventually onto the Baltoro Glacier itself meant the vertical change was continuously up and down, not continuously up like Everest.

"If the porters are up for it," I told Pemba, "I prefer not to have rest days in between."

I sat watching a group of boys playing in a field nearby, always keeping one curious eye on me. I made eyeglasses with my hands and looked back at them, as if to say, *I see you*. They ran away laughing and hid behind a jeep but returned a few minutes later, making eyeglasses with their hands back at me. So I copied them again, and they ran off again, laughing. I changed the game and pretended to throw something for them to catch, and they threw it back for me to catch. I exaggerated jumping way out of the way, as if they'd tossed a bad ball, and they laughed. It was magical to see the language barrier surmounted by curiosity and imagination.

The next day, trekking to K2 Base Camp, on the move for more than five hours, I couldn't help limping a little. I'd hurt my knee running in the Boston Marathon, and this was the first test of a follow-up cortisone injection, hiking past the pain while the joints oiled up. I strode right along after that, listening to music on low and reminding my teammates to drink plenty of water and pace themselves. They may have thought I was being a mother hen, but I remembered my first miserable trek up this mountain. I knew the importance of keeping every team member strong.

One of the principles Pemba and I agreed on at the outset was the need to be self-sufficient. To be successful this time, we'd have to change things up, stop following and start leading. For our comparatively modest team—twelve climbers with a cook and LO— eight weeks' worth of food, equipment, supplies, oxygen, tents, and other necessities added up to more than seven tons, which required the help of 250 porters. I was grateful to each and every one of them and zealous about protecting their health and well-being.

Years earlier, a revered Chinese astrologer told me I should work for myself doing something that serves women's interests and under absolutely no circumstances tell people my age. He said, "You give a lot to others, but don't ask for help when you need it."

"Anything else?" I asked.

"Keep your nails short, and someone will call you 'mom.'"

I laughed. "I don't think so."

Years later, it came true.

"Thank you, mom," the note read.

"Darling, look!" cried Pippa. "It's all come true." She emailed me a copy of the typo from a Pakistani commenter on YouTube. He meant to say "ma'am" but spelled it "Mom." She obviously considered it a win for the old soothsayer.

I was grateful for cloudy skies, remembering how blazing hot and sticky with humid grit it had been the first two times I made this trip. But then it started raining, which meant some of the porters were stuck in the mud. Still, it felt wonderful to be high in the cool of the evening at 3,170 meters. The next day, we continued to Paiyu Base Camp at 3,666 meters. (*Paiyu* means "salt," attributable to the mineral salts in this region. #funfact) We had the luxury of a shower of sorts—a flat cement area with a short hose that channeled water melting off the glacier. I took turns with Sylvi, our Norwegian, holding the hose for each other so we could wash our hair, gasping at the icy coldness. I told her about a wellness retreat in Austria where the doctor told me to jump in the lake and then thank the lake when I was done. I went out there, thinking, *Fuck. This is going to be freezing cold. Do I run for it? Walk off the edge? Do a cannonball?* I just walked out on the dock and went for it. The water closed over my head. The impact of the cold water all but stopped my heart. Doggy-paddling and mumbling profanities, I struggled to shore and made a beeline for the door. And then I had to go back out in the cold, because I forgot to thank the lake.

Sylvi and I shook off our brain freeze—*Thank you, glacier*—and went in for supper. One of our HAPs, who doubled as a butcher, killed a goat with a mercifully swift, deep cut to its throat in accordance with halal rules, and the meat was distributed to the porters, as a form of thanksgiving and to bring us good luck for our next day's hike onto the Baltoro Glacier. I dreaded the coming miles of rocky moraine: large rocks to scramble over, medium rocks that tested hamstrings, and small rocks just waiting to turn an ankle, all lightly dusted with sand and dirt. There had already been multiple ankle twists and a broken leg so far that season.

The sun rose on the exposed glacier, making the way harder for climbers, porters, and mules, but we moved along at a steady pace, eyes cast down, concentration on the ground, until we came to a brisk river. I'd always crossed shallow streams on my own, carrying my shoes and socks, pants hiked up to my knees. This time, the river was wild and white-capped. Two of the HAPs offered to give Sylvi and me piggyback rides across the torrent, and we didn't waste a micromoment acting too proud to accept.

A final uphill push took us to Urdukas at 3,950 meters, where the bustling camp spread out around and above us, constructed in tight tiers on the side of the mountain. On the lower levels, people cooked and made chapati bread. The midlevels were for animals and traders (like Wall Street), and people selling insanely expensive bottles of Coke and Sprite. Upper layers were dotted with bright yellow and orange tents where climbers slept.

"Earplugs are recommended," I told Sylvi as we made our way up through the noisy compound.

I call Urdukas "Dead Mule Camp" because of all the dead mule bits lying around, animals who have perished from the strenuous work in high altitude. I always try to pitch my tent farthest from the ripest torso, head, or tail. If that makes me "high maintenance," I wear the mantle proudly. I also try to pitch for a good view of the majestic peaks. From here, you can see Trango Towers, Cathedral Peak, and a thousand of their smaller cousins. The strange epicenter of Urdukas is a famous stone that split in two. The top half toppled down, killing three porters, who are remembered with punched plate plaques similar to the ones at the Gilkey Memorial.

Every evening, all along the way, a queue of porters lined up outside my tent to visit with me for relief after the day's travel. They knew I wasn't a doctor, but I did have a medical kit, so one by one, directly or through translators, I talked with them to find out what ailed them—headaches, blisters, upset stomachs, trouble sleeping—you name it. One of our climbers actually was a doctor, but they preferred to come and see me, maybe because I made them laugh. Whatever the reason, I was honored to have their trust, and planning for the evening queue, I always brought extra over-the-counter supplies to share.

At Urdukas, my first two cases were headaches, for which I dispensed ibuprofen and admonished them to drink more water. Then came the parade of blisters, which I dressed with Compeed, a UK brand of second skin bandages I prefer. The translator repeated the same advice over and over until I probably could have repeated the Balti words myself.

"The skin must be clean before you apply it. You must not remove this."

Next came a porter with horrendous gas. He was too embarrassed to tell me until I made light of it, and told him, "It's a good sign. You're acclimatizing well. We should all be so lucky."

My final visitor told me that his mule was not feeling well. His mule! Talk about scope creep. Out of my league, I referred him to the doctor, who listened sympathetically and petted the animal, which may or may not have helped.

The next day we traveled to Goro II at 4,300 meters. This Base Camp showed the Baltoro Glacier in all its glory, a vast sweeping trunk of ice that twines through the enormous peaks of the Karakoram, branching off into capillaries of green, silver, black, and blue. Members of the Pakistan Army had been stationed here for over ninety days. I couldn't imagine the brutal reality of such a long stay in this hostile environment, especially in winter. That evening, several soldiers watched with fascination as the porters queued up outside my tent.

"He says he can't sleep," said the translator.

"That's normal for high altitude. I use melatonin. If it doesn't work, I can give him a small dose of Diamox. Tell him not to think so much at night. Tell him to close his eyes, put his worries on a small raft, and let it float away."

He translated my message, and we all laughed.

The next fellow opened his mouth, revealing an obvious abscess filled with pus. I could tell by the smell that it was badly infected and probably had been for a while. I shuddered to imagine what that must feel like at this altitude and remembered the kindness of my dentist in Islamabad. *Shit. What to do?*

"I need to get the doctor," I told the translator.

"No, he wants you to help."

"I will help, but I'm not a doctor. Just a friend. I'll stay with him. Don't worry." (I was picking up their habit of ending everything with "don't worry.")

I fetched the doctor, who brought a lance and antiseptic gargle. The porter gripped my hand, blinking furiously but making no noise, as the doctor performed the dreadful procedure. I offered up Anbesol, an oral painkiller, and said, "Tell him to keep it clean. He still needs to see a dentist, as soon as possible."

The young man's eyes were haunted with the torment of long

months he'd endured on the glacier, but he smiled and nodded his gratitude.

The next day, in surprisingly balmy weather, I made another rookie mistake, wearing a short-sleeved shirt without sunscreen, incurring a crisp, dry farmer's tan that gradually molted off me like a pale snakeskin. The terrain was hillier than I remembered, a reminder that the glacier had a life of its own, always and never the same. The striated mountains around it told the ancient story of its progress from age to age. This part of the trek is like a museum of ice, hilarious "mushroom rocks"—boulders suspended in the air by narrow strips of ice—and extremely large fins of ice that stand solo as if placed by a mountain curator to be admired by passersby.

We reached Concordia at 4,550 meters, the Throne Room of the Mountain Gods, where the Baltoro and Godwin-Austen Glaciers merge. For the first time this season, we could see K2. I enjoyed watching those on our team who'd never seen it up close. Jet stream clouds formed a moving crown at the summit. All around us, peaks rose up like majestic organ pipes or pyramids. The air was steely and bright, the sky cobalt blue.

Ten days after we'd arrived in Islamabad, we rounded a bend on the Godwin-Austen Glacier and saw Russell Brice's camp in the distance. How he builds these camps before anyone else, I will never know. His team would be climbing the Cesen route, and our team would be climbing the Abruzzi Ridge route, which was accessible a bit farther down the glacier. Pemba and I passed his camp, yelling our hellos, and marked the spot for our Base Camp in roughly the same location where we'd made our camp the year before. Our home for the coming month featured a large kitchen tent with an attached supply tent, dining tents, a communications tent, and about two dozen sleeping tents. We had two shower tents with buckets and cups, a pee tent, and two poo tents.

I organized and reorganized my sleeping tent with the single mattress in the middle, clothes neatly arranged by type on one side, and on the other side, a smorgasbord of snacks, medicines, and toiletries. In the corner, I posted my little collapsible butterfly chair, a perfect spot to read and write. Outside, I had two large solar panels from the previous year's expedition, which would have been more useful if it weren't always overcast. I used the tent strings inside to hang *khata* scarfs and miniature prayer flags.

June 27 was a spectacular day for our Puja. We flew country flags for our international team, plus the UN Women and Red Cross flags, and a "Pathway to Paris" flag for climate change, given to me by Jesse Smith, daughter of Michigan's own Patti Smith. Standing beneath the brilliant colors and clear skies, the lama asked for permission to climb and forgiveness for our footprint. After celebrations and *tsampa* mustaches, we had an official day of rest, but following dinner, we started planning our first round of acclimatization hikes. Each rotation would be different for every climber, because some had pre-acclimatized on Nanga Parbat. On my way out of camp the next day, as is the custom, I stopped by our Puja altar to offer rice and burn juniper for good luck and a safe return.

By now you are a mountain master, so you know the acclimatization drill. Climb high, sleep low. Two steps forward, one step back. For four weeks, we hiked up and down, up and down, building camps and carrying supplies, nudging our red blood cells and lungs to evolve. In between I monitored the weather, checked in with our Base Camp and liaison officer, read one book after another, consulted with the other teams, planned the occasional game and film night, and drank copious amounts of tea. I did my laundry in a bucket and tried a hundred different tricks to coax it to dry in the overcast cold. The rarefied air of Base Camp was a world unto itself as we all bustled here and there in the shadow of the Savage Mountain. Members of our team visited other camps, and members of other teams visited us.

One of our visitors was Fredrik Sträng, a Swedish climber who was on K2 in 2008 when eleven people were killed. The movie *The Summit* is based on that incident, and I asked him about it when I first met him, but tears welled in his eyes, and he wasn't able to go on. I could see how deeply the tragedy still disturbed him, and yet, he was here again now, determined to summit. But he was in need of rope.

"I can pay," he said, "or I can carry. Whatever you need."

"No, don't pay," I said. "There are a lot of single climbers here. If people start offering money, especially in different currencies, it's too confusing. I wouldn't know how to distribute the funds."

Pemba asked, "Would you be willing to carry some of the ropes to higher camp?"

"Certainly," said Fredrik.

This is usually the protocol for teams who decide to cooperate. We were the largest team climbing the Abruzzi Ridge route, so individual climbers would naturally end up using our fixed ropes. It was proper etiquette for them to volunteer something in return. Not everyone did, but Mexican climbers Badía Bonilla and Mauricio Lopez also collaborated.

We weighed the avalanche dangers daily, watching the snowfall and checking the wind forecasts. Between fresh powder and twinkle lights, at night the camp was like Christmas in June. We monitored the ice conditions, which shift throughout the season and from year to year, sometimes solid and dry as concrete, sometimes wet and slippery, cracking and shifting with the movement of the glacier. Crossing the frozen glacier was tricky. There was a mini icefall right before ABC, which was just a storage facility for crampons, not a place where teams actually stayed more than once. Stake flags marked the path through the icefall pillars. Now and then we had to jump across a chasm or shimmy down a steep slope, taking extra care.

The climb to Camp 1 was a relentlessly steep five-hour slog. Pemba decided to have Sylvi acclimatize on K2, even though she was here to climb Broad Peak. I wasn't entirely comfortable with that strategy, but neither of us felt we had enough resources to split the team this early. I coached Sylvi whenever I could, especially past the Japanese camp when it became steeper. I suggested a pace we could all be comfortable with.

"Let's use the rest step technique," I said. "Five steps, rest, five steps, rest. Stay focused. If your mind wanders, you'll slow down."

We reached Camp 1 and moved up to Camp 2. The wind howled with fresh fury, and we tucked our heads down, pushing into it, doggedly adapting to conditions, adding and shedding layers as needed until we reached House's Chimney.

Pemba made the decision to build our Camp 2 tents below House's Chimney, even though other teams put tents above. The howling gales above the Chimney proved almost unbearable, unlike anything I'd seen in previous seasons. Beneath the Chimney was no picnic either. We could feel the tents, animated, clinging to the mountain for dear life as the individuals inside—two or three per tent—practiced their favorite mantras. In the morning, everyone was more than ready to head back down to Base Camp.

When bad weather moves in, spirits decline. The mountains turn into great shaggy triangular sheepdogs who will, sooner or later, stir, shake off the extra snow, and resettle. People get nervous, listening for the next distant—or not so distant—rumble and hiss. Every avalanche raises two equally terrible possibilities: 1) the expedition is over, or 2) the expedition will go on. Sometimes it's hard to know what to pray for. Every weather report is a prophecy of doom, one way or the other. This is when physically weak team members will fall ill. Stress to the body breaks down the immune system and saps energy. When someone decides to go home, there's often a sigh of relief underpinning the disappointment. They just need the pain to stop.

Harder to combat is a weakness of heart that begins to whisper to the head, listing a thousand excellent reasons to call it quits—a child's birthday, an aging parent, an imperative business or social function—all of which facilitate a constant recalculation of the shrinking prospects for a successful summit bid as the weeks wear on. Some purposefully manly men will assert an "executive decision" to tap out at this point. And I love how a man who taps out because he simply *must* be home for little Madison's ballet recital is lauded as a super-amazing dad, but a woman who "abandons" her children to climb a mountain is judged to be less principled than a feral cat.

Whatever is lying dormant comes out at high altitude, and a lot of it has to do with fear. Fear is the witch trial that happens in our own heads, a judgmental voice that decrees *you have no right, you don't deserve, you aren't enough* for something this good to work out the way it's supposed to. It's de rigueur for climbers to mentally and physically cop out. I've seen it every single year. Fear spreads, but I wasn't going to let these climbers wallow in it. It would be better to distract the team with films and games than to have their minds wander.

Time to get back up the hill. The snow was deeper, the rocks were slick, and the wind was as ferocious as ever. I worried about a couple of the climbers who were taking longer than usual to get into camp. By the time we reached Camp 2, one climber had turned around. I was starting to cough, praying this wouldn't turn into a sinus or chest infection. I spent the next day in my sleeping bag, reading and forcing myself to drink a gallon of water. Dawa

Gyalje Sherpa, who was climbing and sharing a tent with me, offered me some Tiger Balm and asked, "What do you think about tomorrow?"

"Let's get up at six and climb up House's Chimney. Then we can head toward Camp 3 and check out snow conditions," I said. "Pemba and Fazal want to go to Camp 3 and check if the fixed lines are still in place after all the avalanches."

In the morning, Dawa Gyalje and I climbed to Upper Camp 2 and found the same wind-scoured ghost town I'd seen earlier: mangled tent frames and tattered neon yellow fabric, some weighted with fallen rocks, some flapping in the wind. We continued up, slowly and cautiously, halfway to Camp 3 before heading down. By the time we reached Lower Camp 2, Pemba had radioed to tell us he and Fazal had reached Camp 3. They were going to spend the night and see if things improved. Having spent two nights at Camp 2, Dawa Gyalje and I decided to head back down to Base Camp. It was getting dark, and that's the worst time to try to get through the ice-fall maze, but I could feel the air, thick and scratchy, rasping in and out of my lungs. All I wanted to do was get to my tent.

"Do you see a light ahead?" I asked Dawa Gyalje. My eyesight sucks when I'm tired, so it could have been the moon falling from the sky, for all I knew.

"I think so." He called out, waving one arm. "Hello!"

If there was an answer, the wind took it, but as the headlamp bobbed closer, I could see it was one of the cook boys coming out to meet us with Coke and biscuits. I could barely croak my gratitude. My arms were suddenly so weak, I couldn't hold the cup straight. I skipped dinner that night. Went straight to bed. Started a course of antibiotics before I fell asleep with my socks on.

The next morning, I gave in to a climbing ritual I hate, sticking my head under a towel over a bowl of hot water with menthol oil.

The trick is to appoint a reliable timekeeper who doesn't hate you by now. People often do this in the dining tent, which is disgusting, and I promise you, if one does it, you might as well bring out bowls for every climber, as that is how fast this shit will spread. Within minutes I felt the vapor rising from the potent elixir, and I barked uncontrollably, expelling horrifying eels of bloody snot into the bowl.

It was mid-July now, and it looked like another season of no summits on K2. Rain turned our camp to a swampy quagmire that became an icy menace as soon as the sun went down, but the downpour gave me a few days of rest and antibiotics. As the team became nervous about time and real commitments back home, we started hypothetical planning.

"Two questions," said Pemba, sitting across from me in the mess tent. "First, what do you think about partnering with Russell Brice for a summit toward the end of July? And second, would you be open to attacking Broad Peak first and K2 second? Sylvi has to leave by the end of July."

I felt all eyes on me as the rest of the tent waited for me to answer, and I was taken back to the moment of uniquely feminine leadership on Mount Rainier. *I need a decision. Do you want to see how far we can make it as a group? Or do some of you want to stay here and allow others to go for a summit push?*

"Look," I said, "from the very beginning, the most important tenet of this expedition was that we were self-sufficient. That is why we brought seven tons of equipment, tents, supplies, and oxygen. That is why we have over four miles of rope. We have the talent and the experienced climbers to see to the summit. What we need is a weather window, and the one we are looking at is like threading a needle. Russell's team is one camp and one day behind us on a different route. I think it's a bad idea."

"But the two routes join at Camp 4."

"Only if they catch up. If they don't catch up, or if we wait for them, we lose our weather window, and no one summits."

I studied my teacup, choosing my words carefully. I had climbed with Russell on Manaslu. I liked him as a person and I respected his expertise. I'd even pulled strings this season to make sure he got his Pakistan visa in time because he came off Everest so late. But in three years on K2, I'd never seen anyone summit via the Cesen route. K2 was and will always be about risk and return trade-offs. My appetite for risk can be higher, but not without the appropriate return, and this proposition was only lowering that return while adding risk.

"Let me ask you this," I said. "What is it that you need from another expedition that we don't already have?"

Pemba thought long and hard about this and shook his head. "Nothing."

"Then I vote no. Why introduce additional risk factors without improving our chance for a summit? We already have an incredibly risky undertaking. All we have to do is fix ropes from Camp 4 to Summit—and keep ourselves healthy."

"True," he conceded.

"As for Broad Peak," I said, "I'm afraid that if we switch our efforts entirely away from K2 to Broad Peak, we'll lose focus on the main goal for everyone except one climber, which doesn't make any sense at all. We'll wear ourselves out, and miss the next K2 weather window. Again—too risky."

A general discussion took place, but as far as I could tell there was no refuting the facts. Pemba would either be focused on this summit and align his resources accordingly or our attempt on K2 would fail. I said good night and left, hoping people would sleep on it and come around to my way of thinking.

"It's time for Sylvi and me to go to Broad Peak," Pemba announced the next day.

I've read too many climbers' obituaries that feature this sort of haggled, please-all-the-people decision. Pemba was a seasoned climber who had just started his own company, operating on a business model that included running individual clients up and down the mountain. I resolved to sit back and watch it all unfold. At four in the morning, Pemba left with Sylvi, a HAP, and two Sherpa, aiming to reach Broad Peak Camp 3 the following day and summit the day after that. At noon, we received word that the Broad Peak party was turning back. Pemba agreed to let Sylvi and her small team give Broad Peak another go without him, and we made plans to make our K2 summit bid in two days' time to catch the weather window.

Out for a walk on the glacier the next day, I found a frozen mass of shredded clothing. I carefully extracted it from the ice and found the initials BG on the back of the tattered shirt. I took pictures and notes to compare with my K2 death list. About an hour later, Lt. Shabbar ran over with pictures of a skull still connected to a spine. There was a severed arm nearby with a wedding band on one finger and the wiry remains of a bangle bracelet on the wrist. Definitely a woman. Probably from an earlier climbing date as we wouldn't wear jewelry on fingers and wrists today, knowing about edema.

"If we can figure out who it is," I said, "we could return the wedding band."

I put on my reading glasses, and we used our headlamps to look closely at the ring for any identifying engraving or initials. As this was a wedding band on the fourth finger of the right hand, the person would likely have come from Northern or Eastern Europe, potentially Russia, Poland, Bulgaria. Maybe Denmark or Norway.

Not that many women died on K2, and not all of the names of those who did were public, because some who died didn't summit. As I searched through my list and went online to look for pictures, trying to see if any of the women were wearing jewelry, I remembered Jim's singular ring, added to the lucky charms around my neck, and the way he made me promise to bring it back.

I secretly prayed, *Please let there be a summit window. Please let me stay healthy long enough to witness the summit of K2.* Sometimes these prayers would be in short sequences and even game-like: *If we get to Camp 1, we'll summit. If we get through the Black Pyramid, we'll summit.*

Now there were no ifs, only the possibility of when. The summit window was approaching.

I sent Wingman a message: "QUO NON ASCENDAM."

To what heights can I not rise?

Code for the summit bid.

26

If ever man sets foot on that crystalline head of K2,
it won't be a climber, it will be an aviator.
—LUIGI AMADEO, DUKE OF ABRUZZI, AT A 1910 LECTURE IN MILAN

SUMMIT BID

In 1909, the Duke of Abruzzi reached 6,199 meters on K2 but was forced to turn back when he found the ridge too long and steep for the Balti porters. We pass by the ghost of that endeavor at Camp 1. At Lower Camp 2, the wind kicks up, trapping us inside our battered tents for two days. I hear two of my teammates coughing and throwing up in tents on either side of mine. I run over 4 mg of Zofran for the nausea and a couple of Tessalon Perles pills that should slightly numb the throat and lungs to make the cough reflex less active, but the next morning, they both head down the mountain.

We climb House's Chimney and emerge into gale-force winds. Climbers from another expedition behind us declare, "This is suicide," and turn around, but I see Fredrik Sträng huddled in a tent with his Sherpa at Upper Camp 2. We pause there just long enough for one of the Sherpa to have a cigarette.

"Upper Camp 2 is a wind trap," I shout to Fazal. "It has to be better higher up."

He nods, game to try.

Climbing on exposed rock with crampons on the Black Pyramid is incredibly tricky, and this fucking wind—and another cigarette break, seriously? I'm so cold standing there, I have to wrap a bivvy around myself. Good news is, the hideous cold is making me move faster to generate body heat, but there isn't an unused curse word in my vocabulary.

We placed Camp 3 just above the Black Pyramid, to avoid the avalanche risk of the year before. According to radio chatter, the team on the Cesen route had not made it to Camp 3 yet, so I'm grateful we weren't obligated to wait for them. The next day we made our way to Camp 4, where, on the far side of the Godwin-Austen Glacier, the tips of Broad Peak punch through into the sunshine. When word comes through at 10:45 AM that Sylvi is the first Norwegian to summit Broad Peak, we jump up and down, applauding, and Sylvi's group does the same on Broad Peak, somewhere on the far side of a hazy sky. This major success for the expedition puts us all in a great mood. One down, one to go.

I check my gear and try to sleep, but with five of us in one tent, it's impossible to stretch out your legs without kinking your neck. You have to choose one position or the other. My skin is crawling with chilblains, every capillary from thigh to ankle inflamed from weeks of constant cold.

"Stop thrashing!" my teammates groan.

"I promise it's not fleas."

I'm relieved to get up and get going. We begin the ascent of K2 at 11 PM, scaling a snow pitch steeper than I am usually ready for first thing out of a tent. Focusing on every swing of the ice axe, every kick of the crampon, I work my way up to a rocky lip where it levels off somewhat.

I've studied the gullies leading up to this ice serac. To avoid going under it, the Italians in 1954 climbed rock farther to the left.

The last teams to summit in 2014 chose a mixed rock and ice gully farther to the right. We decide to split the difference and choose a gully halfway between that which should leave us less exposed during the traverse under the ice serac. I look at my watch: 5 AM. Gray dawn tints the clouds. A heavy snow begins to fall, and I take it as another sign from the universe.

Two weeks before I left for K2, I listened to Ed Viesturs talk about his summit with Scott Fischer. Ed said if there was one mountain he didn't feel he deserved to summit, it was K2. Why? Well, on the summit day, it started to snow. Ed had a lower risk appetite and focused on the future, where he worrried about the pileup of snow and eventual avalanche risk. Scott had a higher risk appetite and focused on the present, and in the present, you wouldn't see snow accumulate. Ed said that without Scott's influence, he probably would have turned around. Instead they summited. The thing is, years later, only one of those two men is still alive, and it's not the one with the appetite for high risk.

The wind slings snow in our faces, creating near-whiteout conditions. Fucking weather forecasts—the only thing you know for sure is that they will be wrong. Conditions swiftly deteriorate. Scrolling through my brain is a list of climber deaths due to swiftly deteriorating weather. Churning clouds and raging wind sap the energy and suck the will until there's nothing left but *just die already*. I use my ice axe to determine a rate of accumulation. *Dammit*. Did I learn nothing from Ed Viesturs's presentation? Am I continuing or turning around? Which of those two am I?

I need to see what's going on with the line-fixing, which is happening in real time right in front of us. I motion to Dawa Gyalje to short rope with me so we can move forward in the queue. There are a few crevasses, so this is good practice. Finally, at the front, I see Pemba has chosen the Sherpa not using bottled oxygen to put in the fixed lines. Fucking hell. We'll all run out of oxygen at this rate.

"Pemba, we can't continue like this. Let's build two fixing teams and have them leapfrog each other. Dawa Gyalje and I are willing to help."

I think he can hear me, but the wind is strong, and the snow is blowing right in our faces. He nods. Dawa Gyalje and I go ahead, short roping each other until it's safe to stop. The wind escalates. The temperature drops. I'm already out of drinking water.

Crampons don't stick well on the slippery blue ice, so I'm front pointing, digging in any way I can until I slip down a pitch of blue ice. As I struggle to right myself, I notice Dawa Gyalje filming, and I give him the finger.

"Oh, c'mon, *didi*," he says. "It is what makes us all human."

"No. I didn't see you filming the Sherpa throwing up back there."

I don't want to be human right now.

I am the rock. I am the rock.

Pemba gestures to his watch and shouts over the wind, "Do you think we should continue?"

I've been keeping one eye on the snowfall, the other on the team. Looking at the line behind me, all I can think of is the game Chinese whispers, which, given the number of Chinese climbers in line, makes this suddenly politically incorrect.

I take the regulator out of my mouth and call out to them, "Does anyone want to turn around?"

No one does.

"Okay. Let's do this."

Climbing up the gully at a snail's pace, I see the deterioration in the serac that towers over us—an evident fracture and a rippled texture called "popcorning." I'm stricken by the unbelievable mass of the thing. It's the size of a tall building. The bulk of it might lend a sense of security. It's been standing there for centuries. Why would it fall? But if an earthquake on Everest could destroy the Hillary Step, an earthquake could shift this leviathan too. Every part of this mountain is made of something that seemed invincible for eons. And then one day it wasn't.

27

It's never too late to have a happy childhood.
—TOM ROBBINS, *STILL LIFE WITH WOODPECKER*

My father and I were never technically estranged. Basically, after my brother's death, he ignored me, and I feigned indifference. It was a functionally dysfunctional relationship, meaning we spoke cordially on Christmas and birthdays but didn't bother ginning up any great emotional investment, positive or negative. His Parkinson's progressed, and he was in and out of the hospital with infections. You die with Parkinson's disease, not from it, a rather unfortunate detail. Unable to swallow, he aspirated food into his lungs, which led to pneumonia or pulmonary complications. He could no longer walk or control his bladder. Mild hallucinations haunted him. His brain fired and misfired a tweet-storm of lies and promises to large and small muscles, creating tremors. During the last few months of his life, he had a hard time speaking, but truth be told, we didn't have a whole lot to talk about. He wouldn't remember it anyway.

I arrived in Lake Placid, Florida, early one morning to visit him in hospice care, and it took a lot of effort for him to ask, "Why're you here?"

"You're supposed to be dying," I said.

"Ivy . . ." He looked around for his wife.

"She's not here," I said. "I'm here."

"Oh." He nodded. Or his head bobbed on its own. I'm not sure. "Let's go."

"What?"

"Let's. *Go*." He kicked his wheelchair.

"Okaaaaay," I said. No one can claim I'm not up for an adventure.

I flipped the brakes off his chair, checked to make sure his catheter and oxygen were disentangled, and wheeled him out of his room and down the hall. I figured we'd go for a little spin around the hospital, but when he saw the exit, he pointed, insisting, "Go! Let's go."

"Dad, I don't know about your meds. I don't know if—" I glanced over my shoulder as we went out the door.

He took a deep breath of the outside air and said, "Where's the car?"

"Dad, I didn't bring my purse. I don't have the keys."

His eyes got wide. "Back in. Get it."

Through all of this, I couldn't help but think, *What kind of hell is this? What does he want? Is he trying to* Thelma & Louise *it? Are we crossing state lines?* I had no idea.

"Dad, if you want to go somewhere in the car, let me talk to the nurses first. They should know we're going. And that we're coming back."

"No. No." He fumbled out words that added up to him not wanting anyone to know.

"Okay. Hang tight." I walked down the hall and spoke to an orderly. "Excuse me, can I take my dad to McDonald's for a milkshake? Is there paperwork or something?"

Of course there was paperwork, but I found comfort in that.

"He can walk," the orderly said, "but he's unstable without the chair, so be careful."

"Copy that."

"He gets agitated. He seriously blew up at his wife yesterday. Sometimes a urinary tract infection makes people go off their nut a little, so keep up with his meds. He should be good for a couple hours or so."

"No worries. It's nine AM now, so we'll be back in an hour."

I wheeled my dad out to the parking lot and got him into the passenger seat—lifting, wrestling, wrangling the pee bag and oxygen tubes—and we drove for a while.

"So where are we going?" I asked.

He waved his hand, directing me to go straight, turn right, turn left. Eventually I realized we were headed for his house. I pulled in to the driveway and called his wife.

"Hi, Ivy? It's Vanessa. I'm out front with Dad."

"*What?* He's not allowed to leave the hospice!"

"Well, you never know until you ask. He wanted to take a ride. I think he wants to see you."

She stormed out the door, loaded for bear, but before she could go completely ballistic, he blurted, "Sorry. Sorry I yelled."

"And you couldn't wait to tell me this when visited later?" She folded her arms and shot a side glance in my direction. "You had to come all the way over here?"

He poked my arm. "Garage."

So off we went to the garage. I paced the cement floor while he messed with his fishing rods. Jesus. This was taking forever. Every movement was a multistep process—form intention, fumble back and forth, cuss, flail.

"Box," he kept insisting. "Need th' box."

I located the tackle box, and he rattled his hand-painted lures onto a workbench.

A proud grin tilted his mouth. "There. Show you."

"Impressive," I said. "You made all these?"

There's an art form there, a craft, for sure. I couldn't imagine the time and patience he'd invested in creating these fishing lures. There was a story attached to each one, the memory of some little adventure. A few of the larger ones went back to those old ice fishing days when Ben and I were little kids.

"Can't fish," he mumbled. "Not fishing anymore."

"Oh, shut up. You can fish if you want to."

He looked up at me, startled.

"Stop thinking like you've got to own the boat or drive the boat." I tapped my own temple. "New frame of mind: you are now the captain. Rent a boat and tell them, 'Take me to the fish.' That's what they do. Stop worrying that you can't do it yourself."

"Huh." He considered this, hands trembling at the end of his rumpled sleeves. "Let's go."

"What—you and me?" I laughed and said, "Okay. Sure."

Ivy wasn't thrilled with the idea and didn't offer any help with his meds or other logistics, but this expedition was on. My dad and I were going fishing. Give me five minutes and a smartphone and I can make a thing happen. I hooked up an excursion with a guy whose son had MS, so the boat was wheelchair accessible, and he was completely cool with whatever. Before I drove away, Ivy insisted I sign a paper saying I was aware my father had Parkinson's and I was accepting full responsibility for anything untoward. I was surprised there wasn't a body retrieval rider attached.

"We're just going out in Lake Placid," I assured her. "I'll have him back at the hospice in a couple of hours."

On the way to the docks, Dad kept saying, "Minnows, minnows," so we stopped for minnows. Inside the bait shop, I saw Arabic writing on a note by the cash register, so I said, "Assalaam alaikum."

"Wa-alaikum assalaam." The gentleman behind the counter

smiled, pleasantly surprised, and we chatted back and forth. I told him about my dad and our fishing mission.

"Wonderful. That's wonderful," he said. "I would like to meet him."

He came out to the car with a bucket of minnows and even put some frankincense on Dad's temples to help calm his tremors, which had gotten worse because he was excited. I don't know if the frankincense actually helped, but it was such a lovely gesture from a kind stranger.

The urinary tract infection was making my dad uncomfortable, but he tried to grin and bear it, and we lasted for a good three hours on the boat. He was the only one to catch a fish. Once a fisherman, always a fisherman. My dad had the catheter for pee, so that was fine, but eventually he started getting agitated, and I correctly guessed that he was needing the bathroom.

"No worries," I said. Back at the dock a few minutes later, I hefted him into the car, telling him, "You're good, you're okay," but he thrashed and wobbled in the passenger seat, getting more and more anxious. He managed to tell me that he couldn't make it back to the rehab center. He wanted me to stop at a gas station.

"R—right. Go—go right."

"Yes, Dad, I see it."

"Right! Fuckin' bitch!"

I flashed back on that day Ben's body was found. The smell in his room. The feeling of my face on fire.

I'm still here.

The men's room in the gas station was cramped and filthy. He didn't want me to see him with his pants down, so I tried to help him with my head turned away, telling him, "Dad, I've seen everything you can imagine on the mountain. Seriously, don't worry about it."

I returned him to his room at the rehab center and left him slumped in the chair where he was when I arrived.

"I'll come back in a few weeks," I told him. And I did keep that promise, but he died at home as I made the two-hour drive from the airport. Ivy waited for me to arrive before calling the ambulance. I literally walked in, saw the dead body, and she called the ambulance. When the EMTs arrived, they asked, "Are you family?"

"Yes," I said. "Family."

"You don't want to watch this."

I went out to the garage where Ivy had already started preparing items for an estate sale. My father's tackle box sported a neon price sticker.

I don't think so.

I stashed the tackle box in the trunk of my rental car and headed back to the airport.

Ivy set up funeral arrangements a week later in Detroit. She'd made two huge boards to display at the service, pictures of my dad's life. Boats, big fish, big smiles, mountains, parks, open waters. In all the snapshots, he was with Ivy. There was not a single photograph of me, Mom, or Ben. It was as if our part in his life had never occurred.

Okay. Whatever.

I decided to make a board of my own. I told you, I can be Martha fucking Stewart when I want to be. I covered my board with canvas on which I could hang his hand-painted fishing lures. They were armed with razor-sharp hooks, but I knew how to handle them without drawing blood. I opened the tackle box and admired my father's handiwork. Each jig was streaked with shadows, dark reminders of everything that lies beneath the ice, and featured a stark, ever-open eye, the unforgiving black pupil suspended in a pool of white. But in the fine lines of their speckled bodies, I saw the greens of Kilimanjaro, the silvers of Rainier, and the unyielding indigo of Cho Oyu.

I sat through mass, eyes as dry as walnuts, but Jonathan was next to me, that crack in the car window that allows you just enough air to survive. He had sent the flowers and rented an appropriate black town car for the funeral. He lent me his arm as I picked my way across the cemetery lawn. Stilettos, I tell you— ten times more dangerous than crampons. When we reached the curb, he opened the door for me, a proper Englishman.

"Where to, Mrs. O'Brien?"

And I said, "Home."

I tried hard to experience this moment as a formality. My parents didn't have to die to abandon me. In the years since my mother's funeral, I had become a different person, living in an entirely changed body, thinking with an entirely rewired brain. I had become more myself than I had ever been or imagined possible. I had learned the last great lesson of the mountains: that a mountain does not love you. A mountain—however magnificent—is not capable of love. Whatever love is there begins and ends within you, so you must love well and without fear. You must not go to the mountain seeking salvation, because salvation is not a thing to find; it is a thing to inhabit. Salvation is not the swing of an ice axe; it's the altitude we achieve with whatever thin air we're given.

28

*We salute the most beautiful kind of heroism,
that which confronts scientifically calculated danger step
by step without hesitation or sensationalism.*
—BARON PIERRE DE COUBERTIN,
FOUNDER OF THE MODERN OLYMPICS,
AWARDING GOLD MEDALS
FOR MOUNTAINEERING

The summit is within reach. Sixteen hours after beginning our ascent, we are at the summit ridge. I hear Pemba's voice on the radio, calling down to Base Camp. "Summit! We made the summit of K2!"

Screaming, shouting, celebration.

For fuck's sake. His Nanga Parbat client is not on the summit yet. And neither am I. It pisses me off, but I push the anger into my gut and let it move me up the mountain.

And then, something extraordinary happens.

As I approach the summit, by some confluence of prayer and wind with sheer force of will, the whole world opens wide. Clouds fall away below us, and we find ourselves in the brilliant light of a bluebird day. Pristine sun and sky appear.

It occurs to me now, of course, that the sun and sky were there all along. It was me who appeared, finally able to see them.

I summited K2 via the Abruzzi Ridge route, 28,251 feet, at 4:40 PM on July 28, 2017.

As I unfurled the Union Jack, Old Glory, and the flag of the Crescent and Star, along with the flag of UN Women, I felt the winds of change.

EPILOGUE

*If you succeed with one dream . . . it's not long
before you're conjuring up another, slightly harder,
a bit more ambitious, a bit more dangerous.*
—JOE SIMPSON, CLIMBER AND AUTHOR OF *TOUCHING THE VOID*

Back at Base Camp, I sent Wingman a text: "The eagle has landed."

Word spread quickly. One of my extended Pakistan families ordered a U DID IT! cake that I would later share with them at an Independence Day air show.

I went to the Gilkey Memorial with Fazal Ali, Farman, Farman's assistant, Sherzad Karim, and Lt. Shabbar to hang the missing plaques. By the time we finished, it looked like a freshly gentrified block in a venerable old neighborhood, but I knew it wouldn't take long for the elements to leave the new plates as weathered and beaten as the old.

Despite my vow to never do it again, Farman, Fazal, and I trekked out via Gondogoro Pass, and it was even more evil than the previous year, full of ice—not snow—with broken shale that slid down the mountain. We walked for three days, during which I did surprisingly little thinking. I had no mental or physical capacity left for anything beyond one foot after another.

Back in Islamabad, I went to the offices of UN Women, the British High Commission, and the US Embassy to return their summit flags.

"I'd like to give you this in return," said the US ambassador to Pakistan.

He signed a cricket ball and handed it to me. I thought this was very odd until much later when another penny dropped. I was home with Jonathan and the BBC reported that there was an election on the horizon in Pakistan, and Imran Khan, former captain of Pakistan's national cricket team, was leading like an opening pace bowler.

I celebrated my K2 summit with friends at several parties on various continents, including a surprise party hosted by the Honorable Alexandra Shackleton ("Zaz" to her friends), granddaughter of Sir Ernest Shackleton. There was a gorgeous cake decorated with white chocolate snow, and I smiled, remembering the little round cake presented with equal fanfare in the mess tent on Cho Oyu.

Zaz and I posed for pictures in front of a statue of Sir Ernest. We'd known each other for a few years. Not long after I returned from the North Pole, I worked with her on an event celebrating the centenary of Sir Ernest Shackleton's Imperial Trans-Antarctic Expedition at the United Nations Economic and Social Council (ECOSOC) chambers, sponsored by the UK Mission to the UN. The Martha Stewart in me thought it would be fun to create an awesome display by changing the names of countries to explorers for the event. When I pitched this idea, I didn't know I would have to come up with four hundred names. I enlisted Jonathan's help, and as he was plowing through various websites and plugging information into a spreadsheet for me, he called me up to his office to look at a listing on Guinness World Records online.

Under "Seven Summits," it said, "British-American Vanessa Audi Rhys O'Brien (USA, b. 2 Dec 1964) climbed the combined Kosciuszko and Carstensz lists in 295 days (or 9 months 19 days),

starting with Everest on 19 May 2012 and ending with Kilimanjaro on 10 March 2013. Guinness World Records 2015."

"Look at that," I mused. "I wonder if Guinness World Records
has a record for the longest time a person went without knowing
they were in Guinness World Records."

The only records that can't be broken are the "firsts"—but in a
way, I was the first to be fastest. (Possibly first to be shortest!) I look
forward to seeing a new generation of mountaineering women set
new records. The importance of a record is that it provides a platform from which to tell a story, and every story is important. Each
one of us has a small piece of the map of human experience. We
help other explorers find their way when we share the experiences
we've gained, the skills we've honed, the suffering that shapes our
character, and the wisdom we take with us.

Change comes, whether we like it or not, to our lives, to our
nations, and to our planet. The eye of history watches those who
are courageous enough to take the difficult steps, unwilling to be
silenced, incapable of turning away from the singular purpose that
drives their destiny.

On an airplane between somewhere and somewhere else, the
Norwegian gentleman seated next to me asked, "Is stubbornness
an important trait for an explorer?"

"Ah." I smiled, sensing a language barrier. "You mean 'determination'?"

"No. I mean stubbornness."

I thought about the negative connotations of that word, as op-
posed to the literal meaning, and then I thought about all the won-
derfully stubborn people I know who might not have changed the
world without uncompromising commitment to a specific desire.
In my exploration of life, I have tried to "choose the harder right
rather than the easier wrong." Nothing is as straightforward as one

would prefer. Life is a messy, sprawling landscape that results from the tectonic collision of obstacle and opportunity, epic fails and occasional redemptions. You stumble. You suffer. You get up and go on.

In the Aeneid, Book 1, following a tremendous storm that scatters the Trojan fleet, Aeneas tells his exhausted men: "Perhaps one day it will please us to remember even this."

Modern-day equivalent: *I can't wait to never be here again.*

A NOTE FROM THE AUTHOR

I find it hard to say what I really fuckin' mean.
—LIAM GALLAGHER, THE MUSIC LEGEND AND
FORMER OASIS MEMBER, *GQ* MAGAZINE, OCT. 2019

This is a personal memoir, written from my personal perspective. No part of this story should be construed or misconstrued as medical, legal, or technical advice. The activities in this book were undertaken at great personal risk. No part of this book should be taken as encouragement or instruction by anyone considering these or any other dangerous activities.

I am very grateful to Lara Jones, my editor at Emily Bestler Books, a division of Simon & Schuster, for taking an initial interest in this story. Her own love of mountains and the outdoors made my experience writing this so much easier. Enormous thanks to my literary agent, Jen Marshall, at Aevitas Creative Management, who understands this industry upside down and has an adventurous family, a twofer in the publishing world!

This book could never have seen the light of day without Joni Rodgers, who is so much more than plot whisperer. She patiently pulls threads and builds trust to help authors like me "dig a little deeper," even when it is painful to do so. Given the number of Post-its she places on the walls during a working session, I'd say she'd make Jack Welch proud, too. Thank you for pushing me, for pushing back on me, and for reaching this book summit with me.

To Jonathan: I am grateful for your support and love you very much. Even though I say we are chalk and cheese, there is compatibility, or we would never have made it to twenty years! No summit is possible without your support, emotionally and financially.

To my friends: you are my inspiration. Your friendship means the world to me and provides perspective and balance. To all those I climbed or skied with—thank you for intersecting your stories with mine. Thank you to all the expedition companies I worked with over the years for making my trips memorable and successful. I am grateful to those who gave me advice, including Ijaz Malik, Sir Humphry Wakefield, Aura Velasquez, Sir Chris Bonington, Phil Erard, Miles Young, Kevin O'Leary, Penny Vizcarra, Kim Bernhard, and Brian Novack. I am grateful to all those who trained me, including Dan Brewis, Gert Koovit, Ross Eathorne, Brett Oteri, Mark Safer, Lisa Gray, and Philip Carpenter Lee. To those who provided medical support, I am very much indebted, including Drs. Aaron Baggish, John Connors, Ralph Metson, Saul Zion, Peter Hackett, Roger Härtl, and Scott Rodeo. I'd also like to express my gratitude to Eric Simonson, Alexandra Shackleton, Diahanne Gilbert, Bryan Oates, Davina Kaile, Lisa Schoening Jertz, Tracy Campion, Patricia MacDonald, Stacey Severn, Meredith Waites, Nils Krebs, the American Alpine Club library, US Nepal Climbers Association, David Greenbaum and Bridget Cunningham at Vornado Office Management, and Catharina Hedberg and the Ashram family.

Many thanks to the people of Nepal and Pakistan for welcoming me and extending your wonderful hospitality. I couldn't have done this without the Sherpa and HAPs who are my climbing partners, including Ang Chirring (Kami) Sherpa and Fazal Ali. The same gratitude goes for the expedition support staff from the wonderful cooks like Kaji Sherpa and Farman Ullah Baig to the many types of porters who help these expeditions around the world. Special thanks to Sequoia Schmidt, founder of the Denali Foundation, Sher Ali at the Concordia Motel in Skardu, and to all of my liaison officers—Major Salman Ali Satti, Squadron Leader Rahim Anwar, and Lieutenant Hasan Shabbar, Pakistan Navy. It was a privilege to spend time with honorable men like yourselves.

I'd also like to thank the High Commission for Pakistan in London, the Consulate General of Pakistan in New York, the Pakistan Armed Forces, the US Embassy in Islamabad, UN Women in Pakistan, Saba Ghori, Yasmin Amin-Jaswal, Air Commodore (ret.) Aamir Malik, Colonel (ret.) Mujahid Umar, Lieutenant Colonel (ret.) Manzoor Hussain, Kristiane Backer, Muhammad Arif Anis, World Congress of Overseas Pakistanis (WCOP), Dr. Abrar, and Arif Aslam Khan at the Shangrila Resort Hotel in Skardu.

Without Lieutenant Colonel (ret.) Hassan Bin Aftab and Nazir Sabir there wouldn't have been multiple seasons on K2, so without you both, no K2 summit would be possible. And without Buckston—my eyes, ears, and mouthpiece—no one would know who I am or what I summited. Buckston is a multimedia genius. He is literally "me" online when I need two hands in the physical world. Remember that, next time anyone flirts online—it might be Buckston! And if I said something to offend anyone online, it was definitely Buckston!

I want to thank all those who read versions of this story, including Jonathan O'Brien, Whitney Vickrey, Mel Berger, Roberta Burrows, Renee Landegger, Jim Clash, Georgie Pomper, Declan Quilligan, and Robert Anderson. I'd like to thank everyone who provided cover quotes, helped with the title selection, and fact-checked, including Jerusha Rodgers, Rosalind Benjamin, Alex Kolton, Gintare Mulerskaite, and Randi Bowe.

To Megan and Lara Richards, my two godchildren, I hope your parents won't give me a hard time about the profanity. To Oscar and Raffi Li, thank you for the smiley faces to the summit; I'm sure you placed a few ahead of me and that helped a lot.

I would like to leave you with one of my favorite messages from the author of *Summits: Climbing the Seven Summits Solo*:

May your hair extensions always be in place and your crampons sharp.

—ROBERT M. ANDERSON, MOUNTAINEER, WISHING ME LUCK ON K2